AF256002

Cross Stitch
Graph Paper Notebook

This book belongs to:

____

____

____

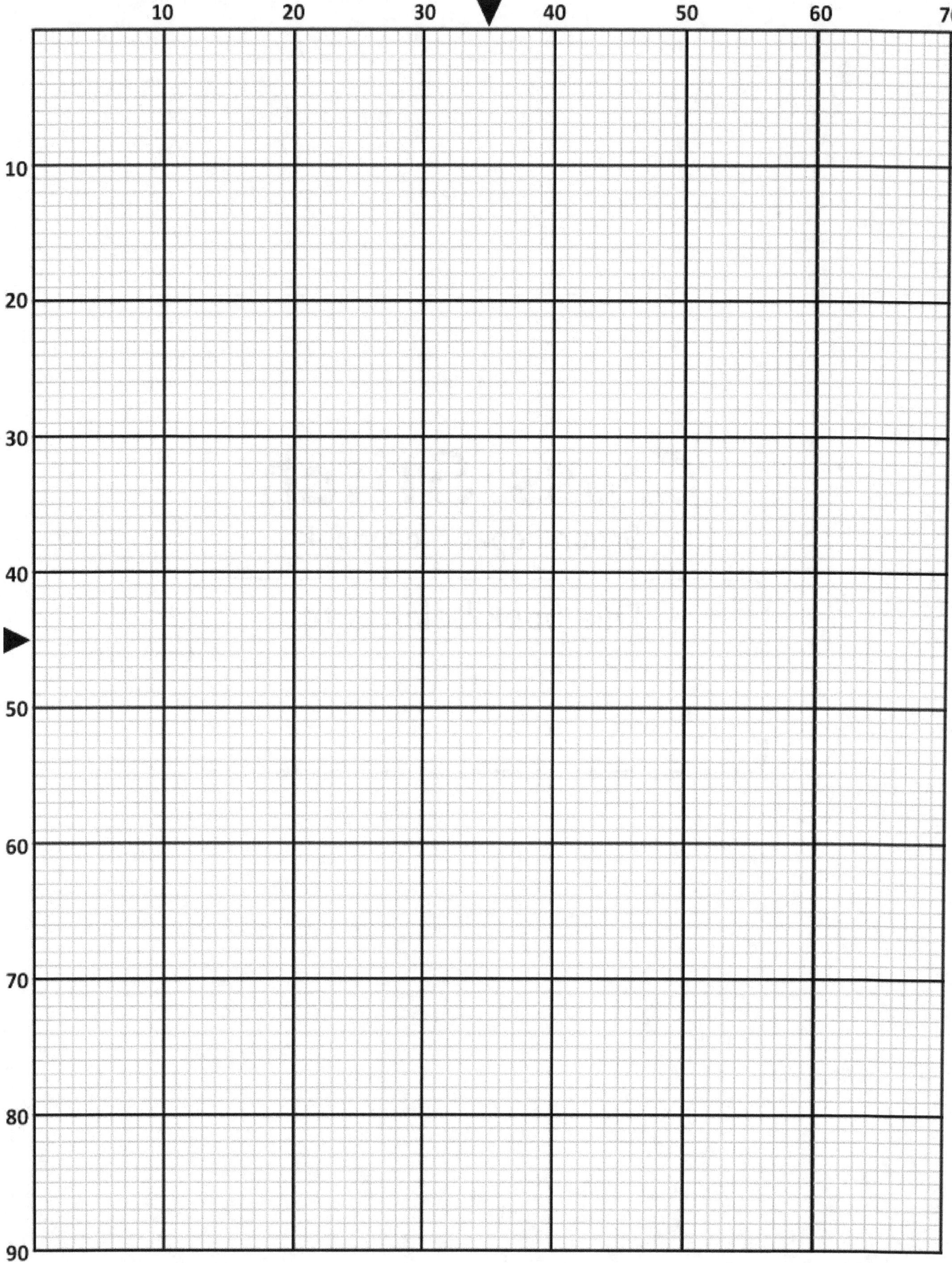

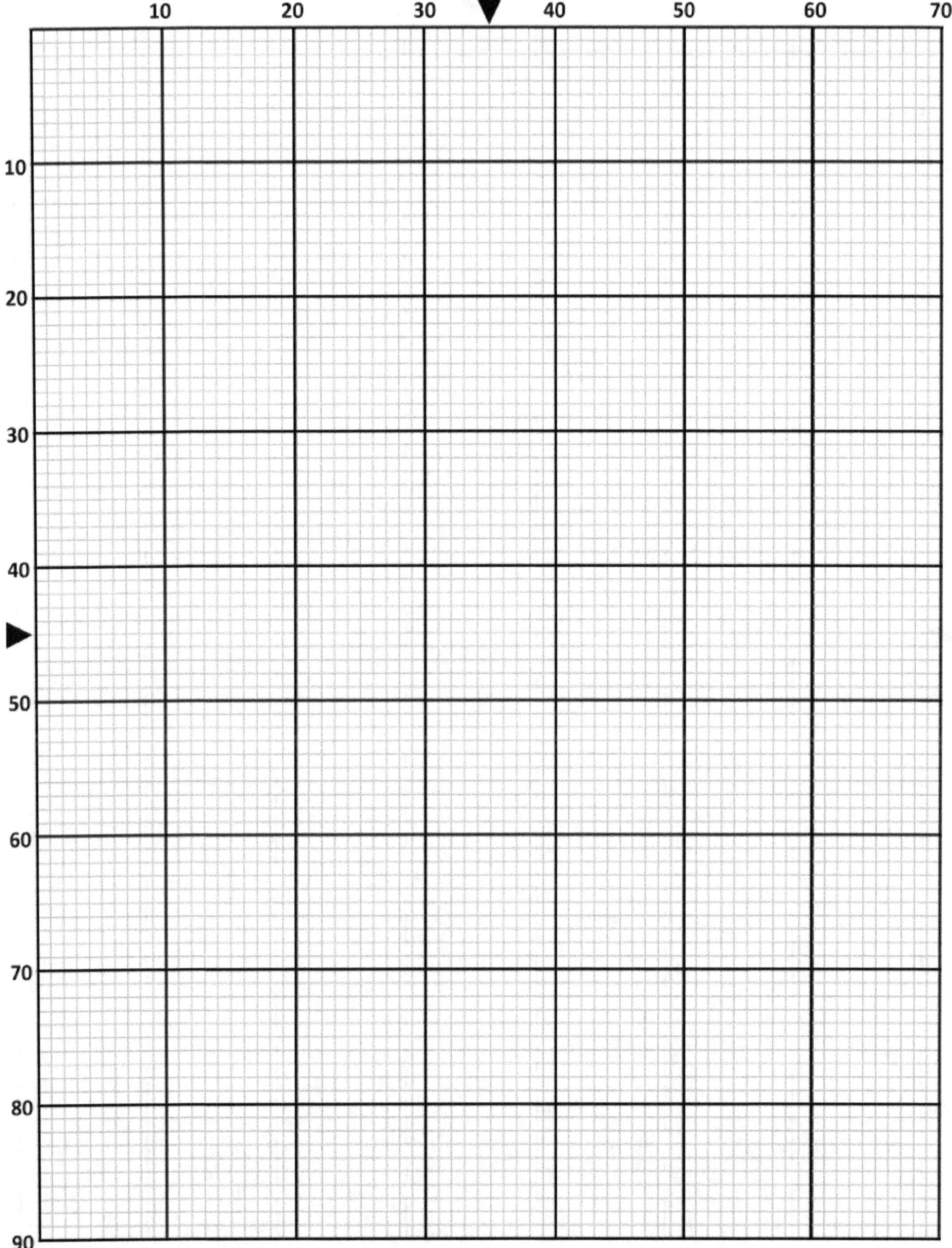

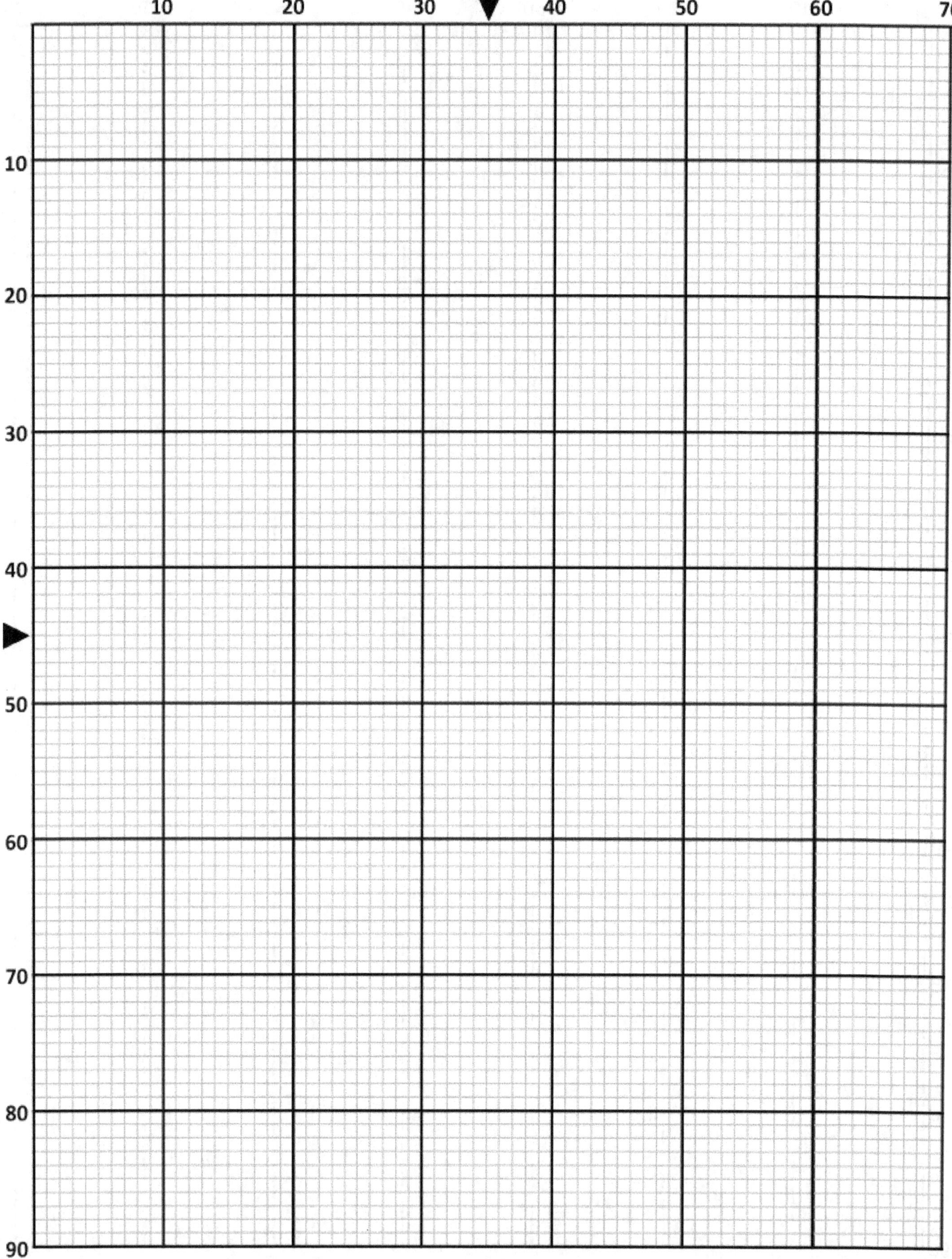

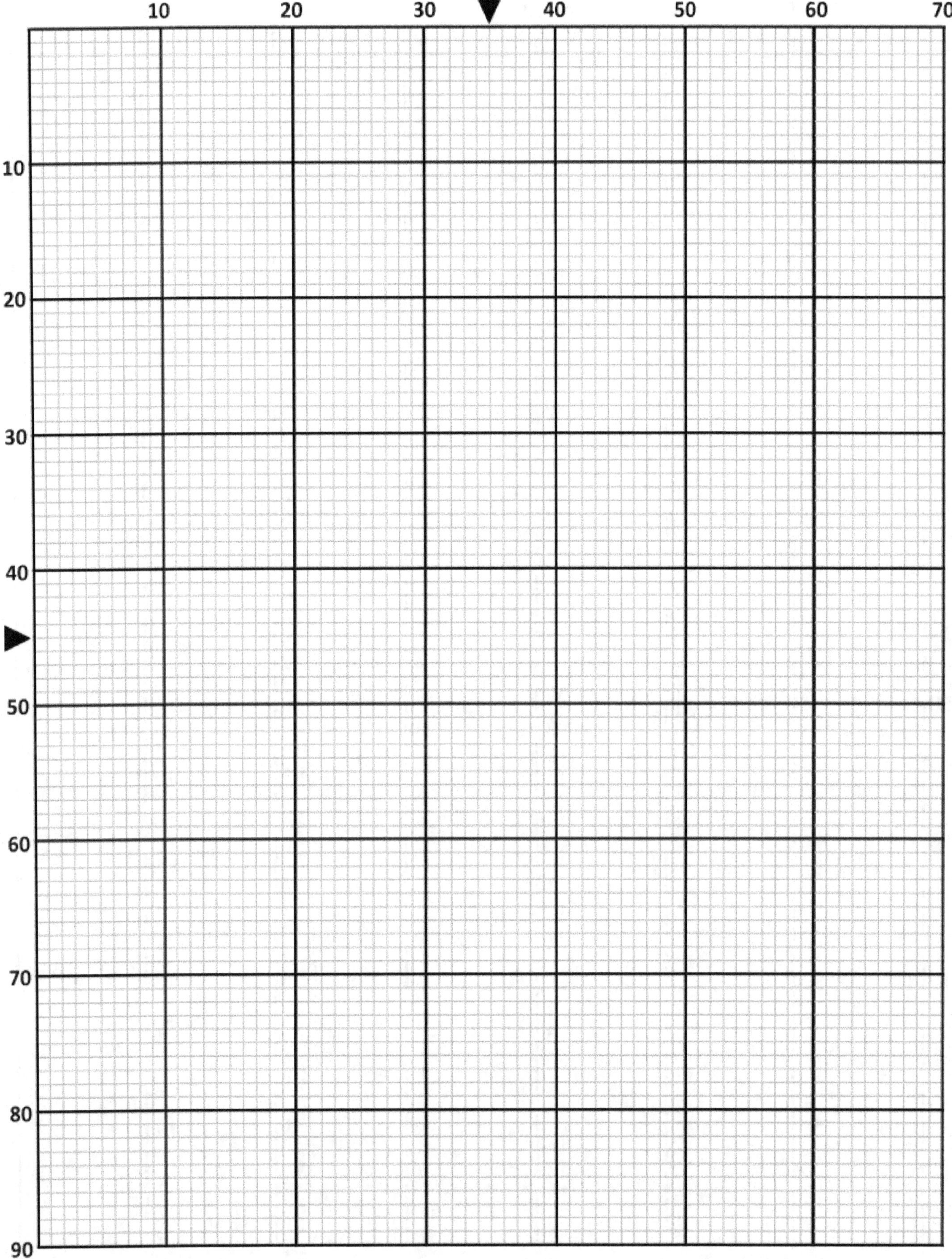

10
20
30
40
50
60
70
10
20
30
40
50
60
70
80
90

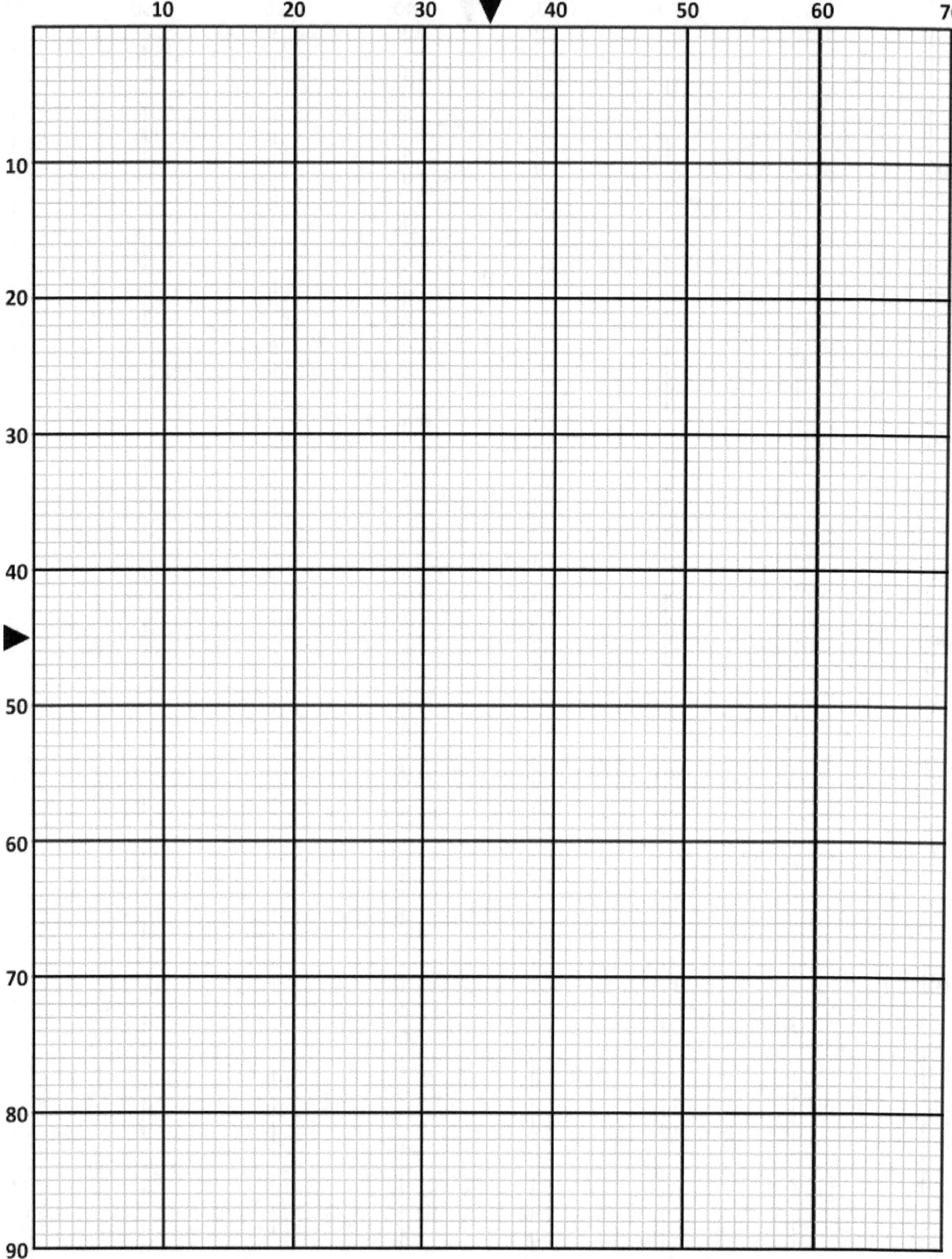

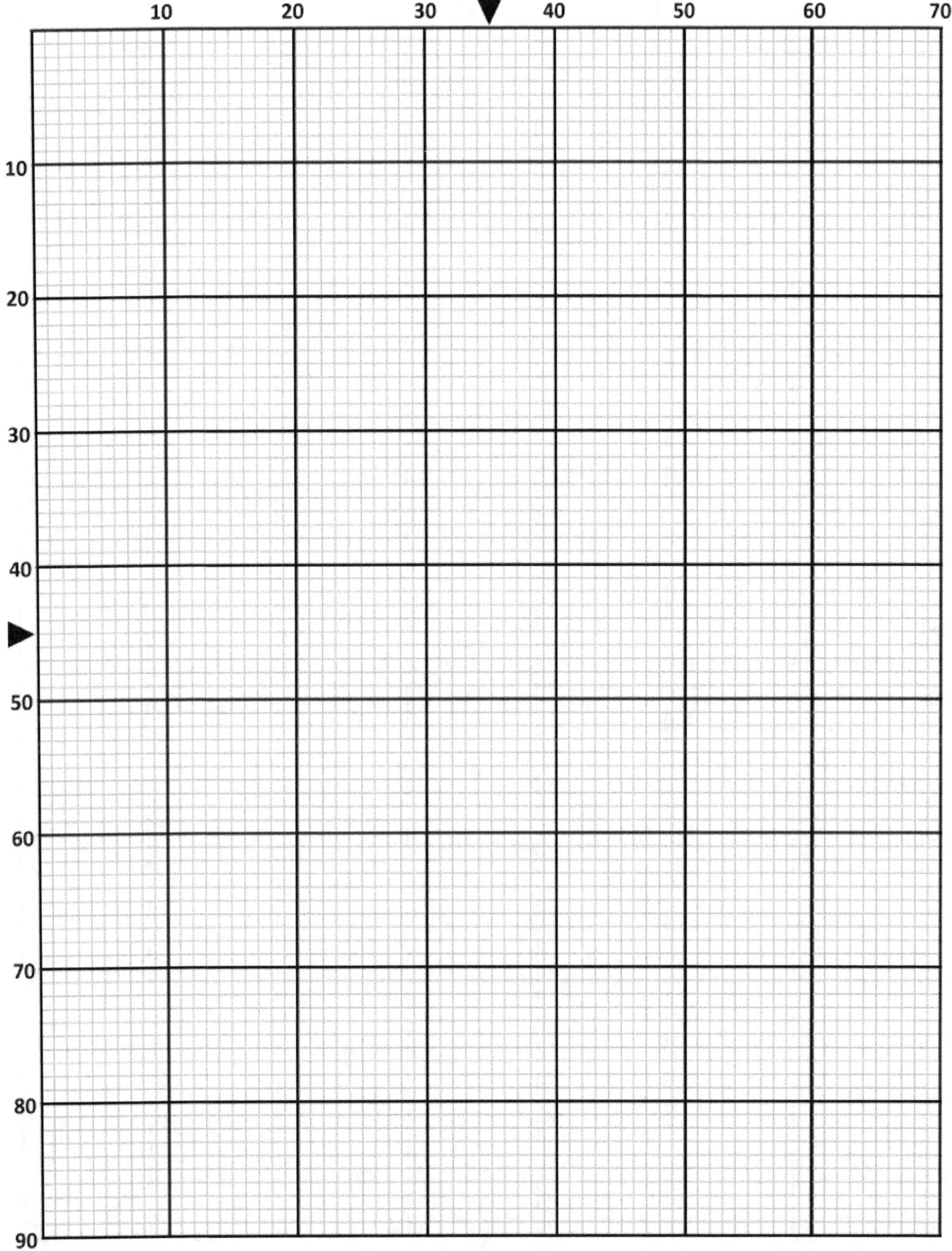

10
20
30
40
50
60
70
10
20
30
40
50
60
70
80
90

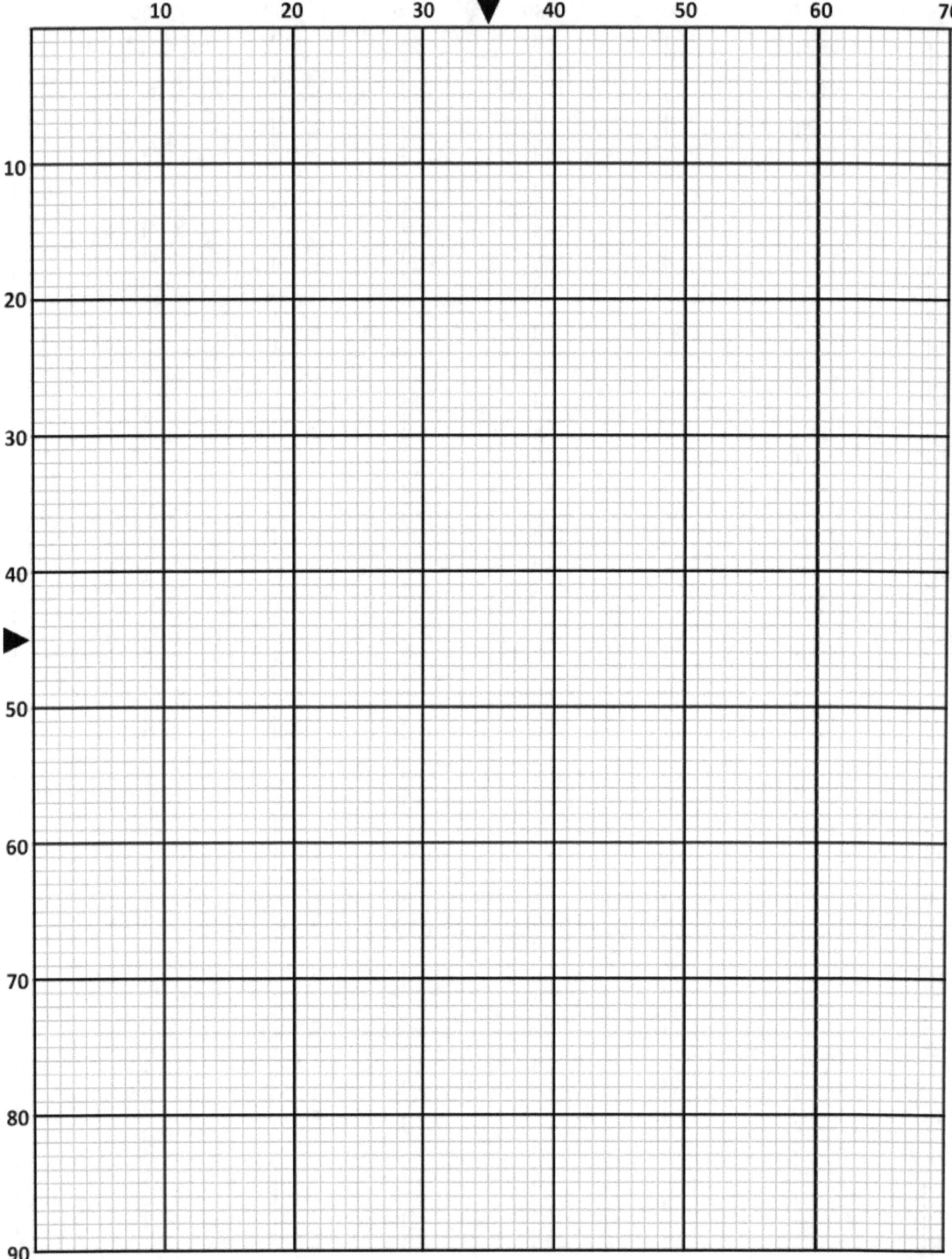

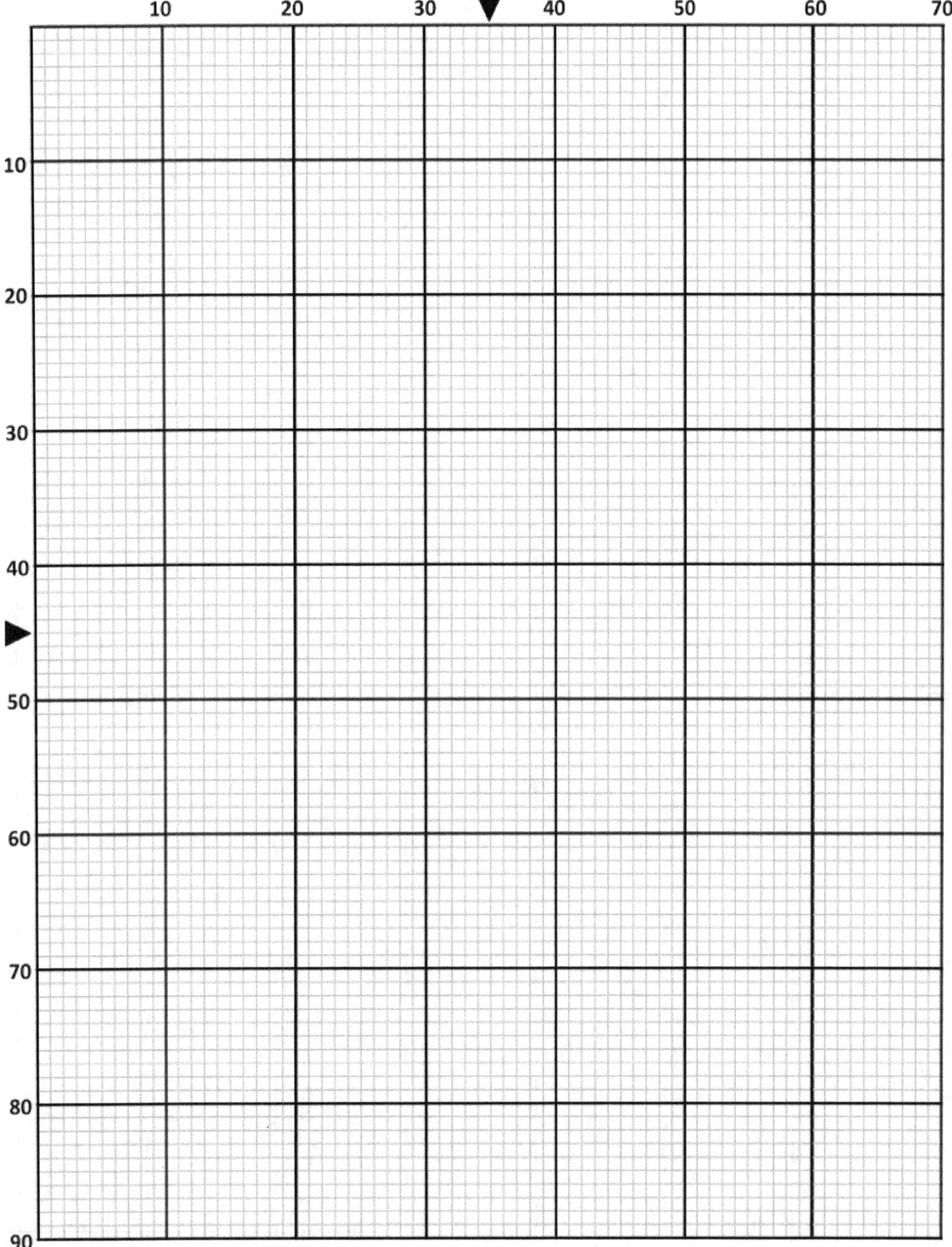

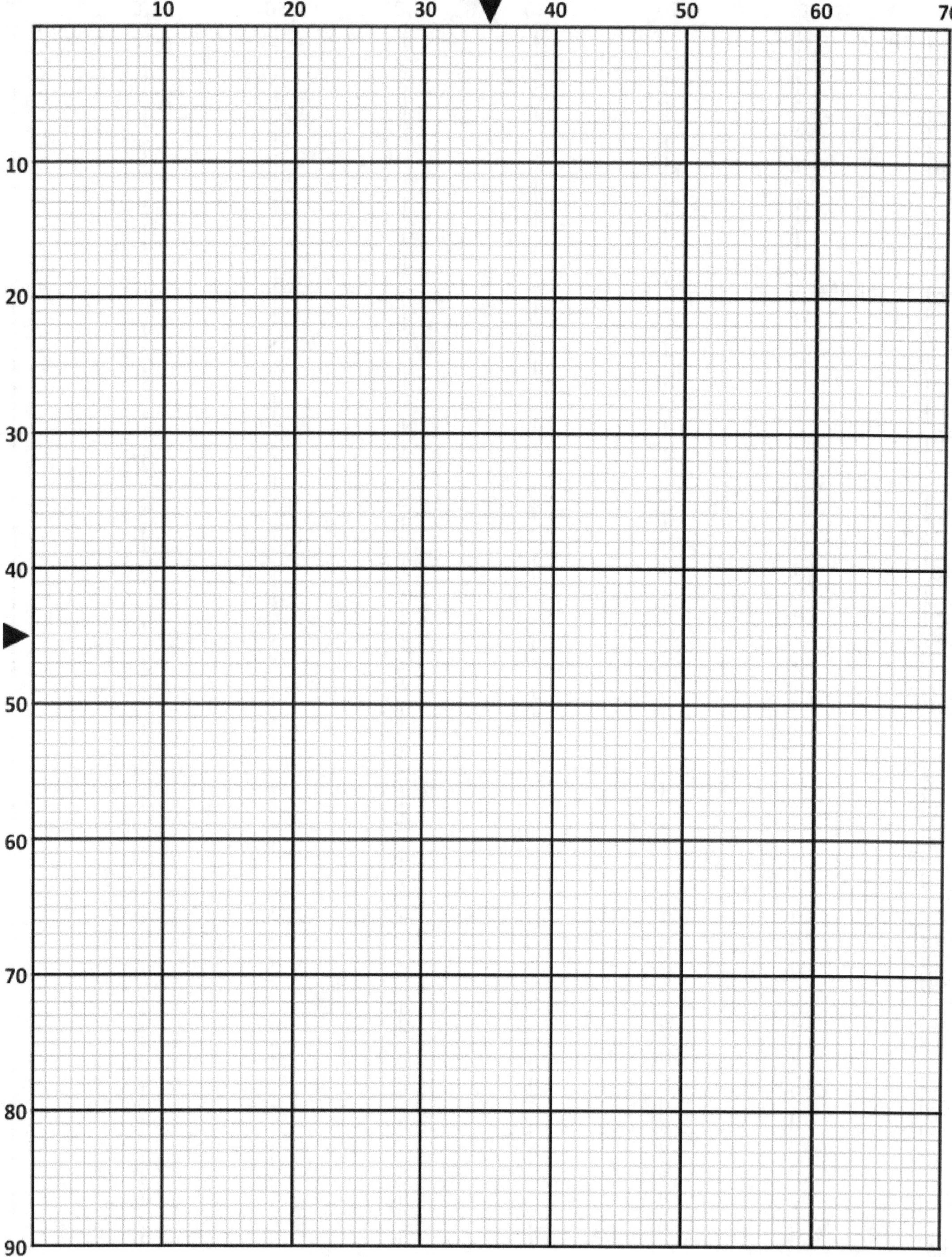

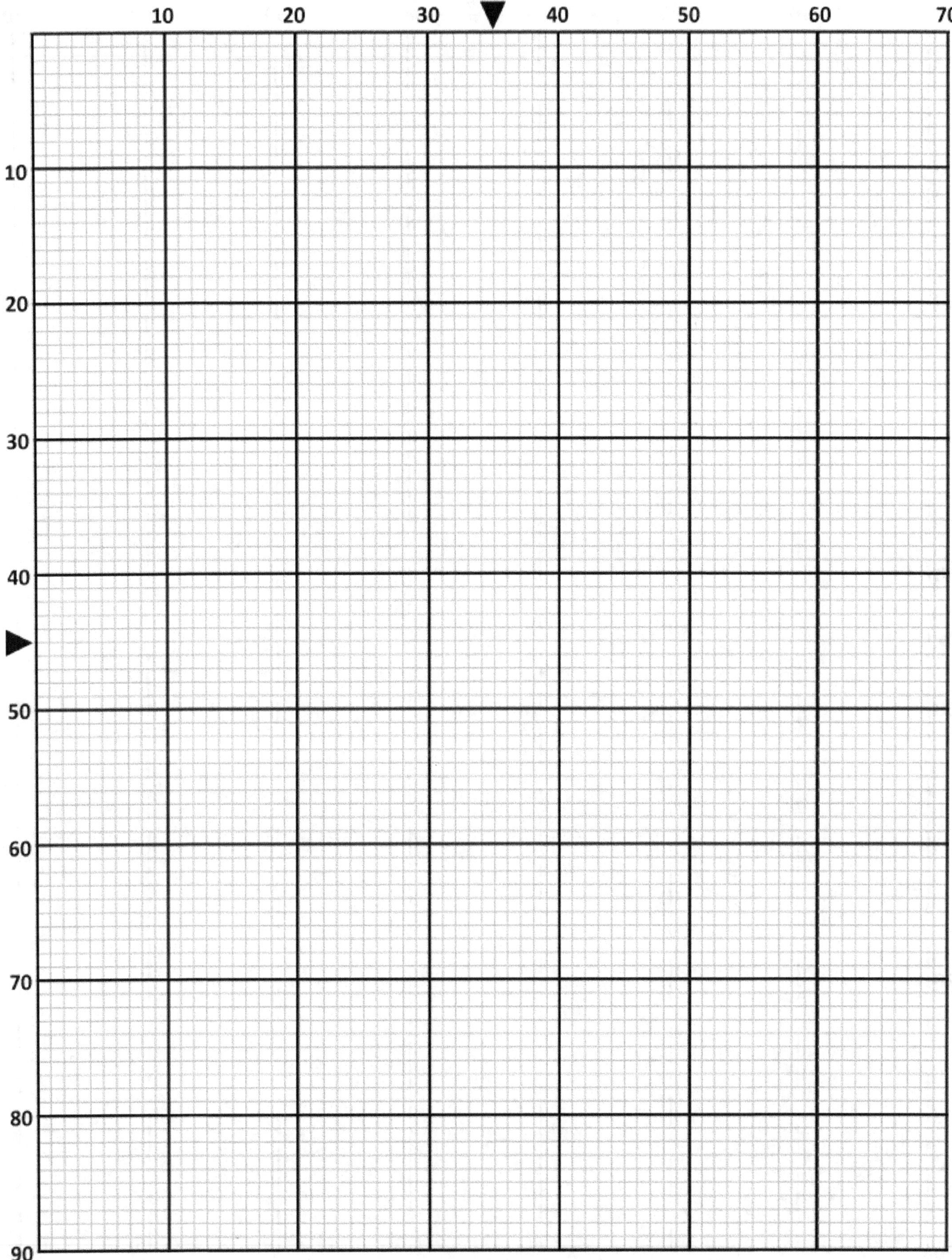

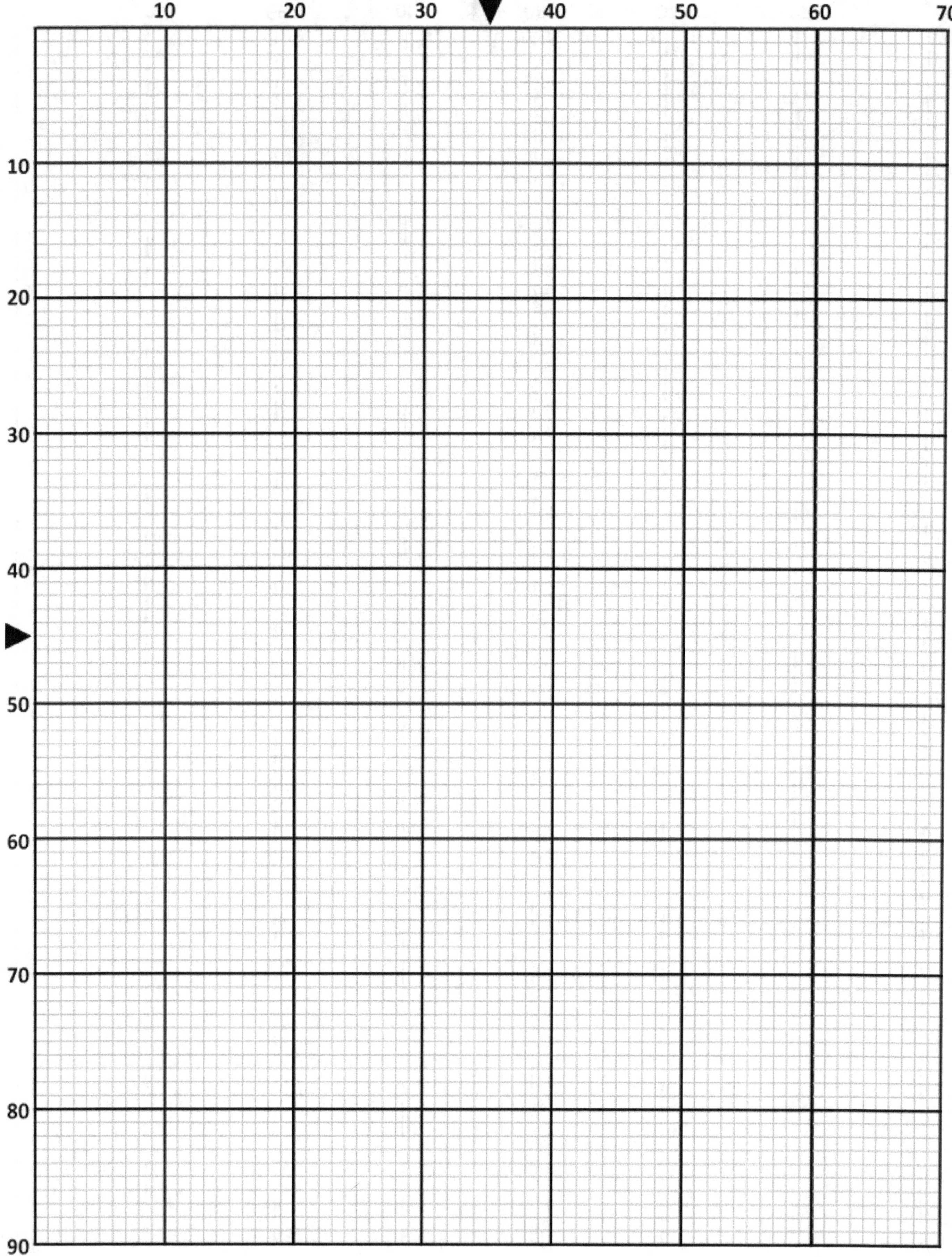

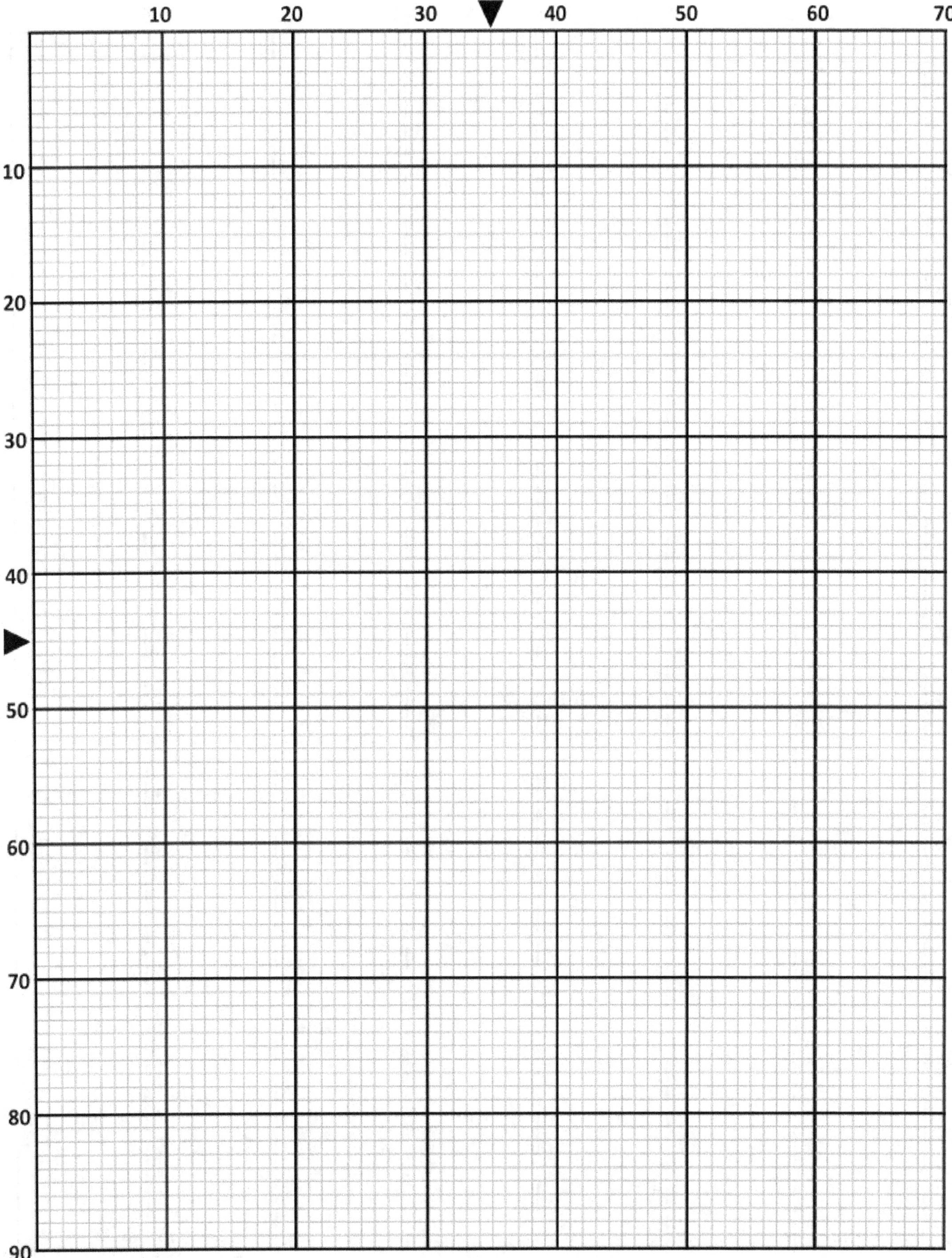

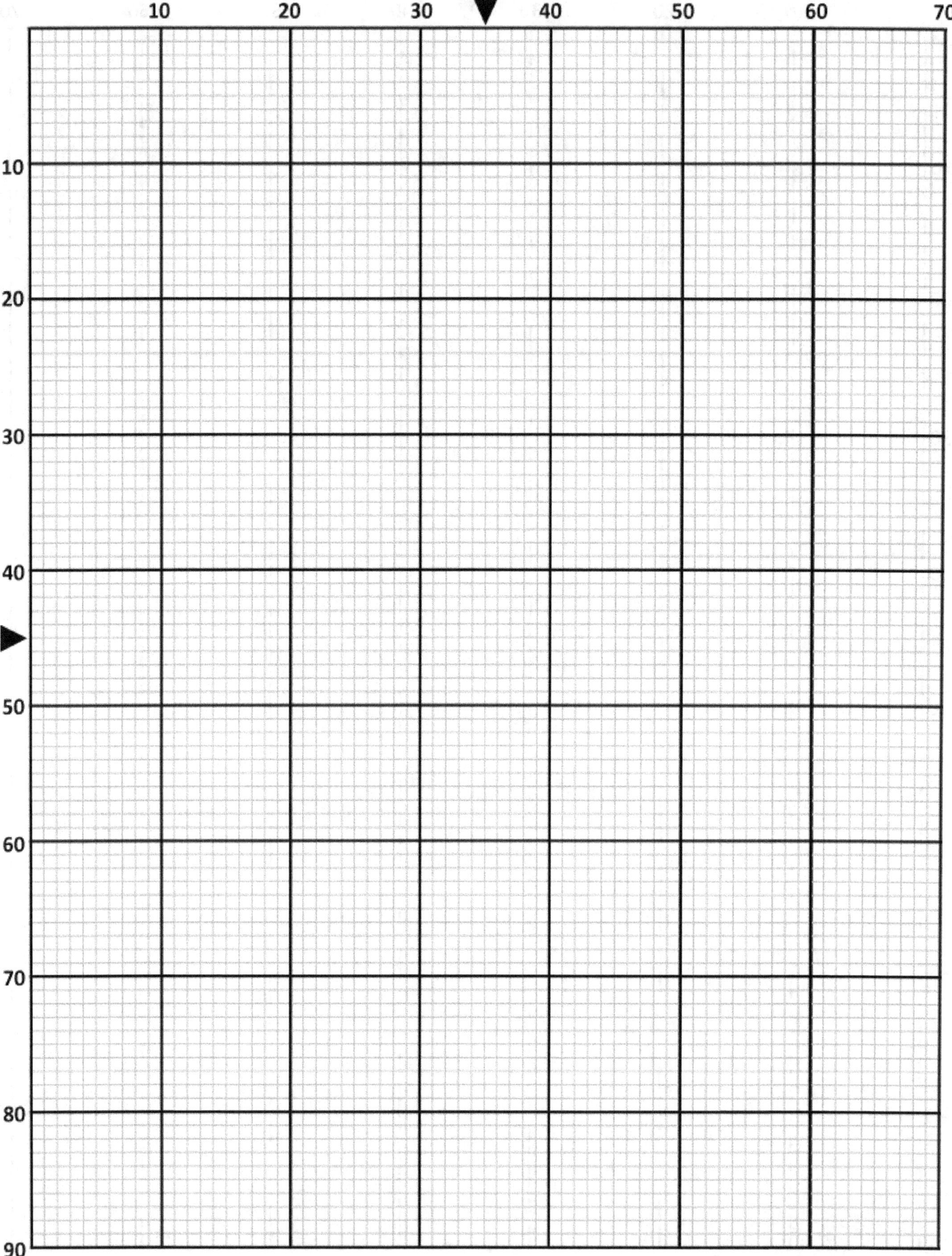

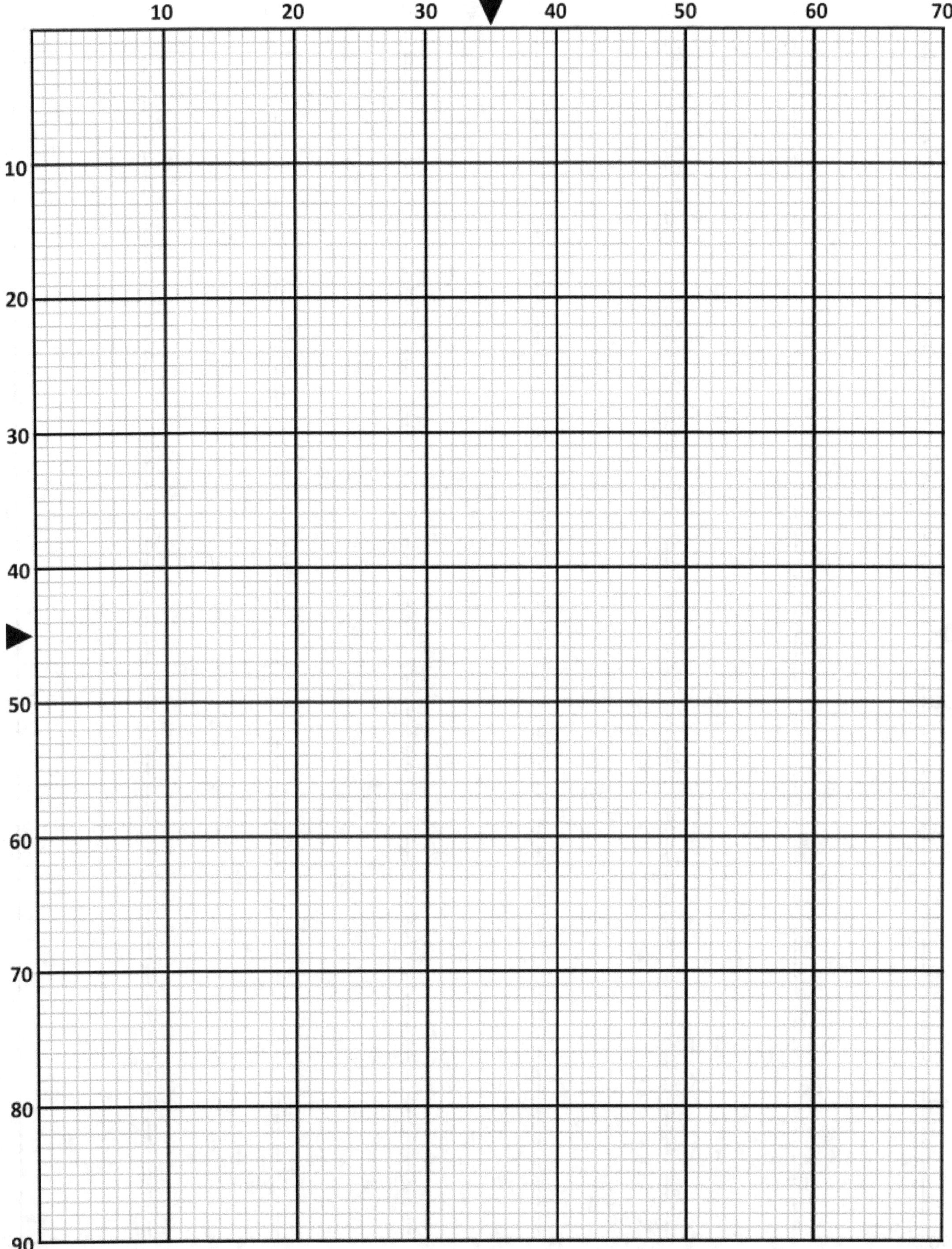

10
20
30
40
50
60
70
10
20
30
40
50
60
70
80
90

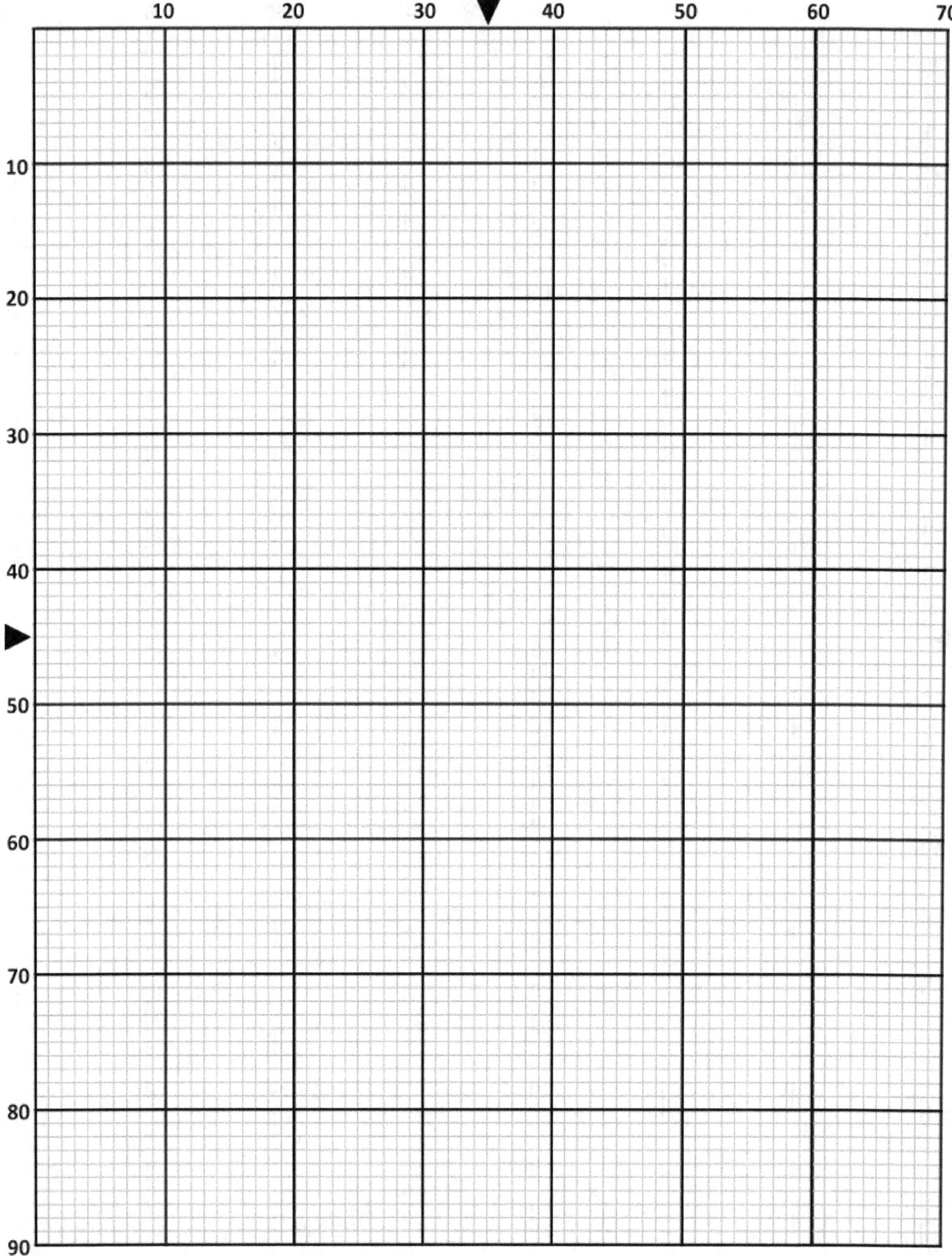

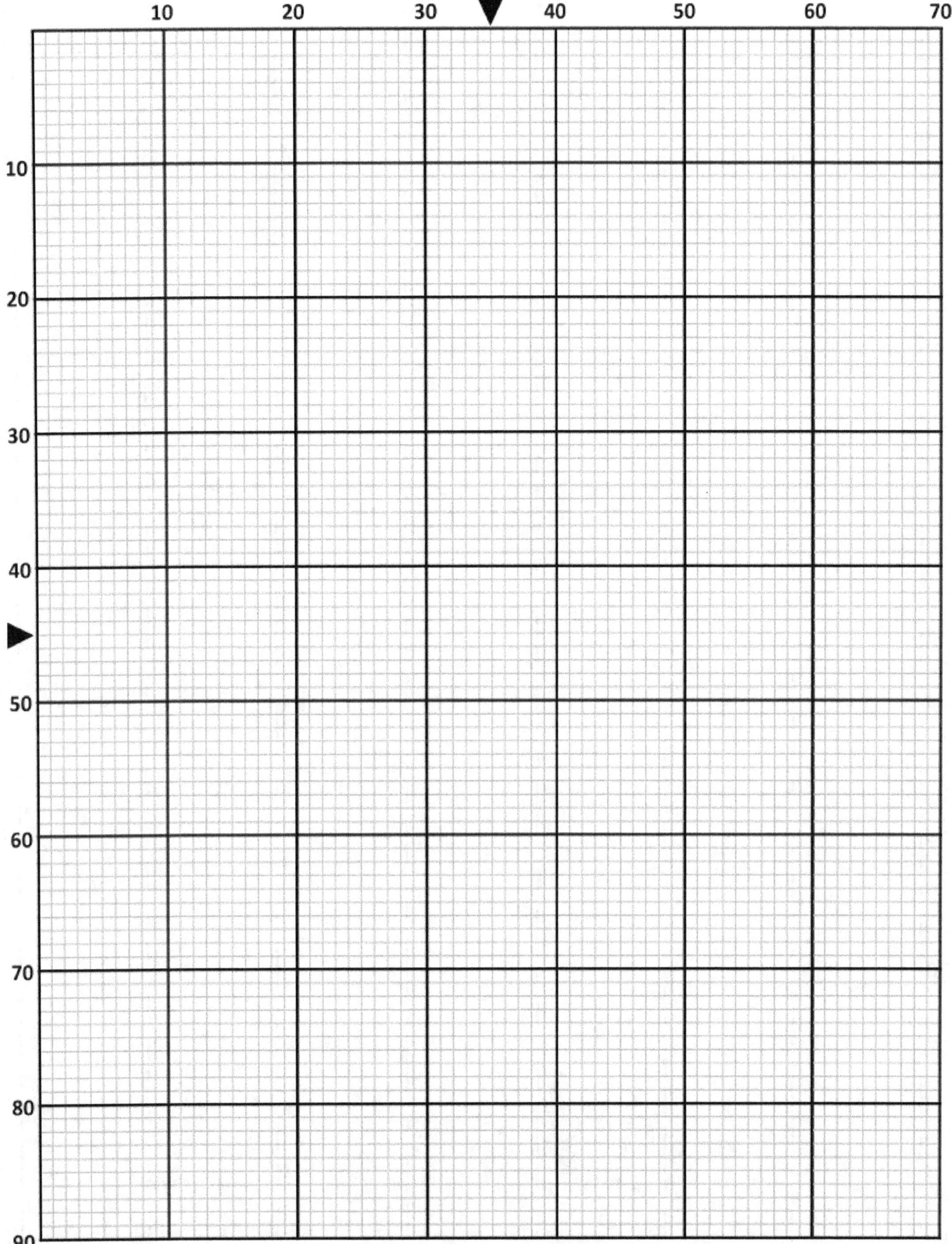

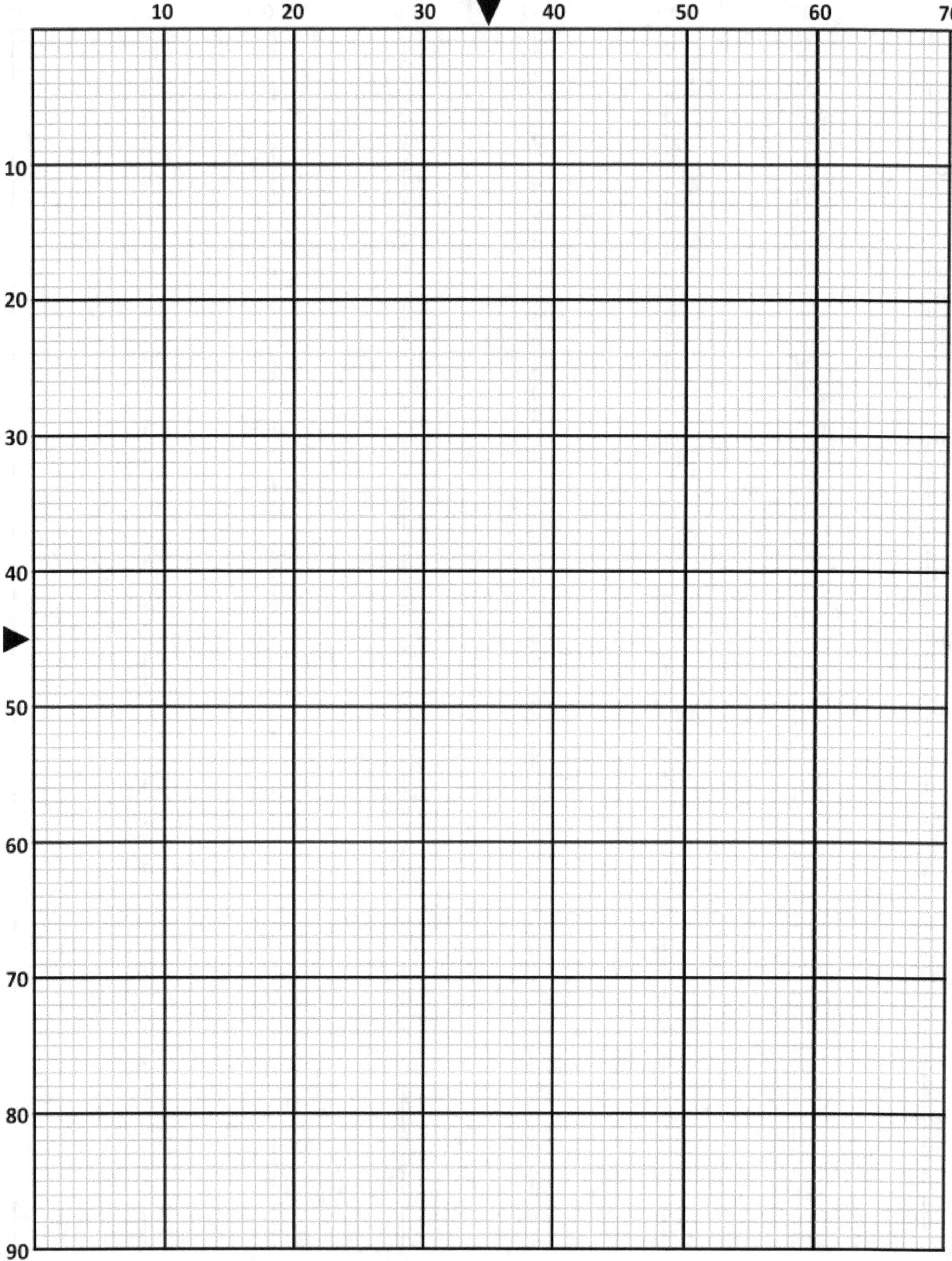

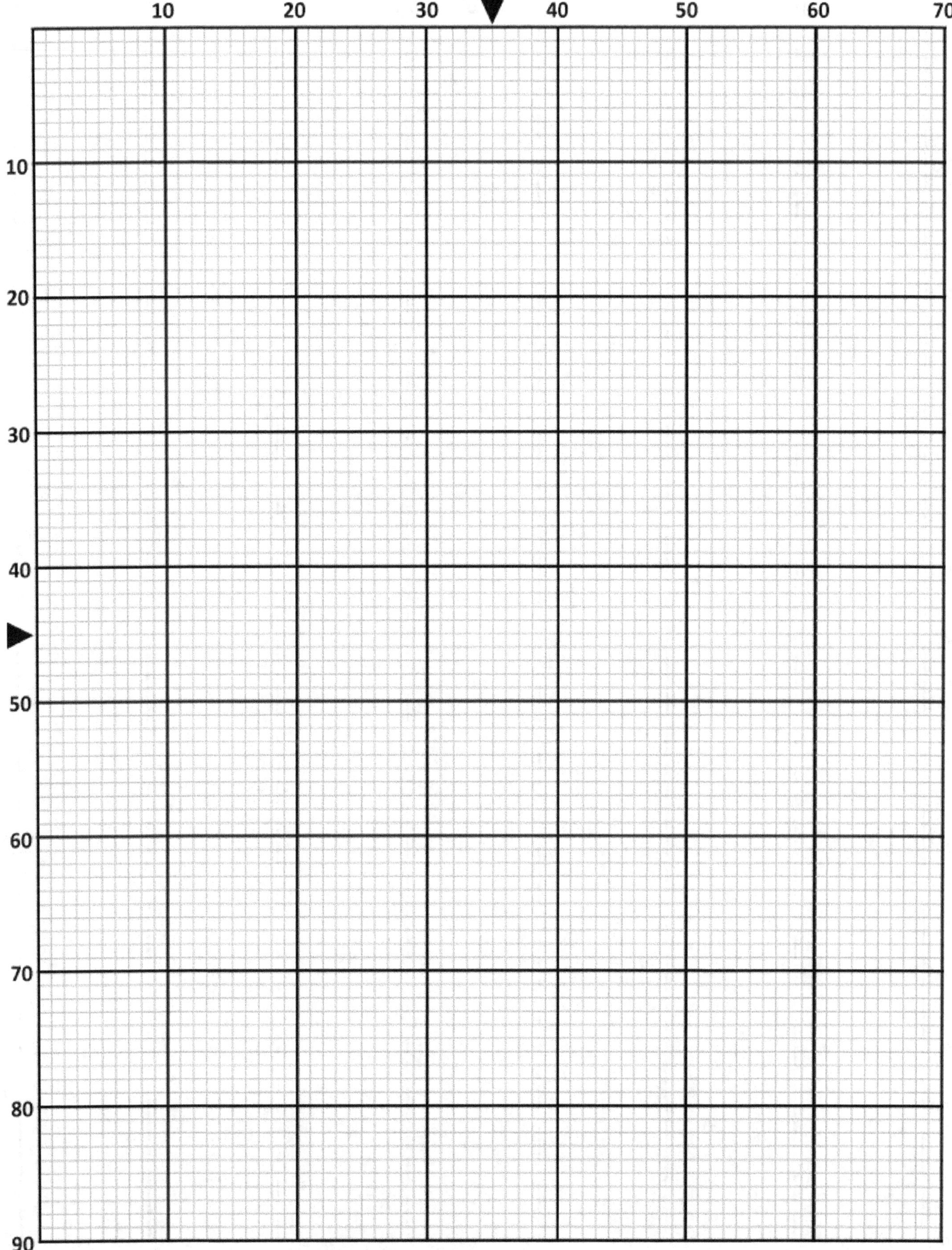

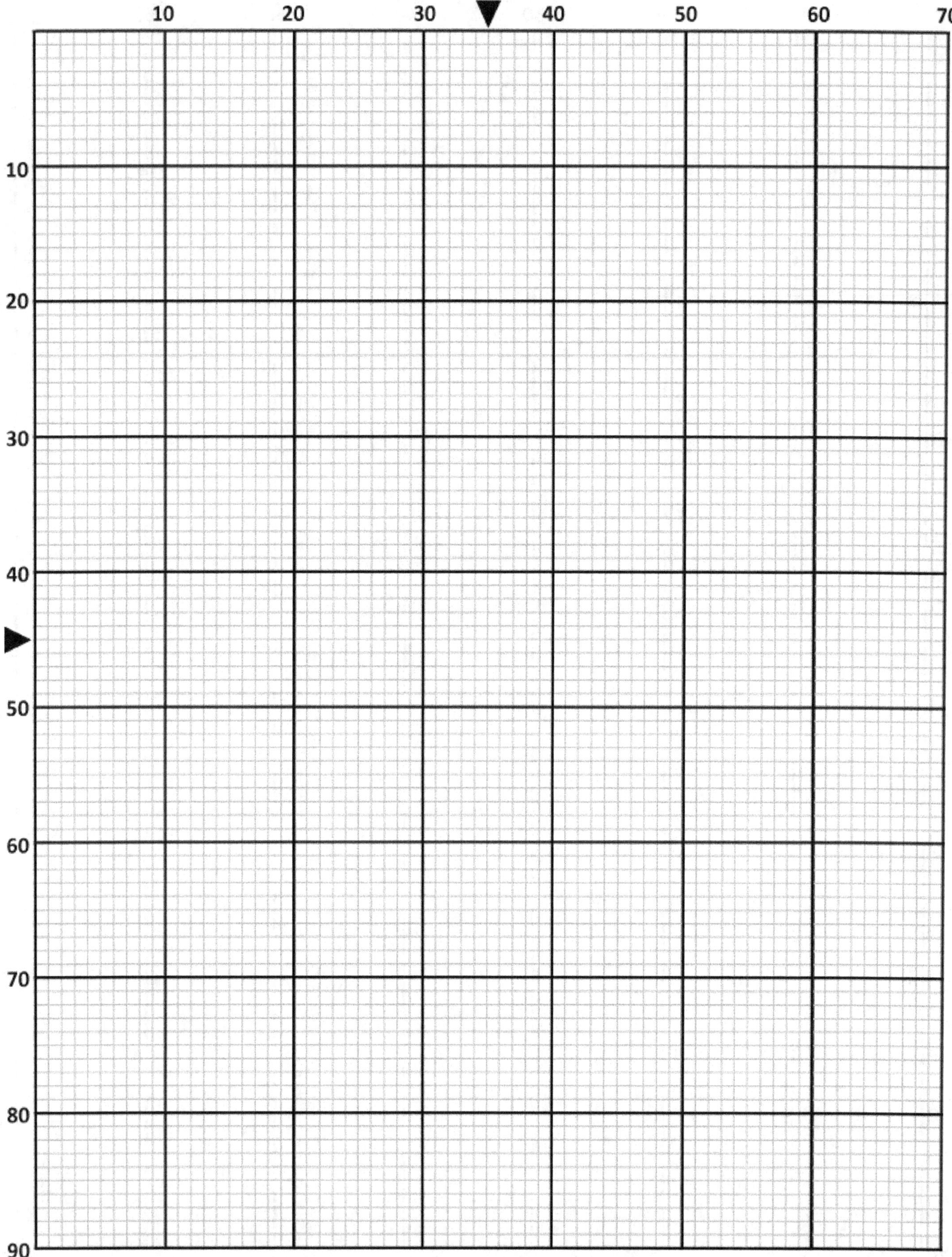

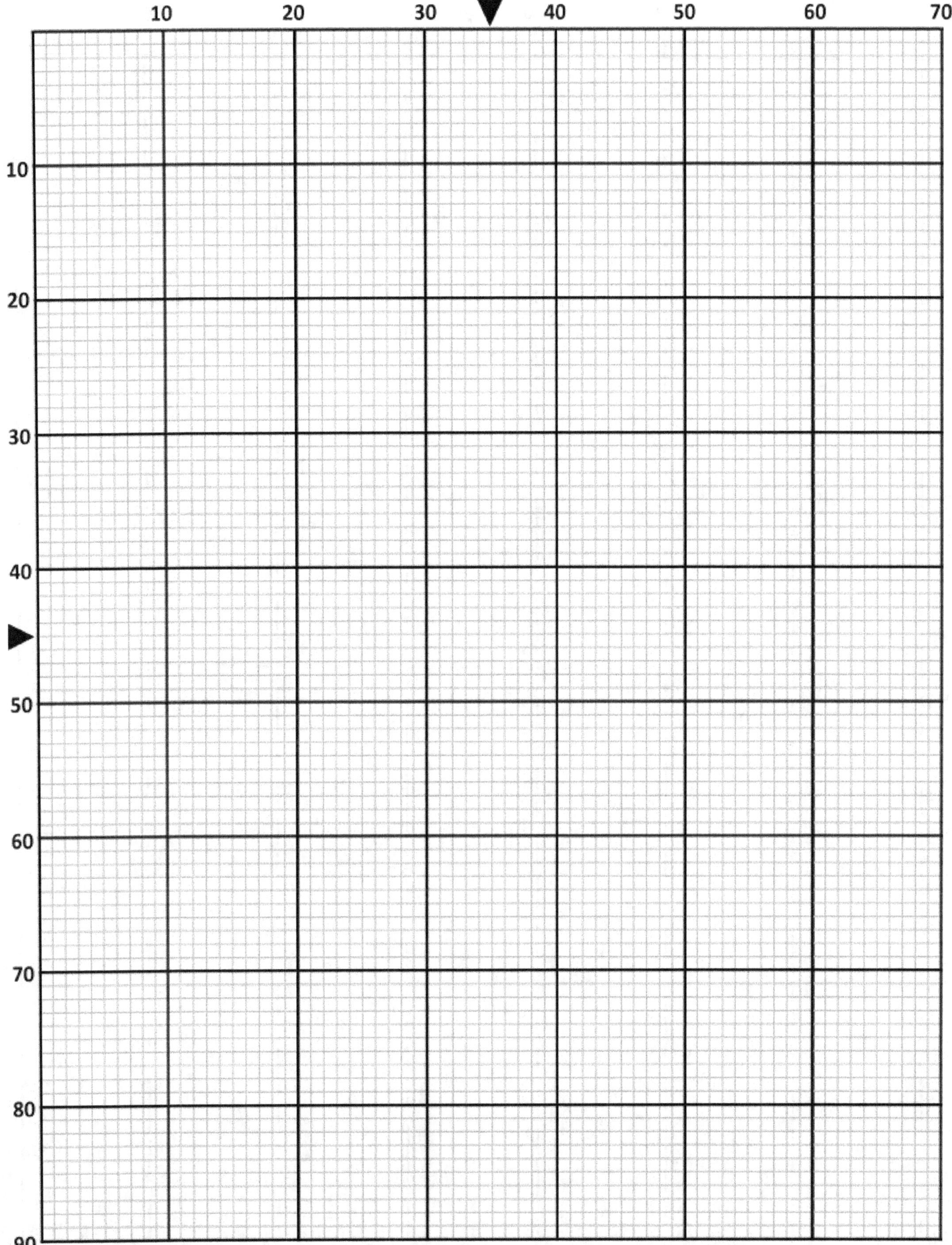

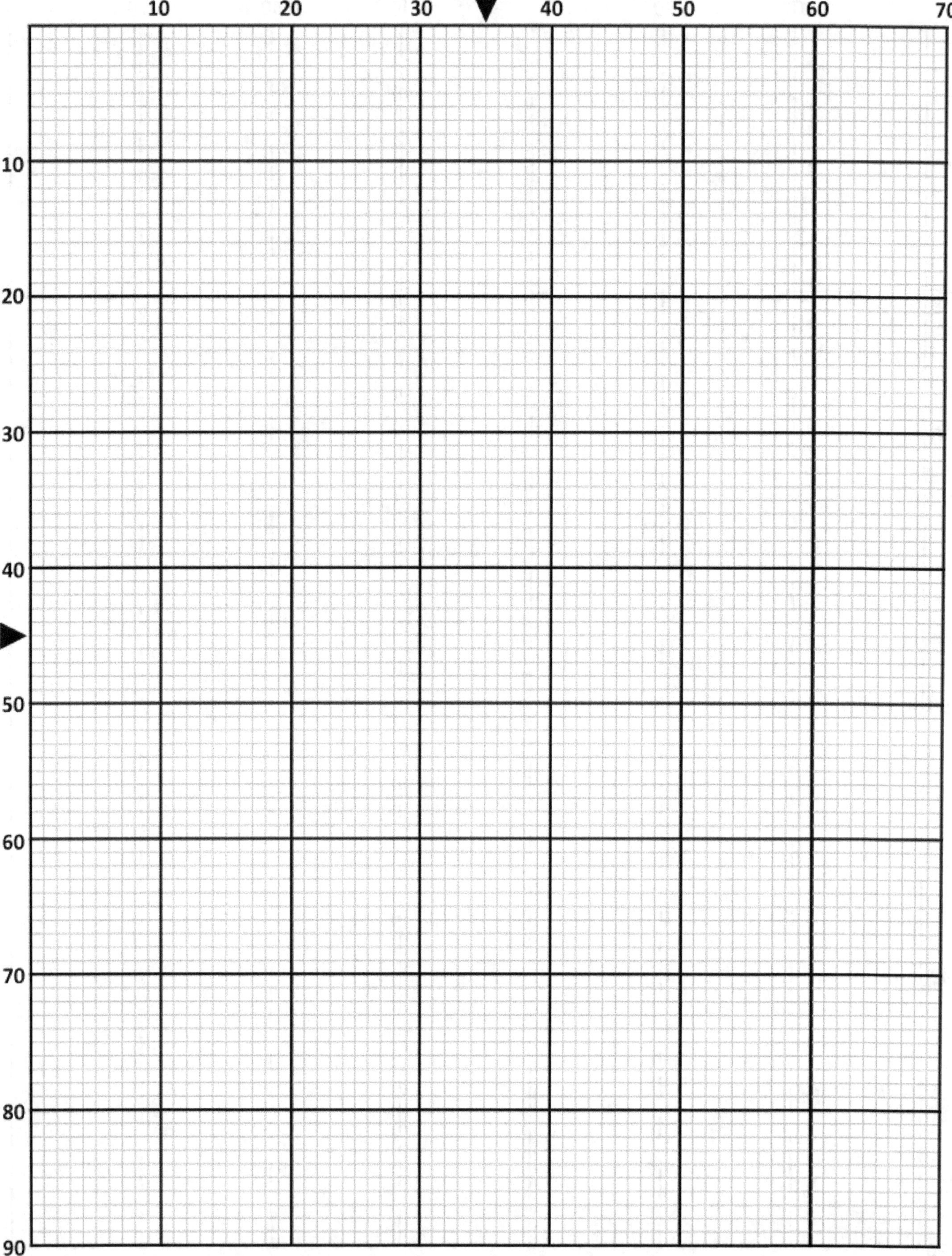

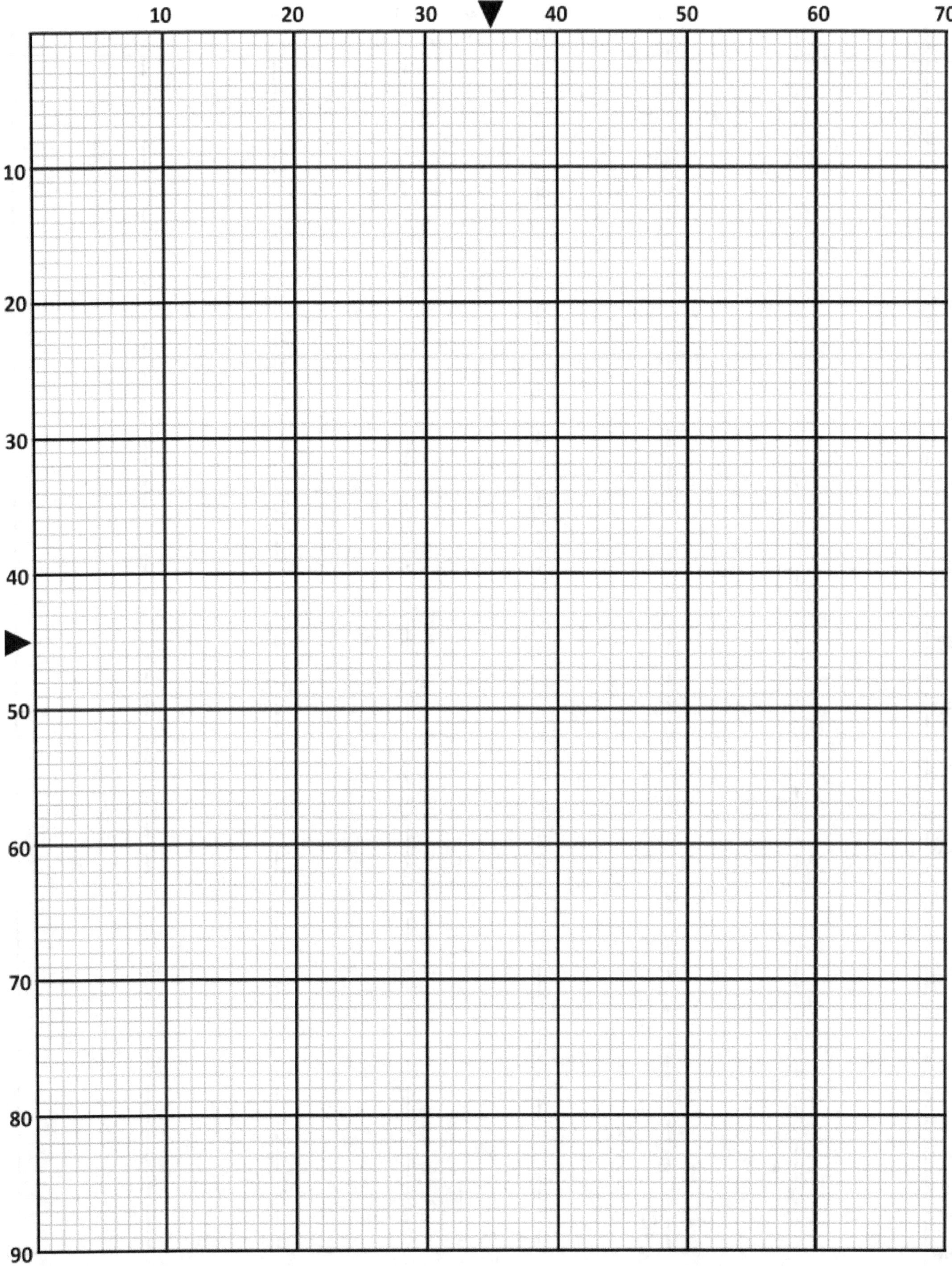

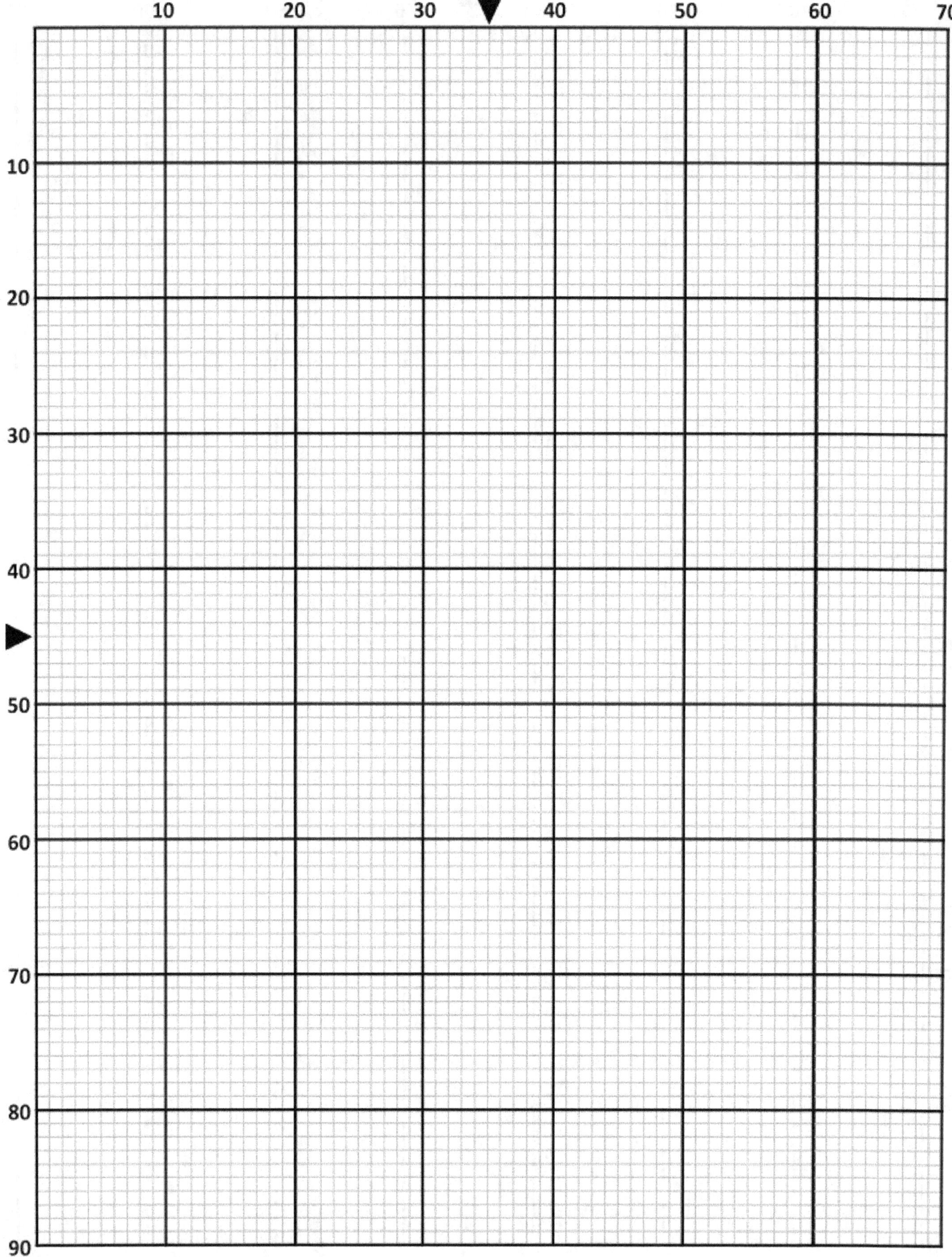

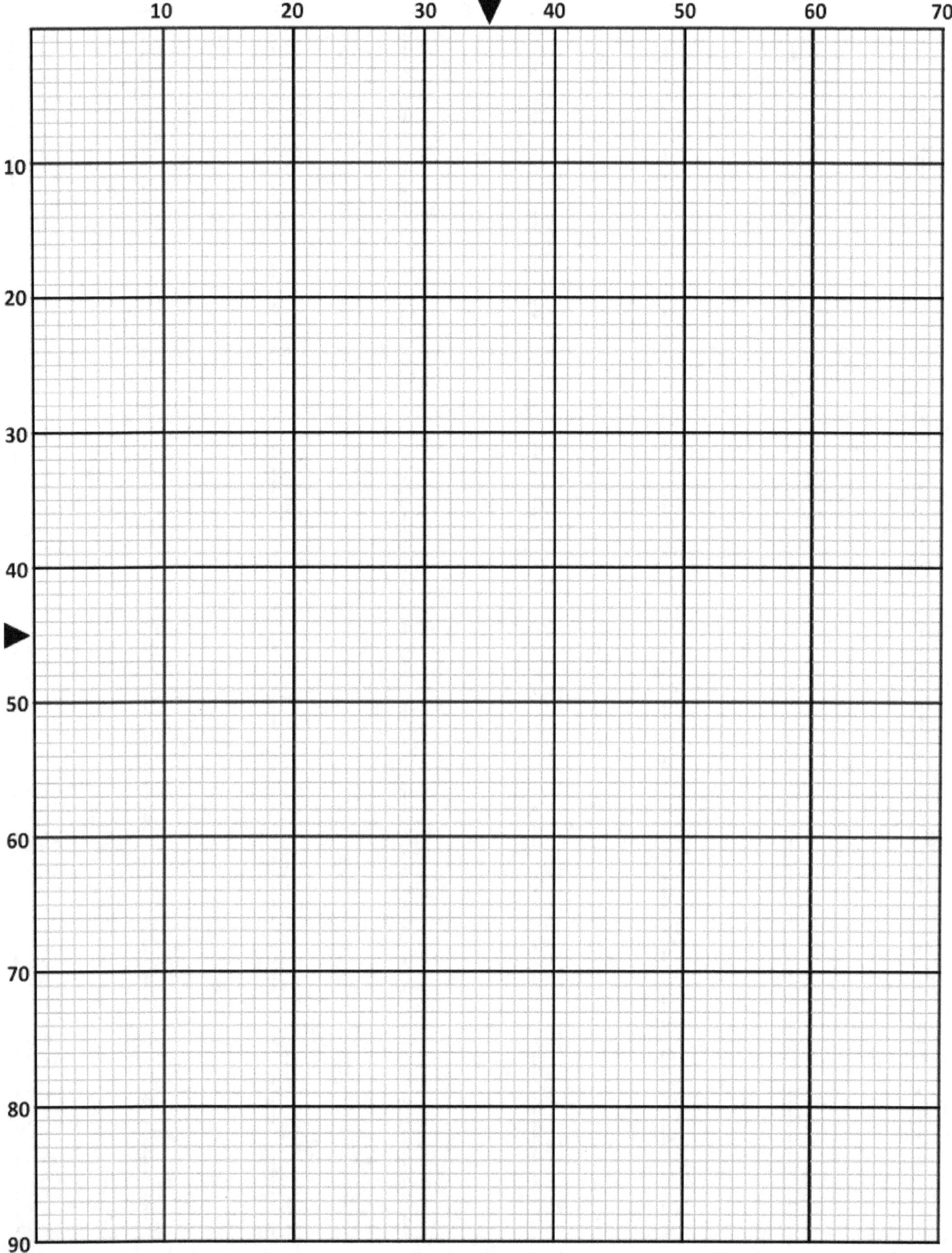

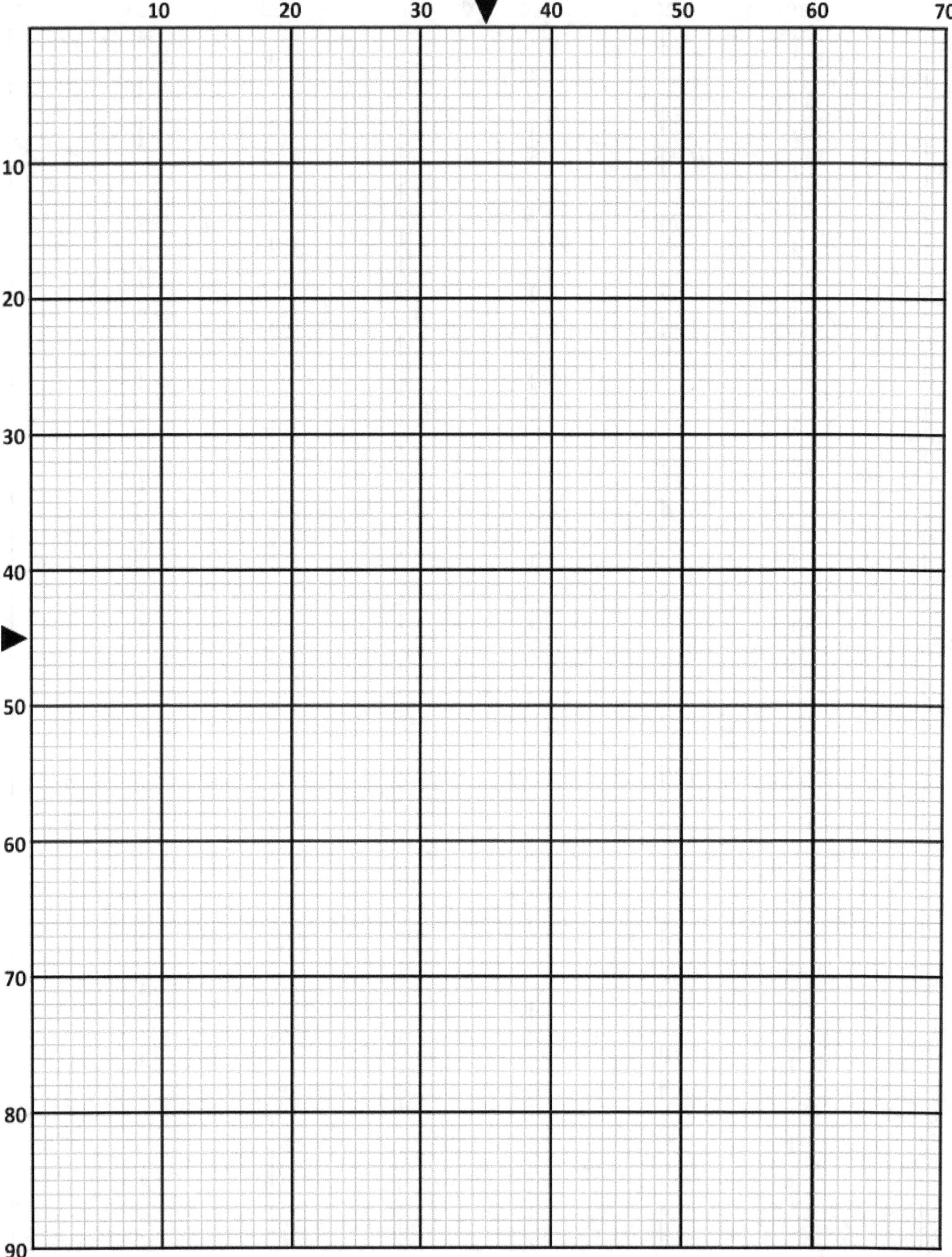

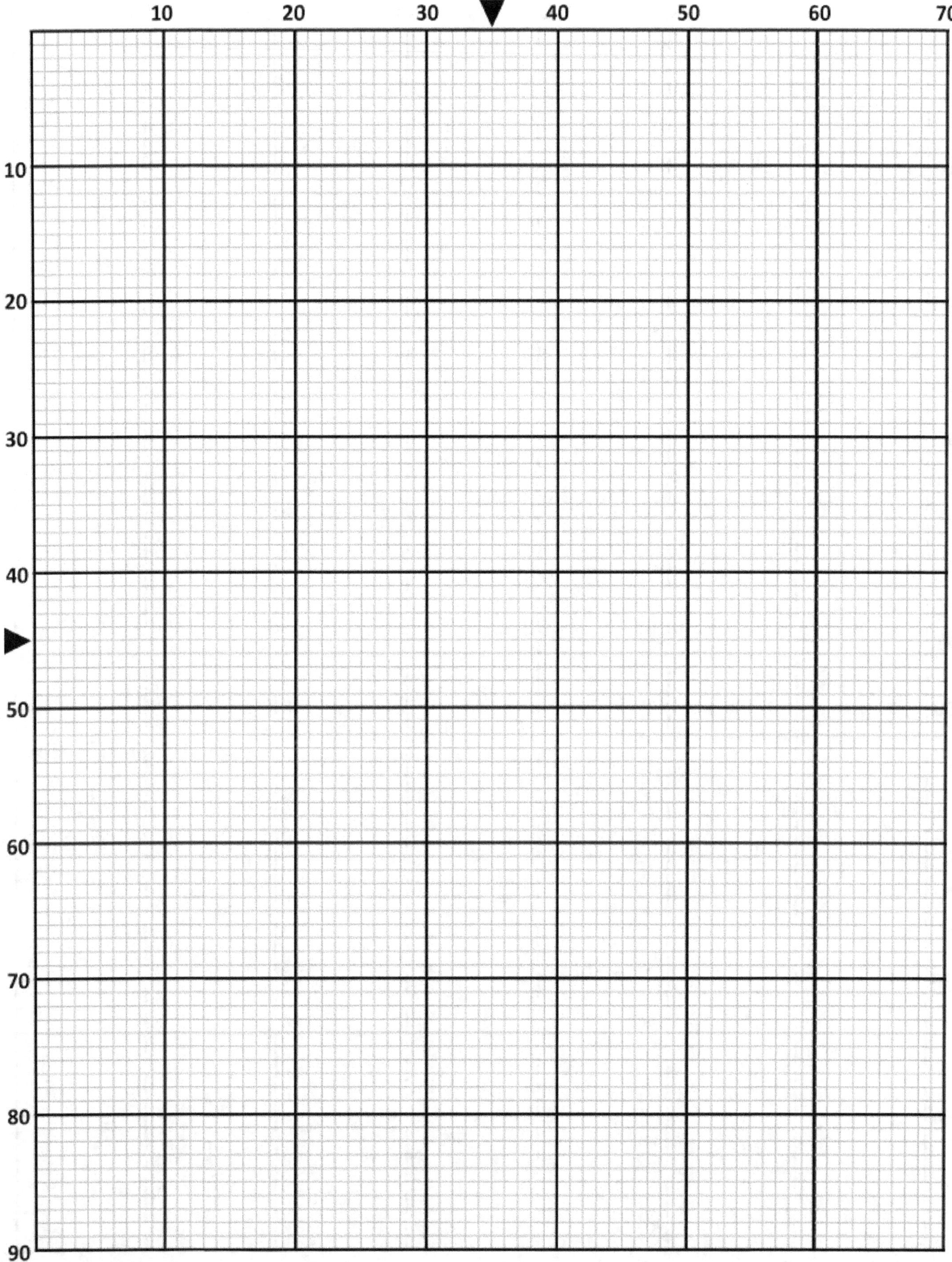

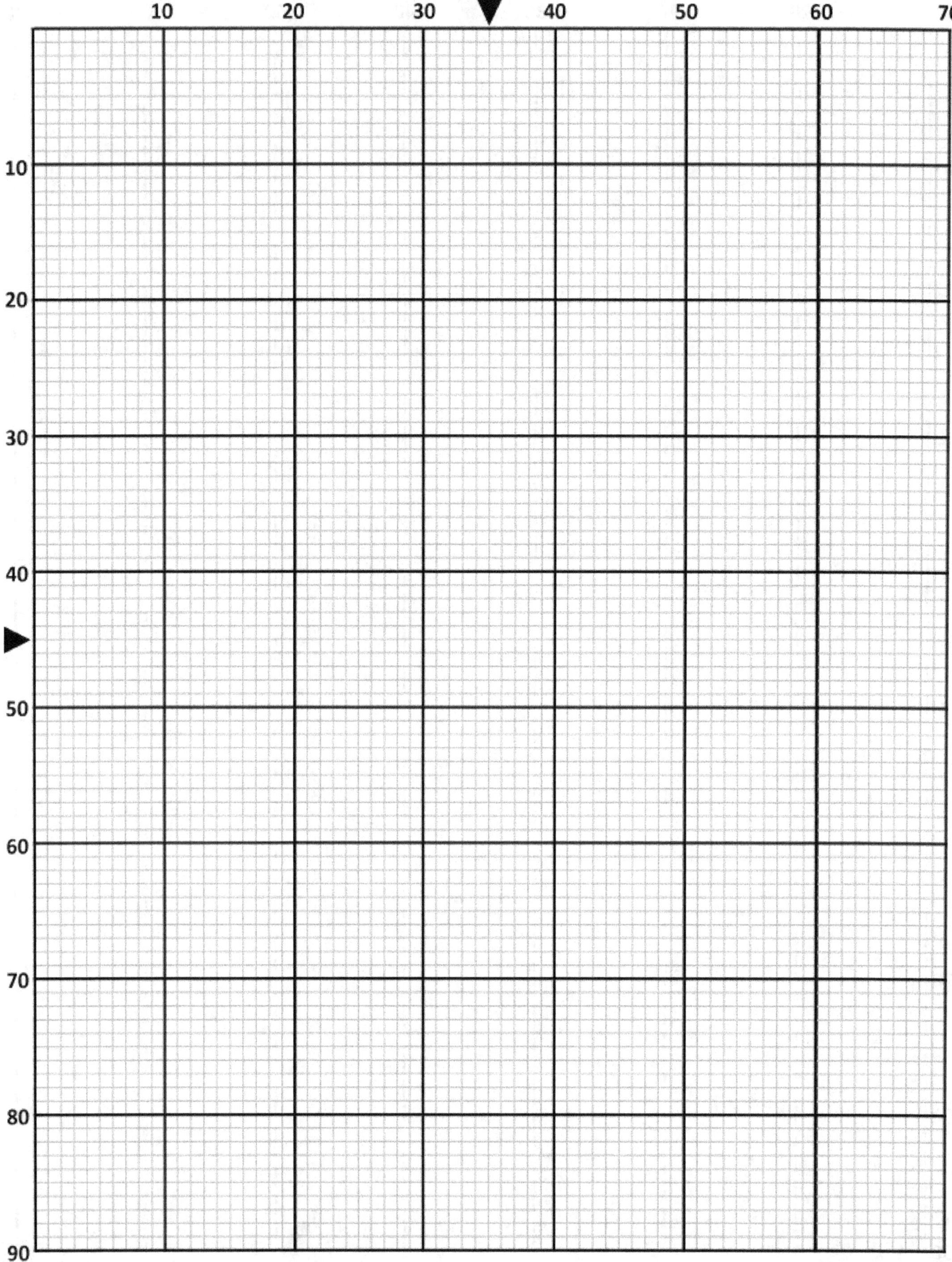

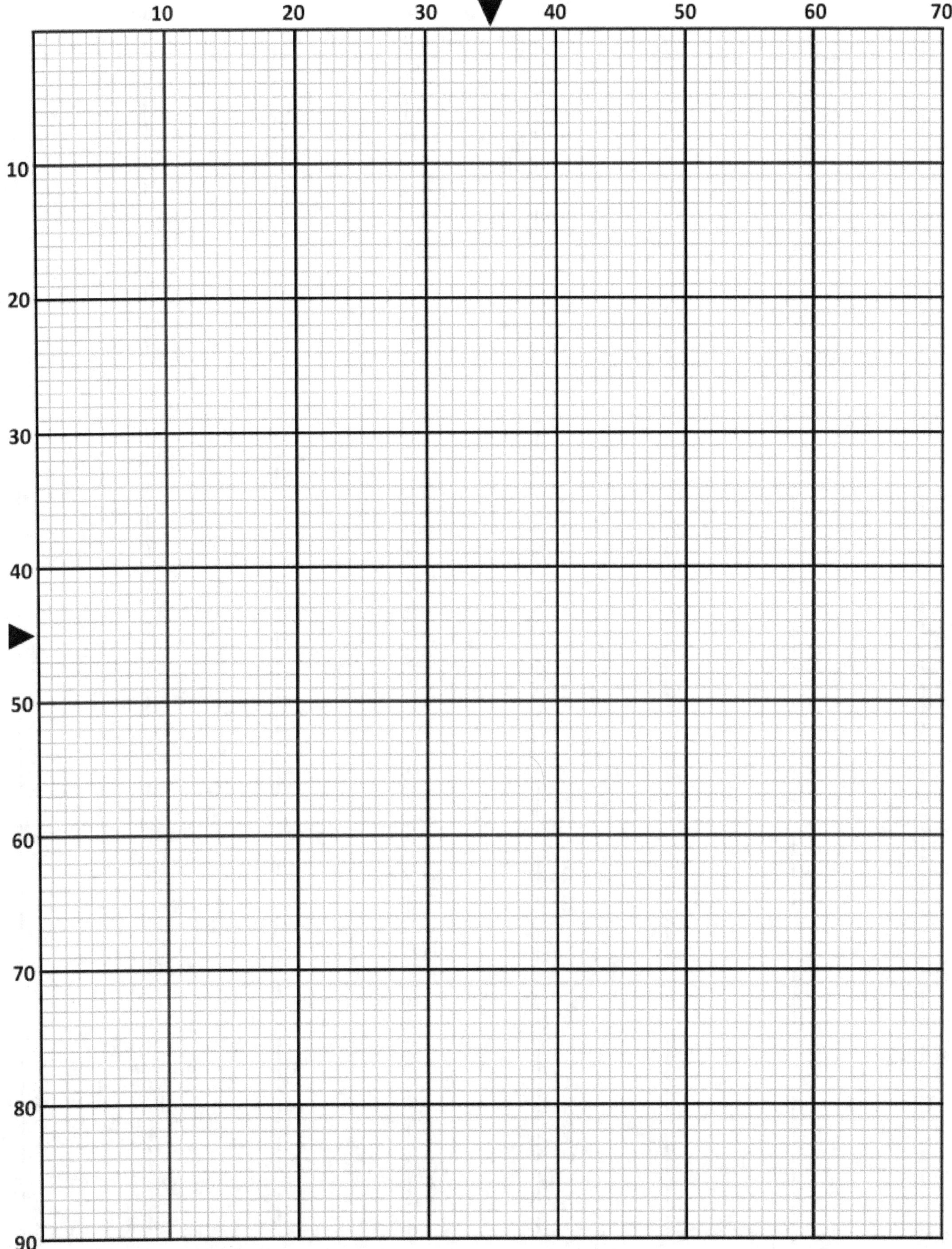

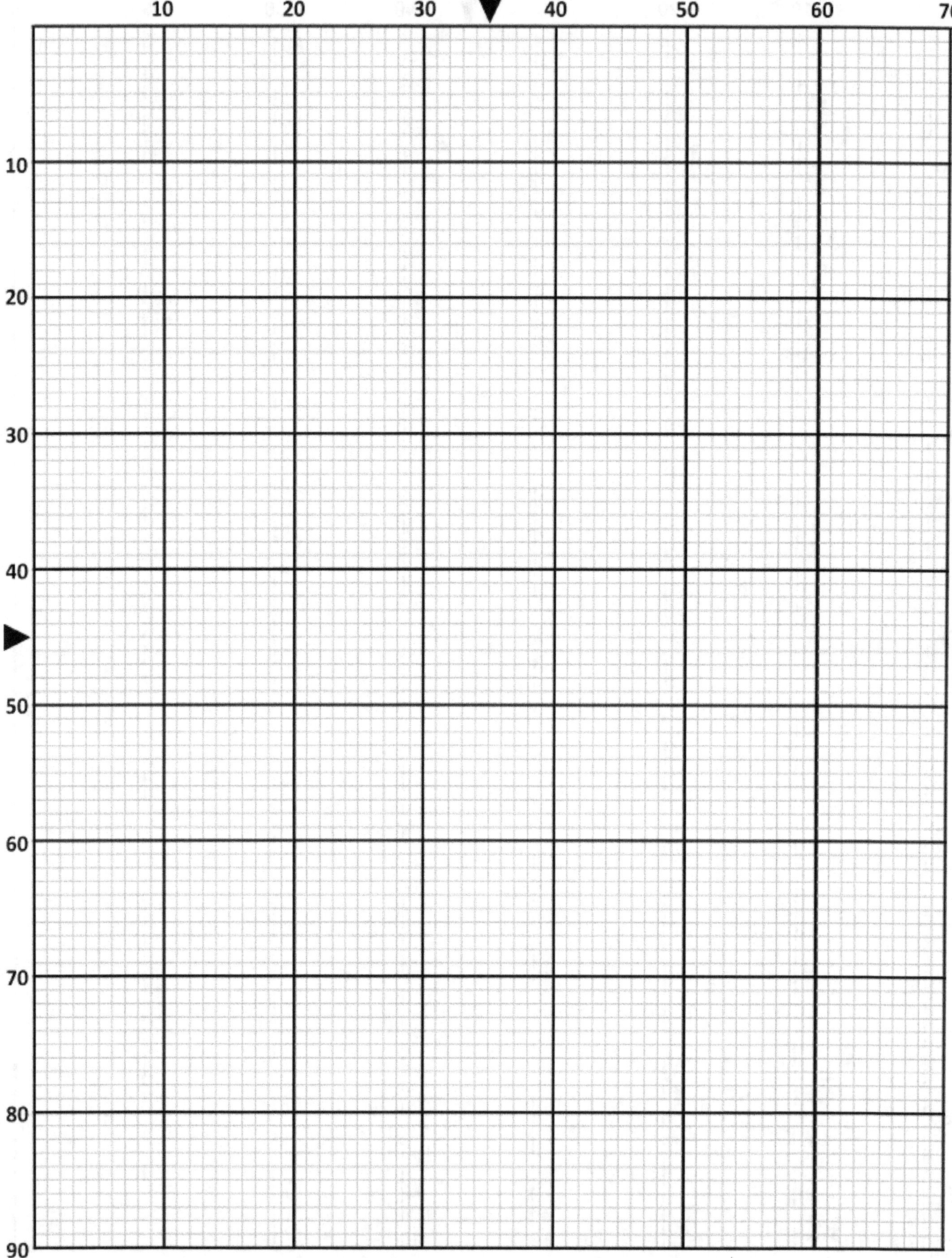

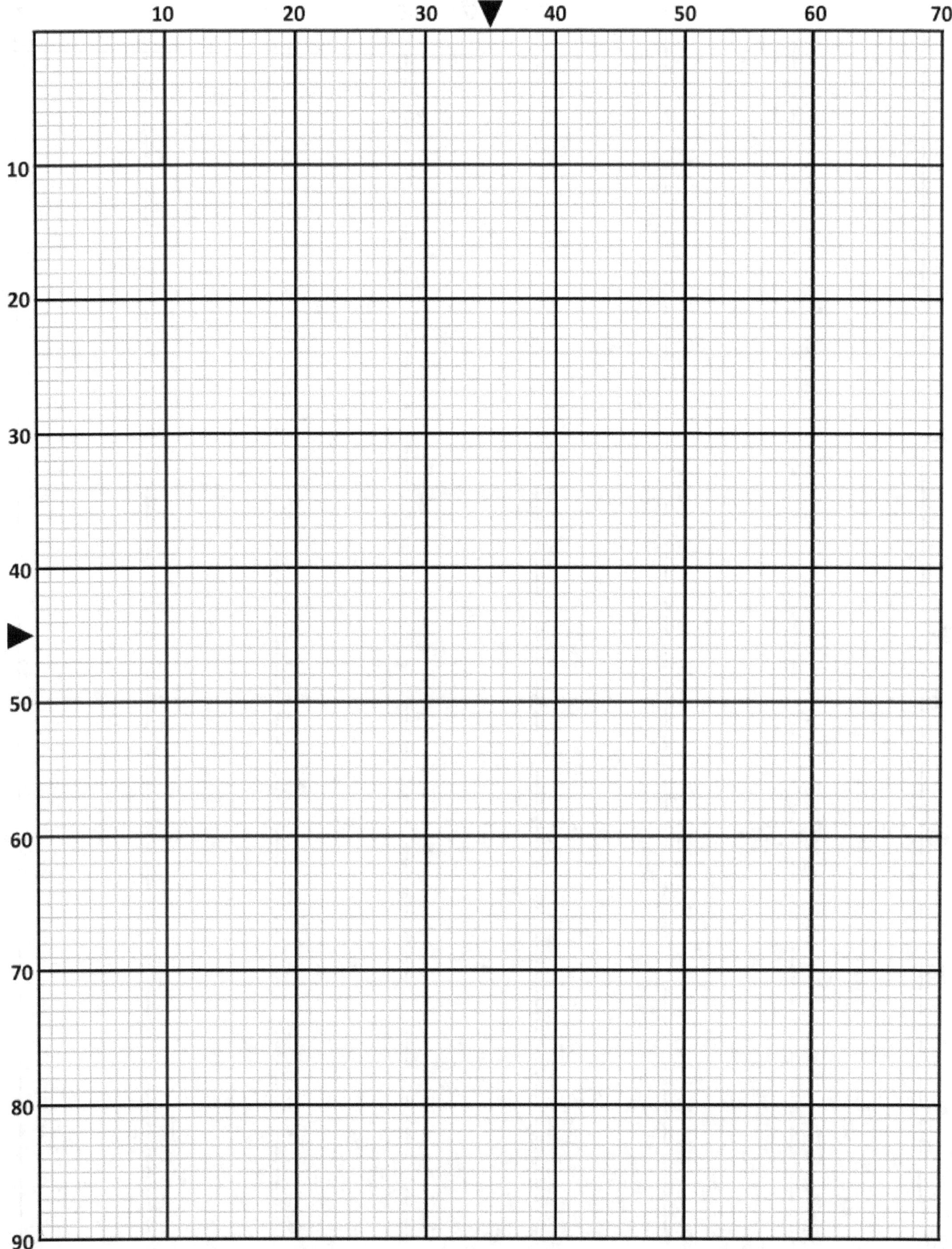

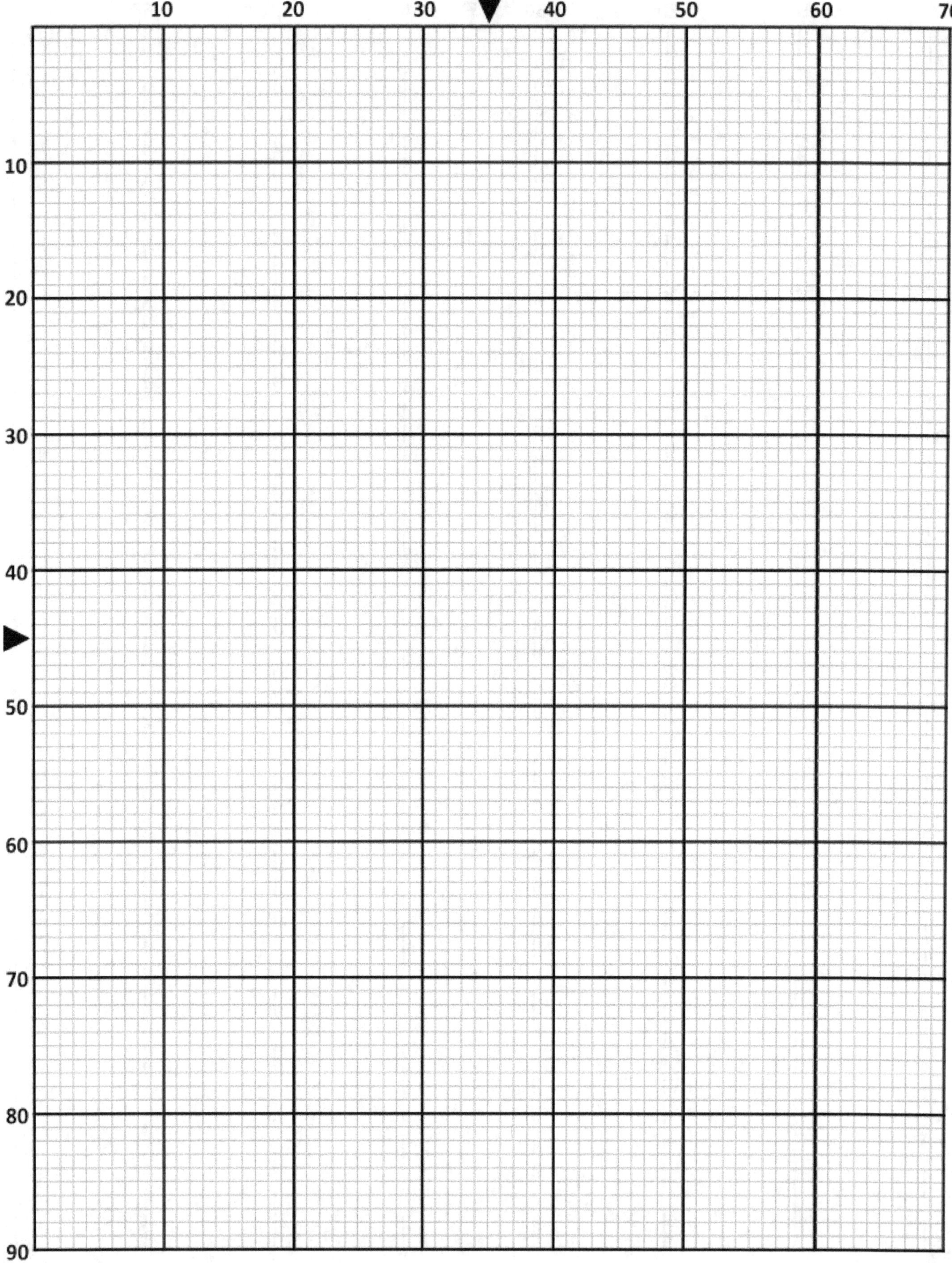

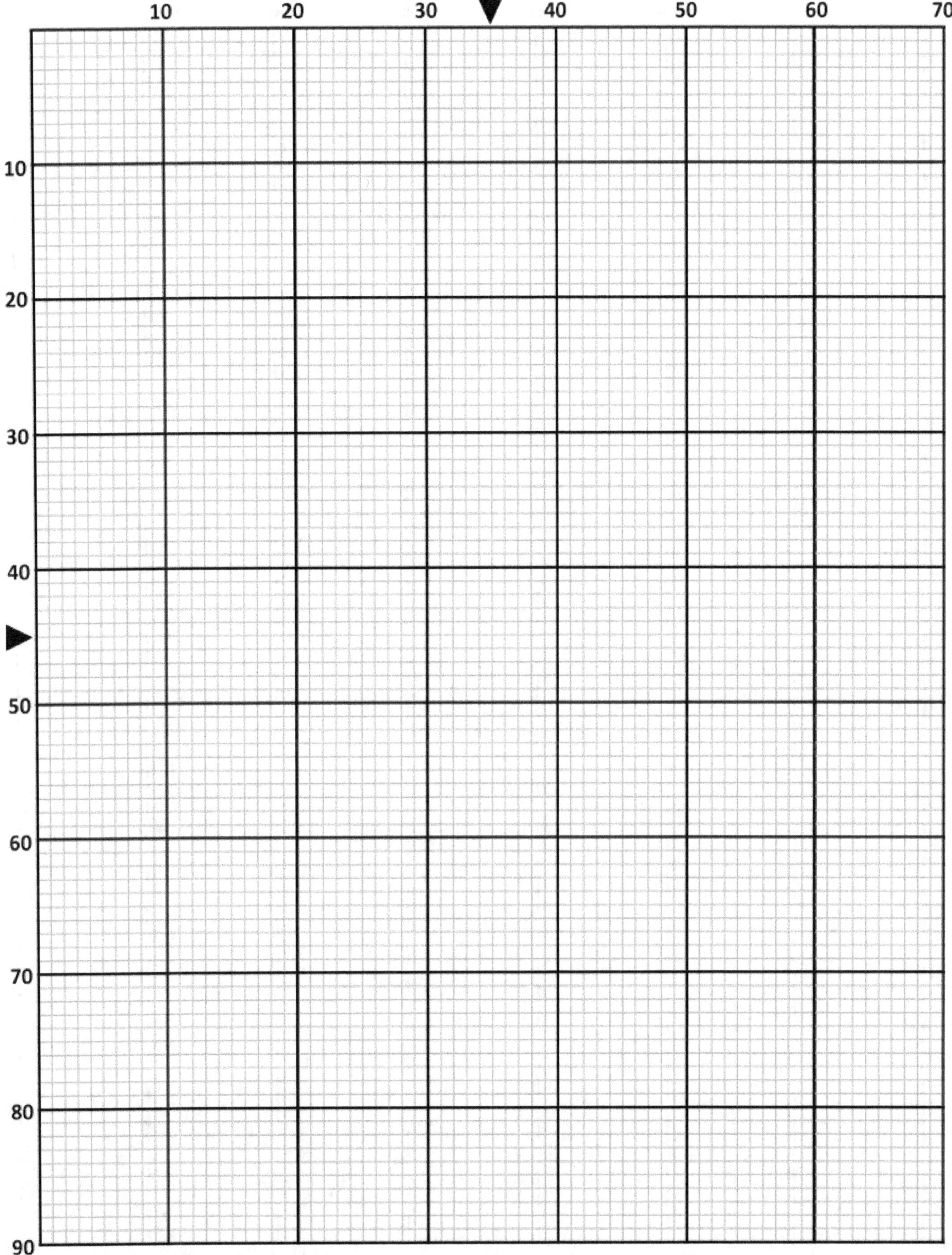

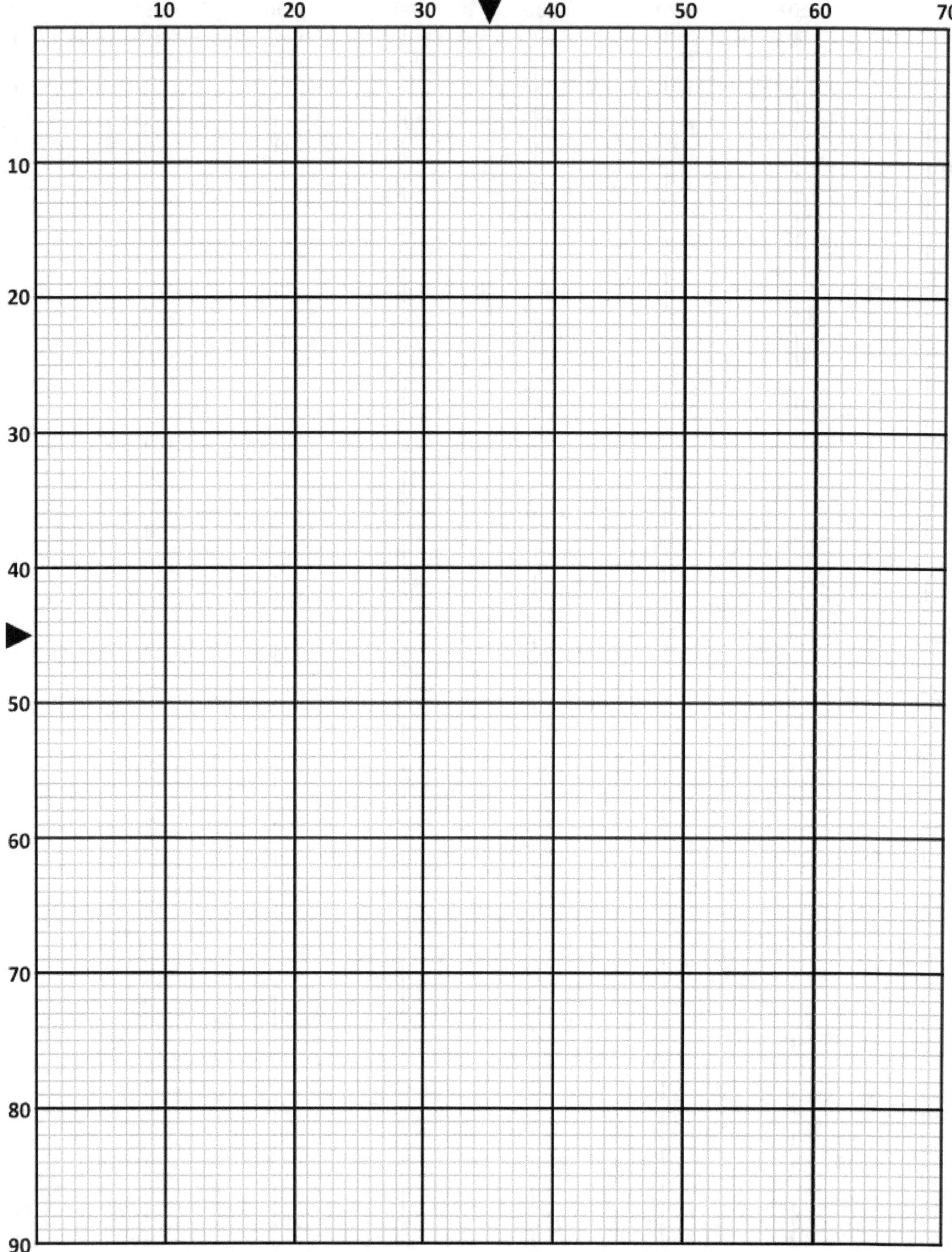

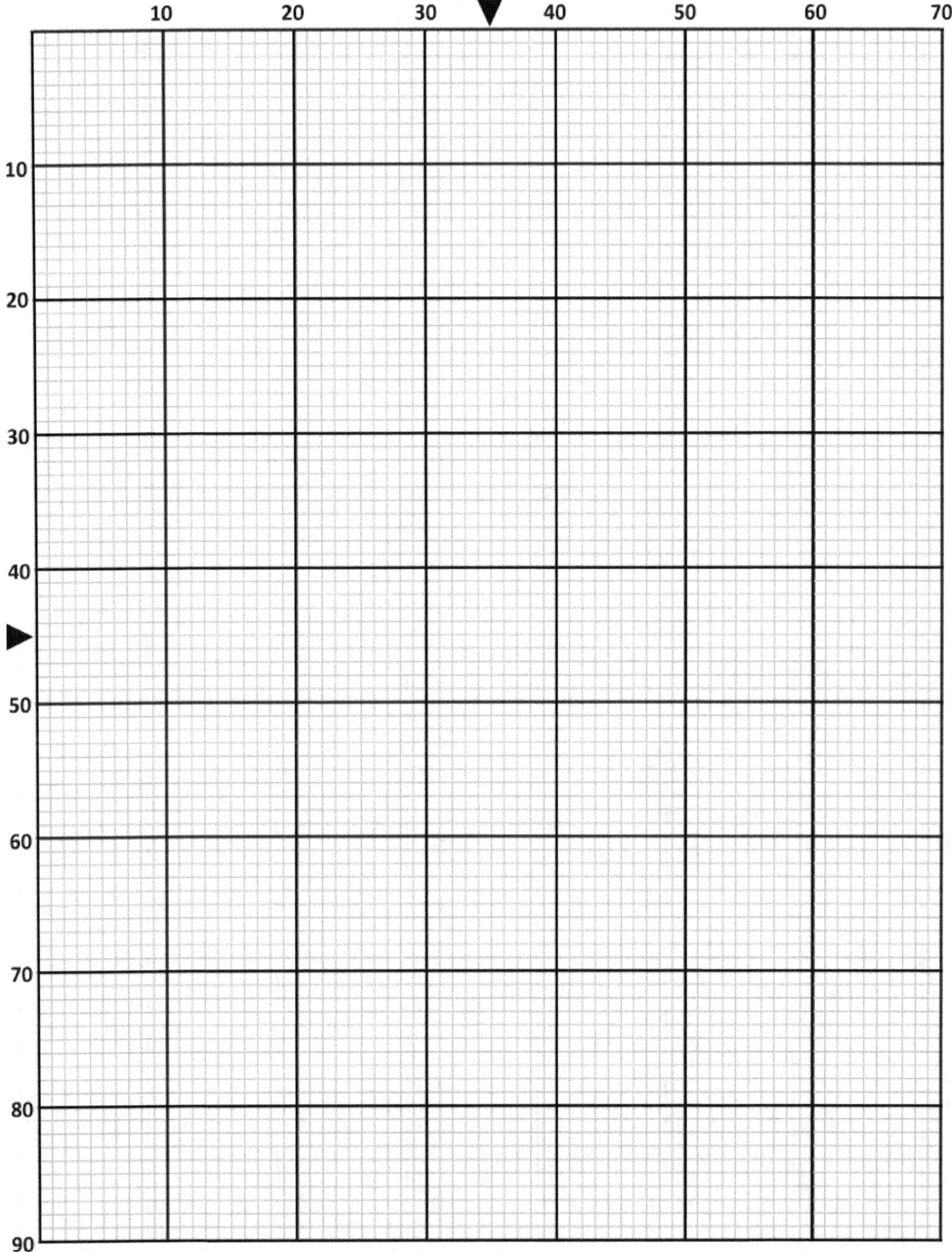

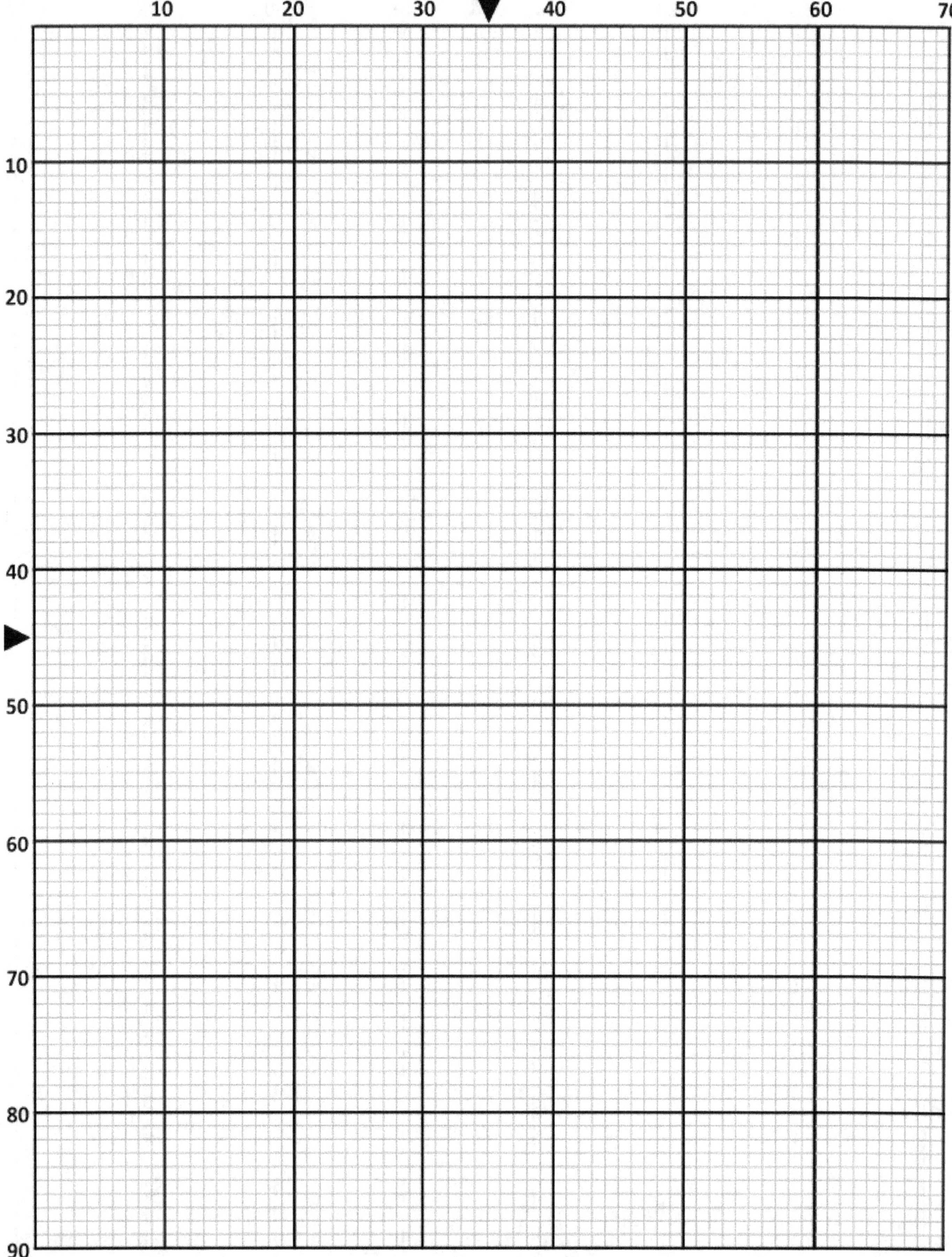

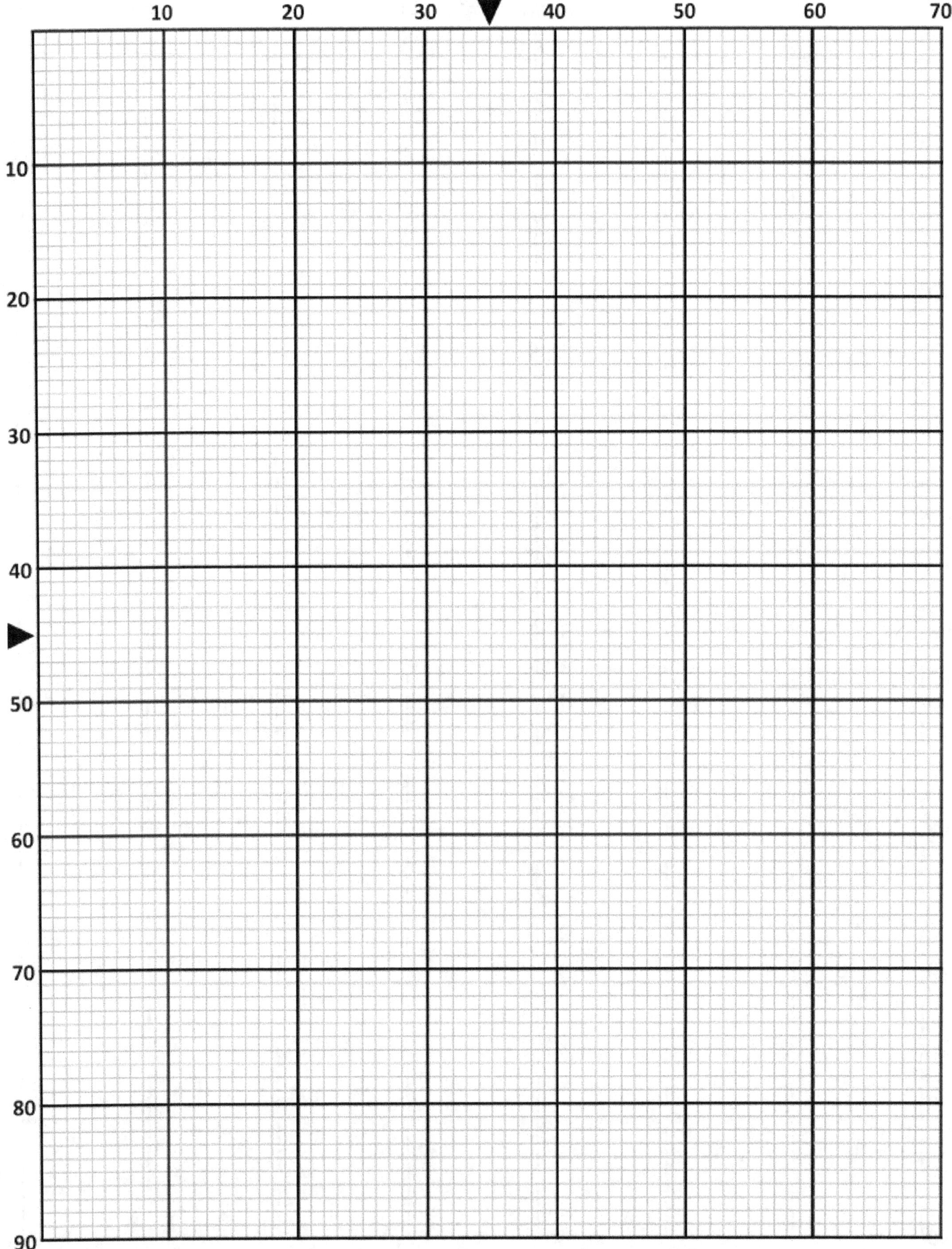

10
20
30
40
50
60
70
10
20
30
40
50
60
70
80
90

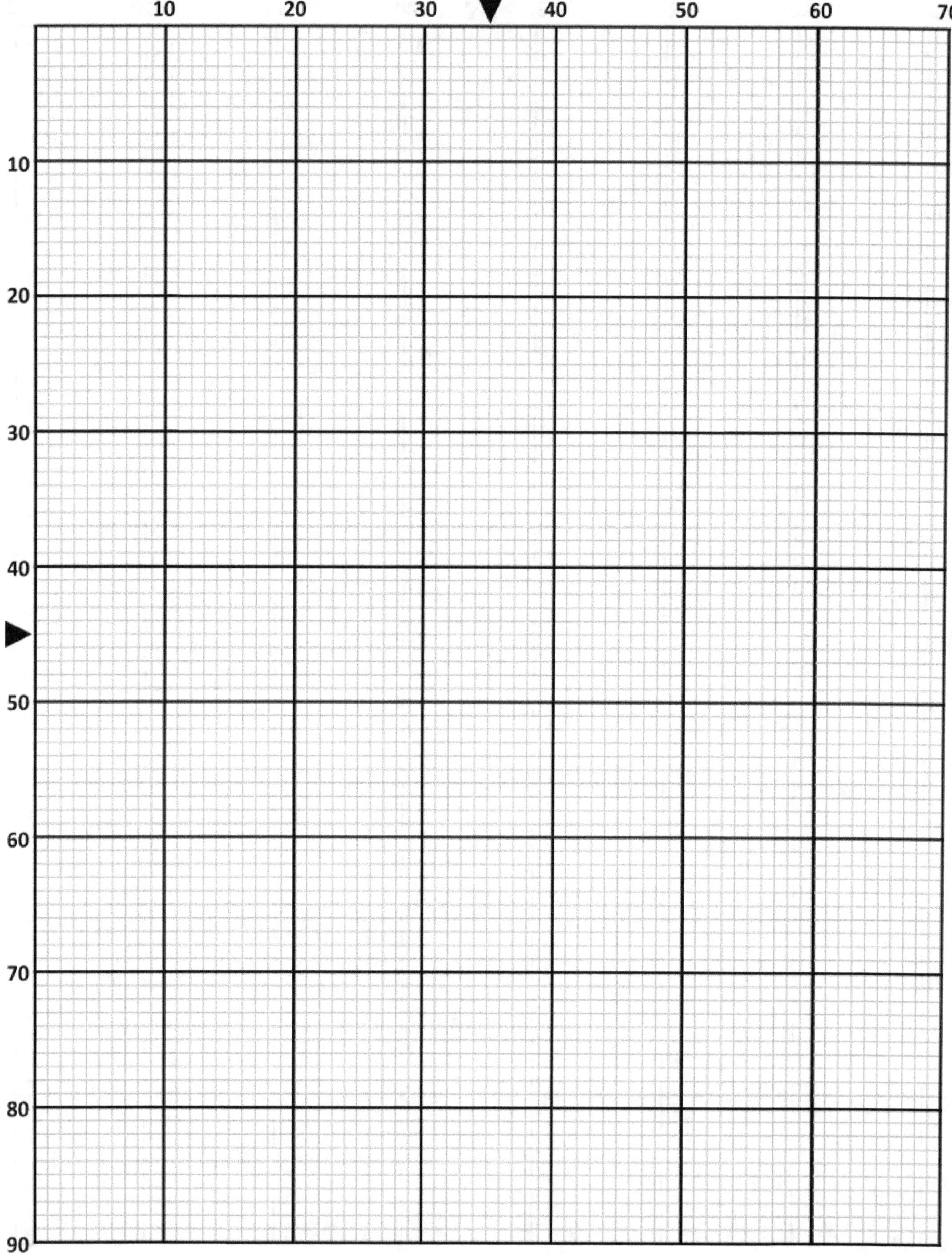

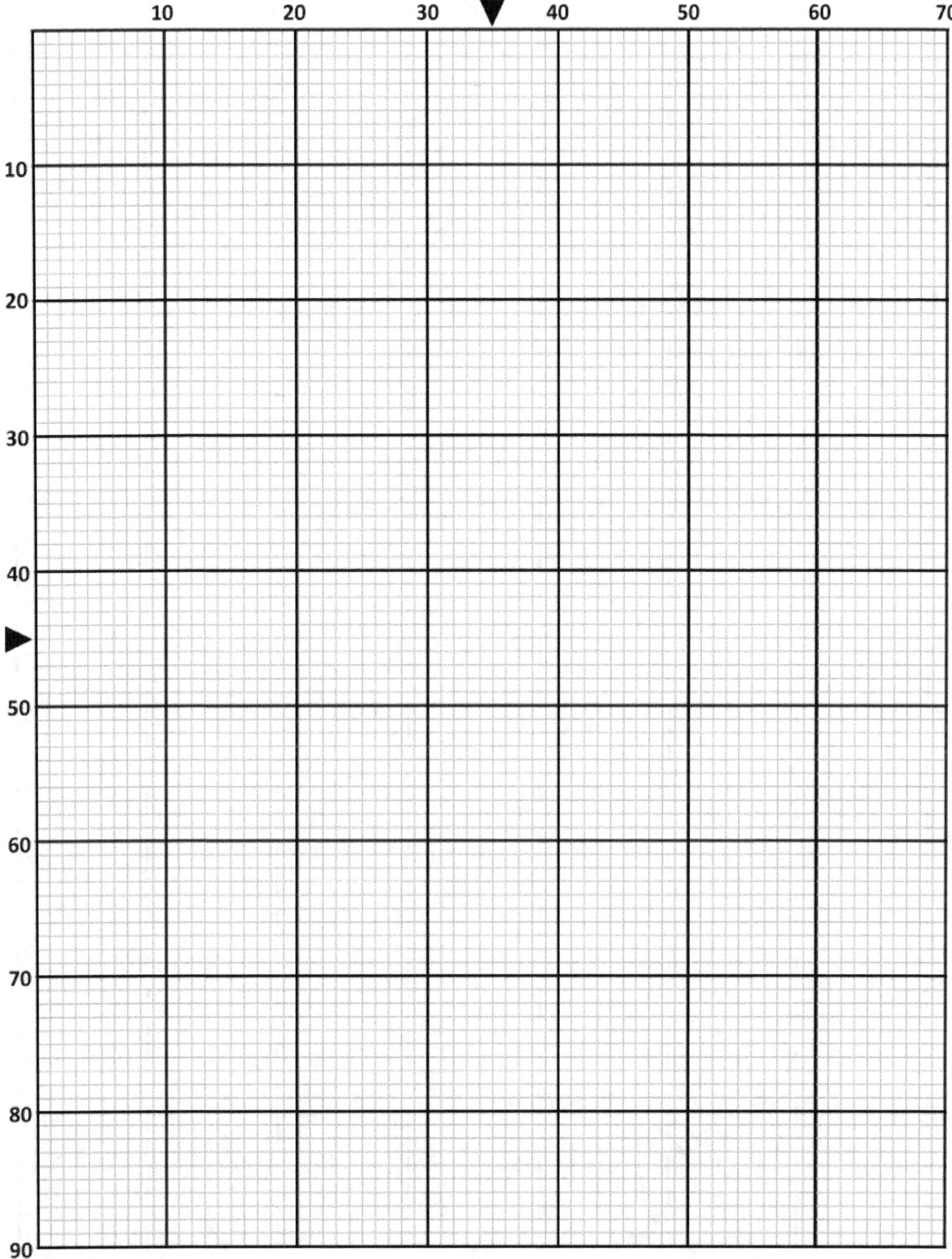

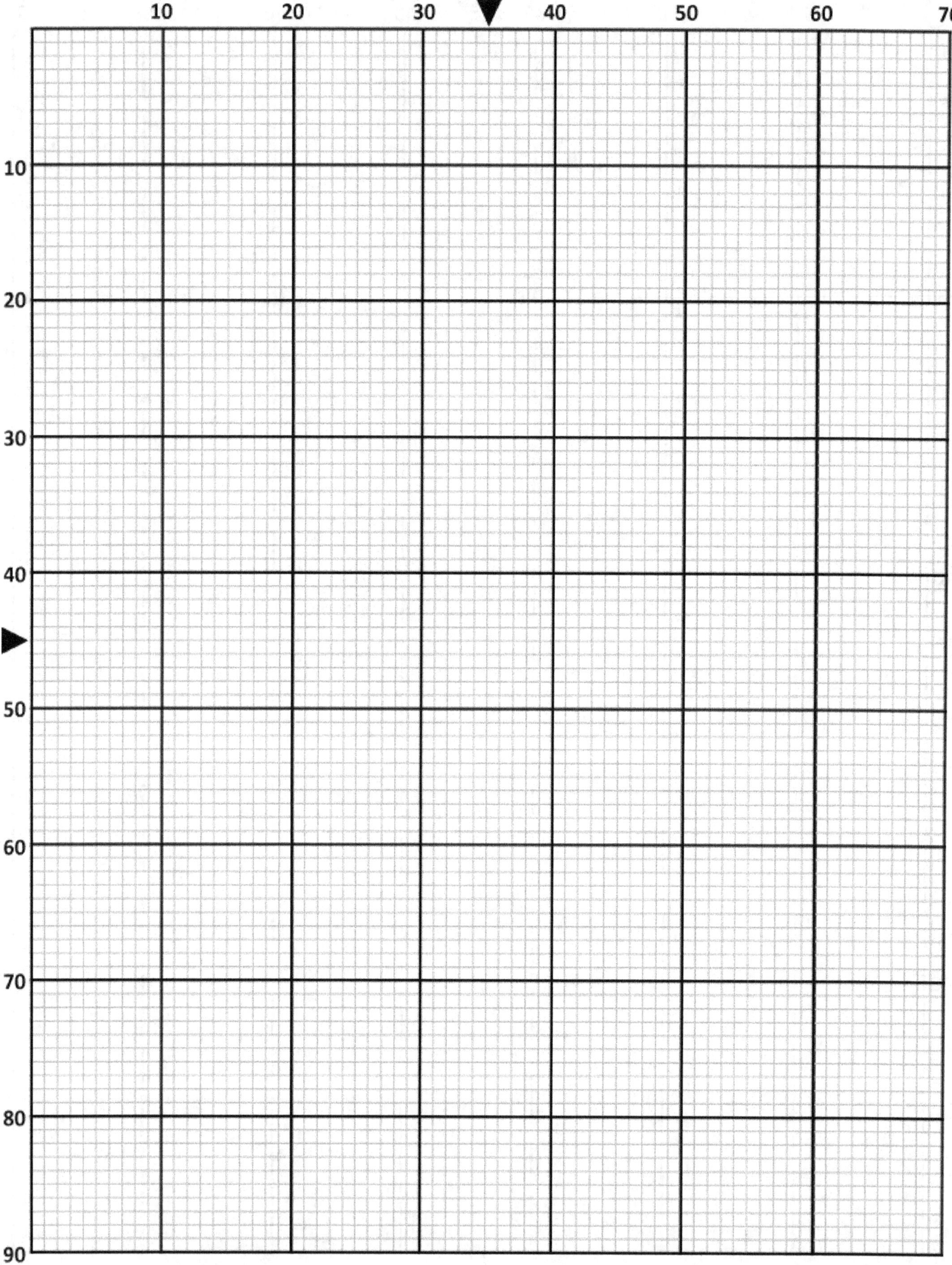

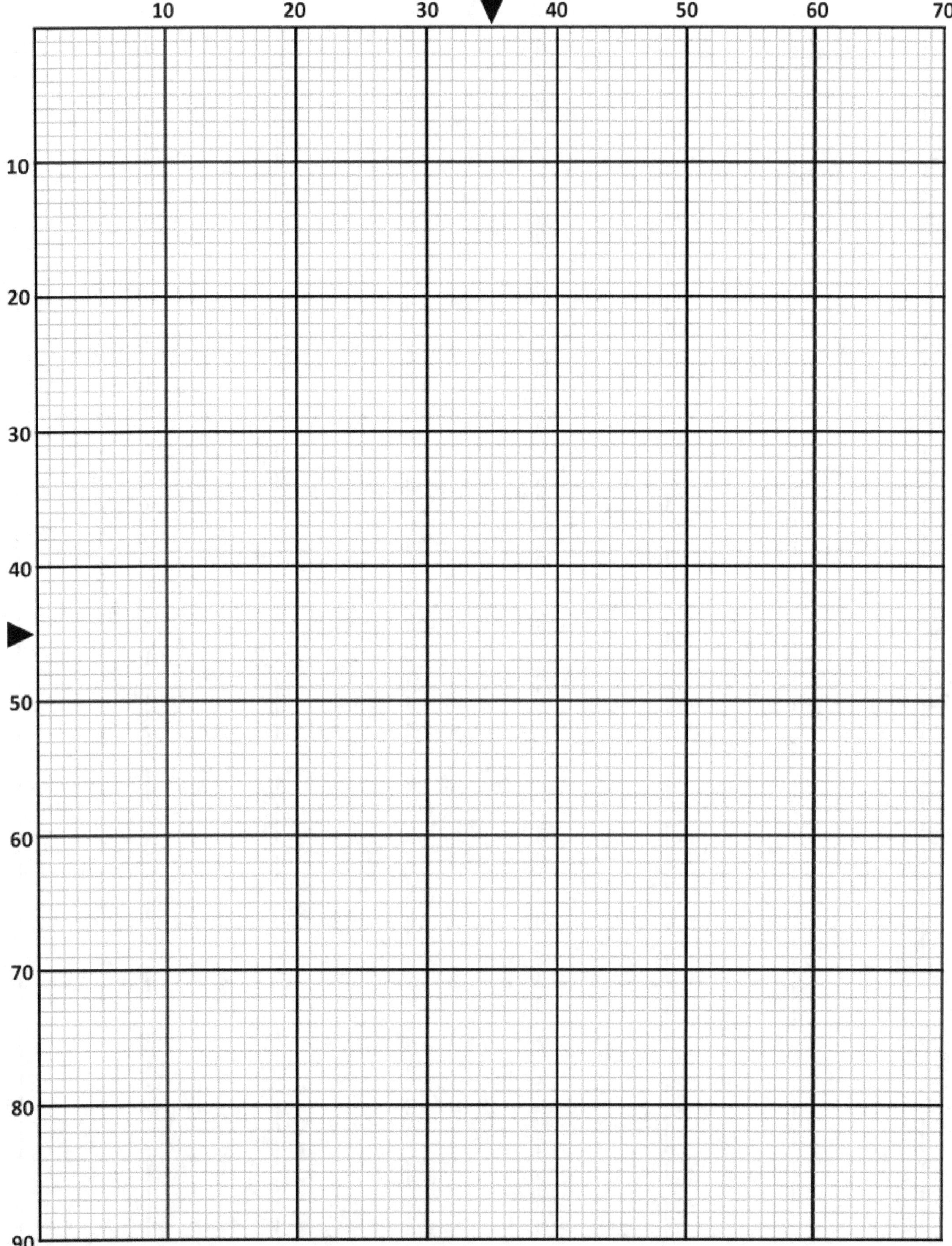

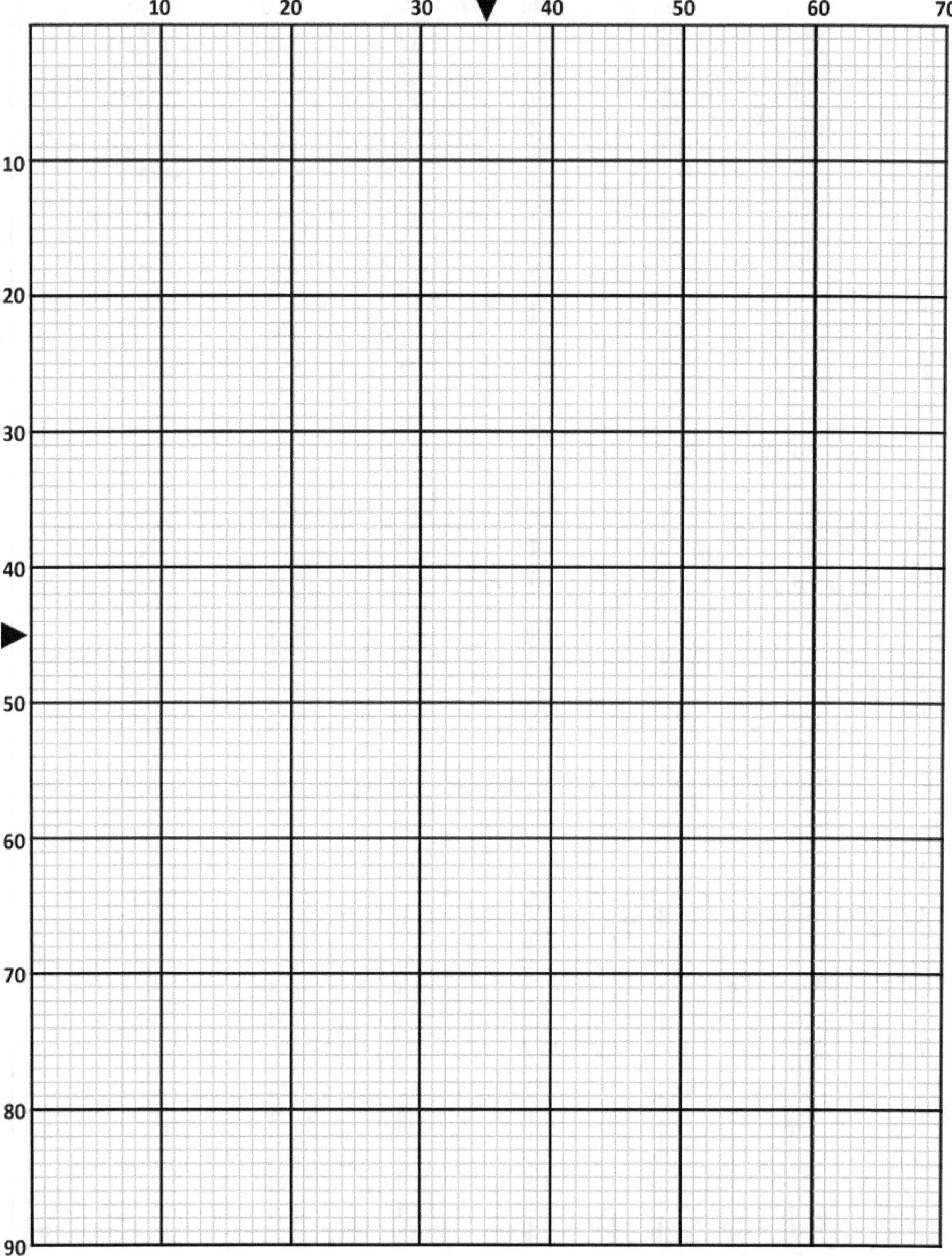

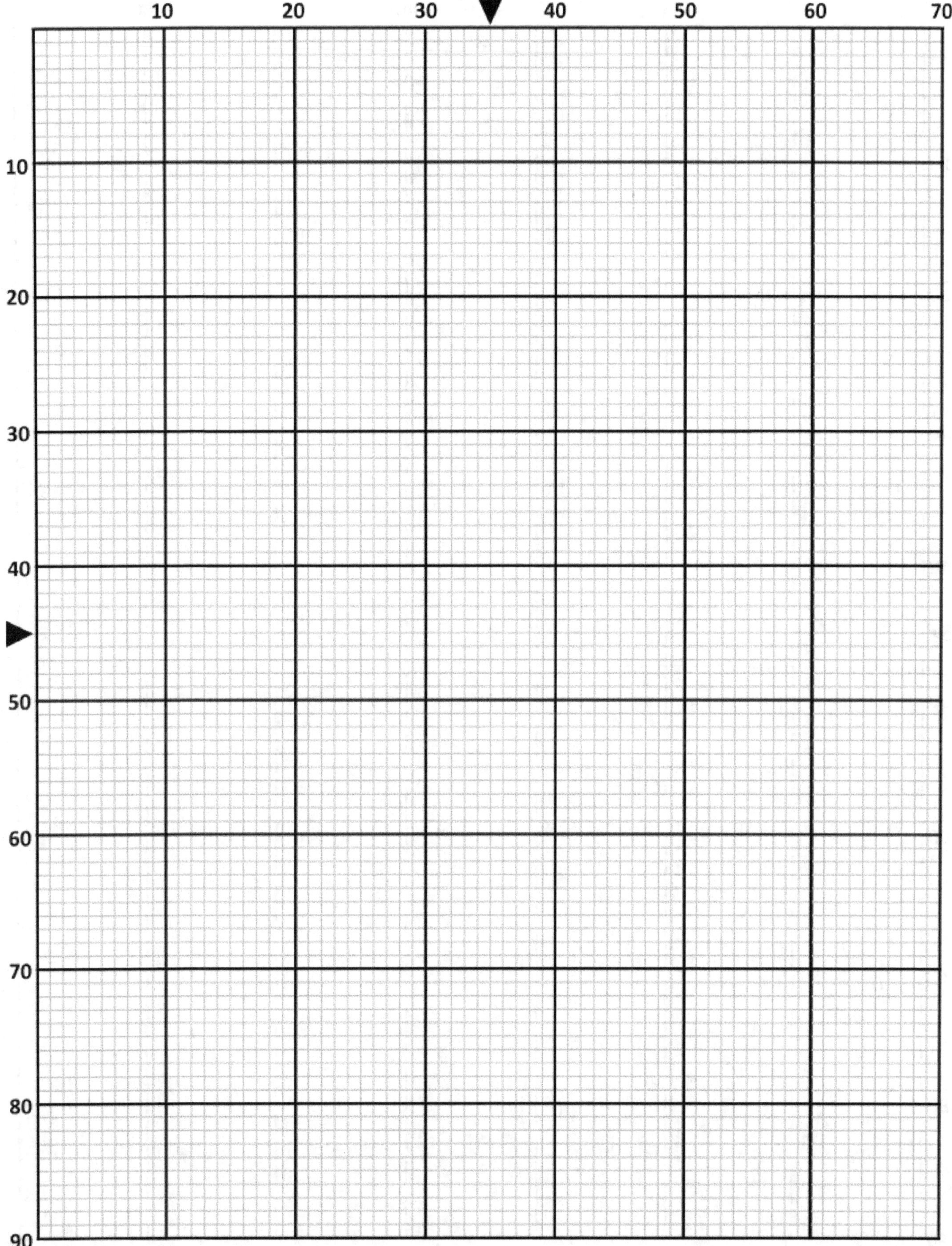

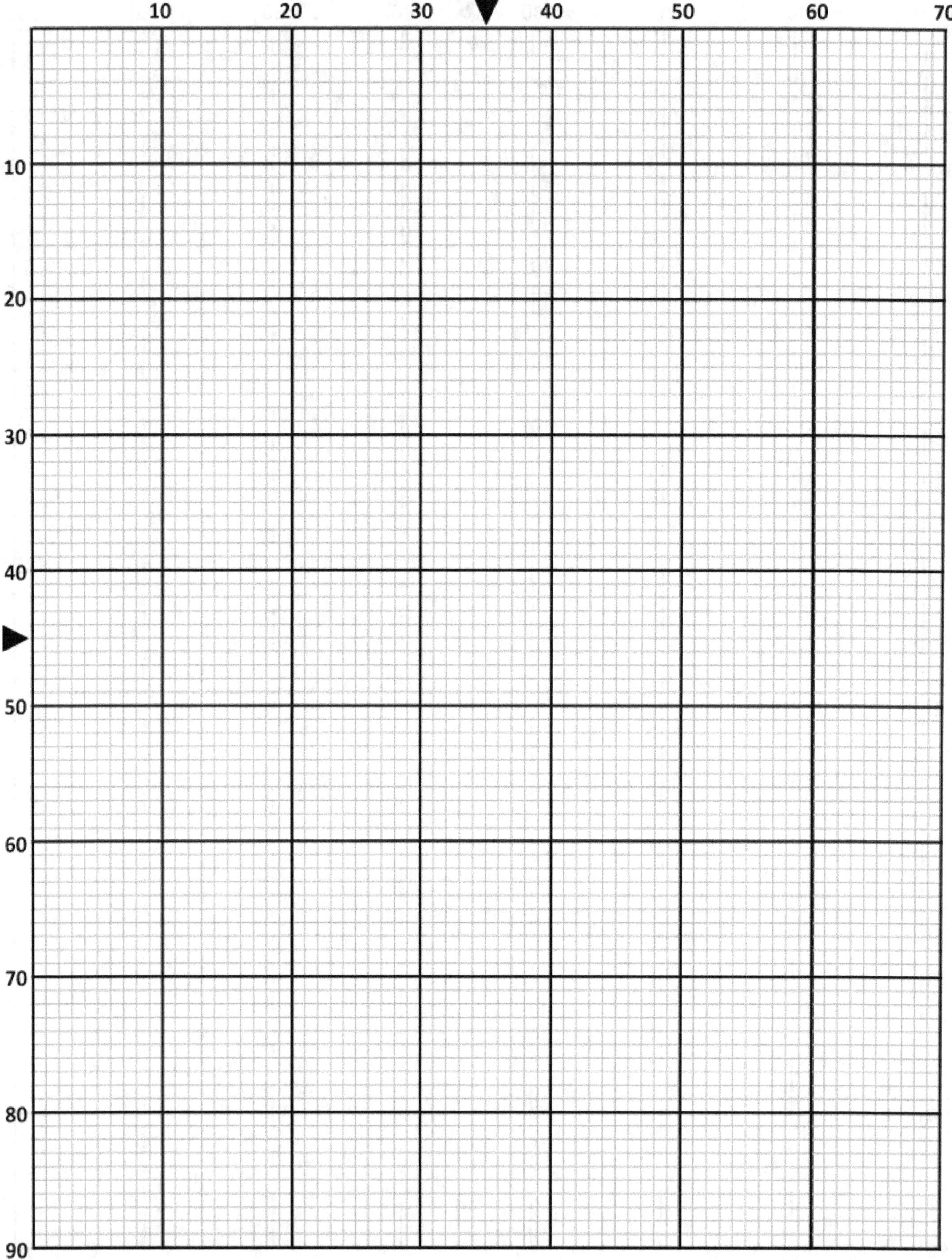

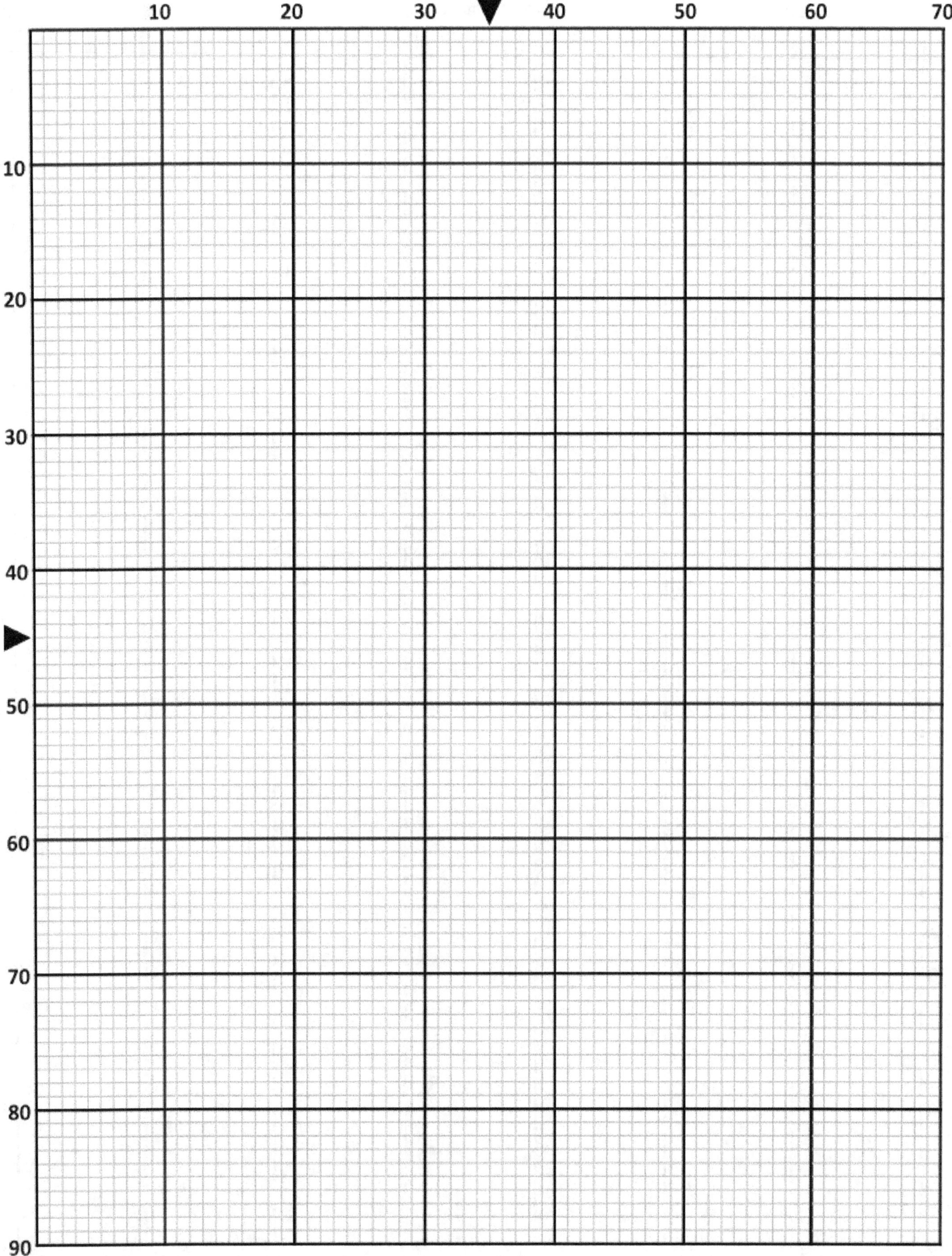

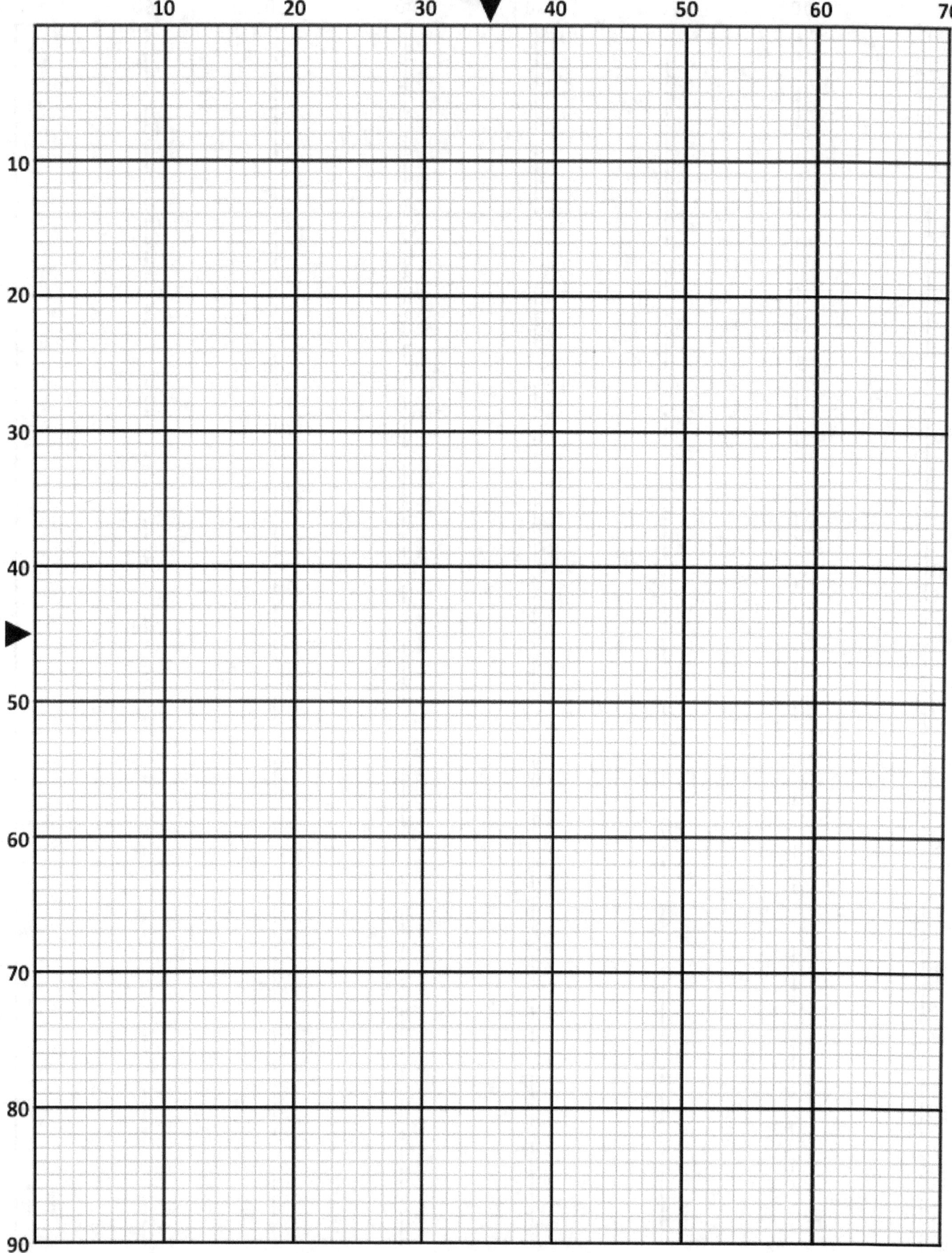

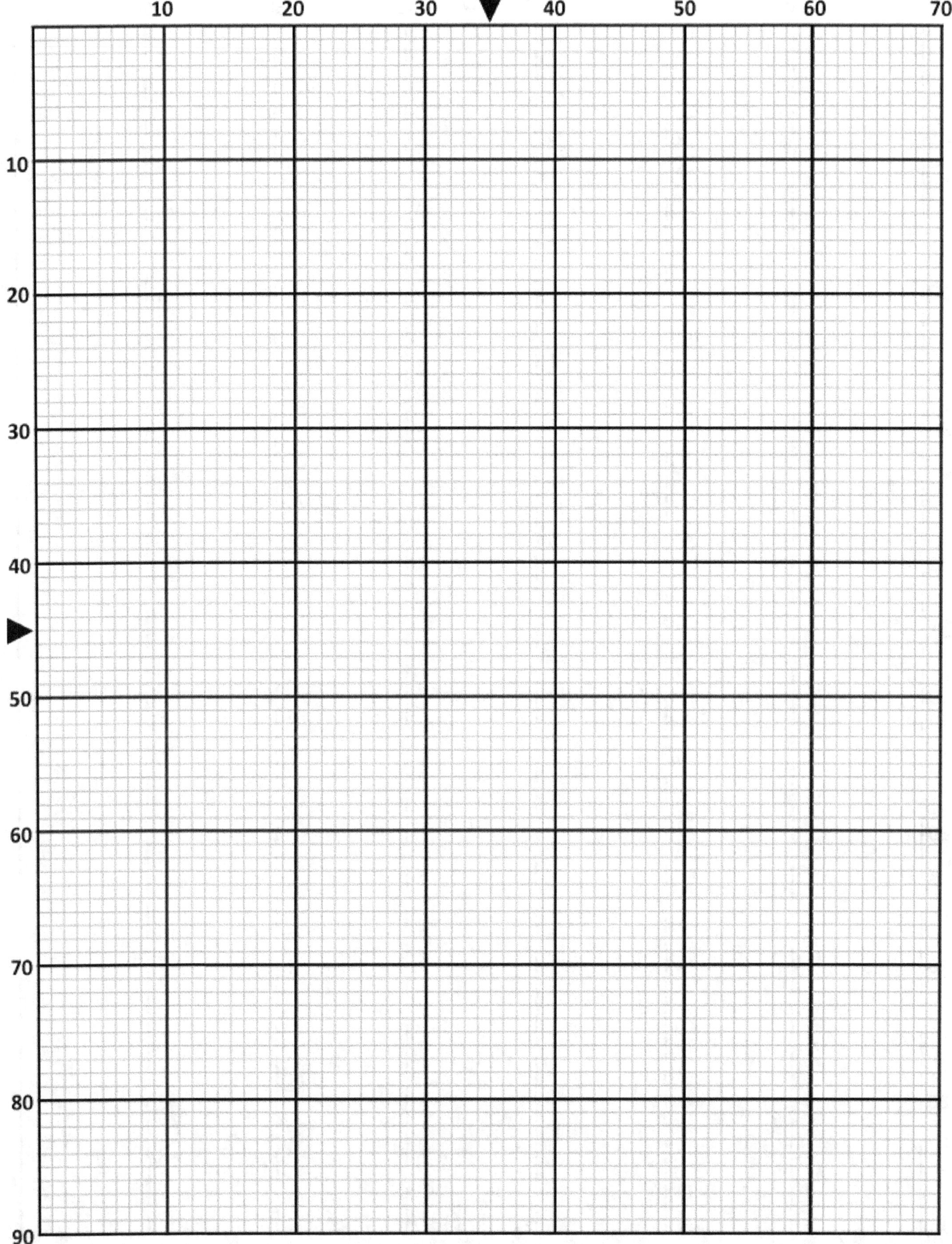

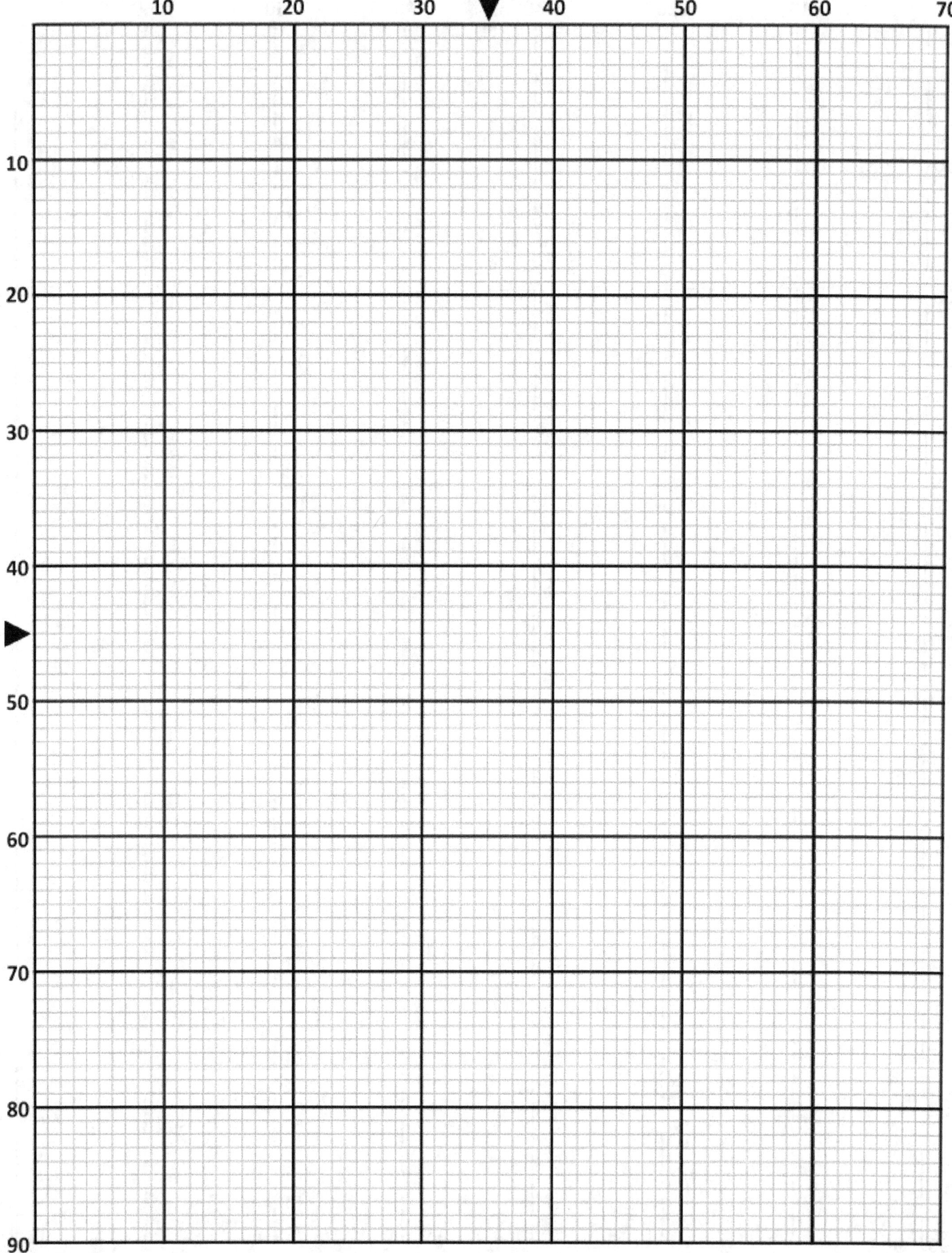

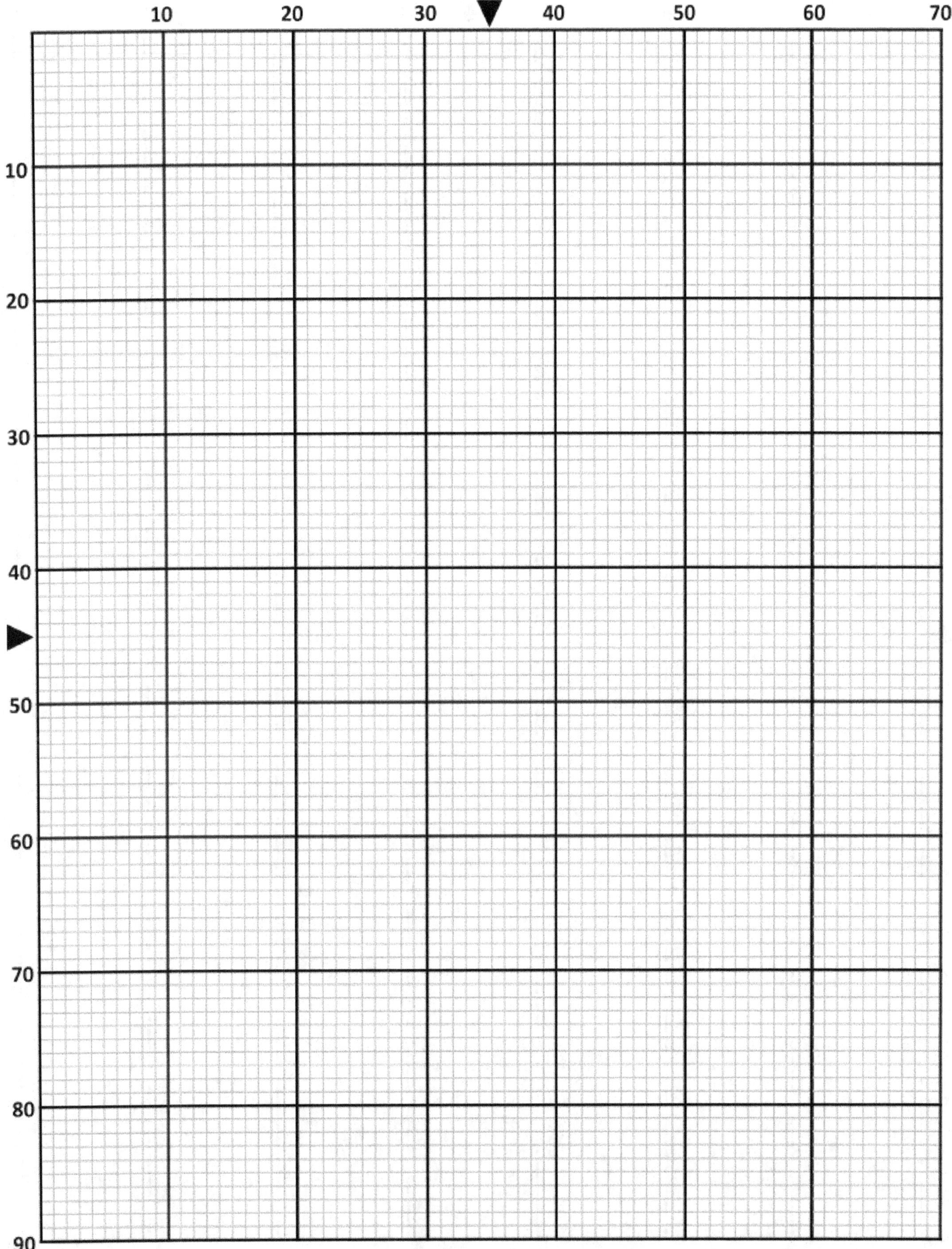

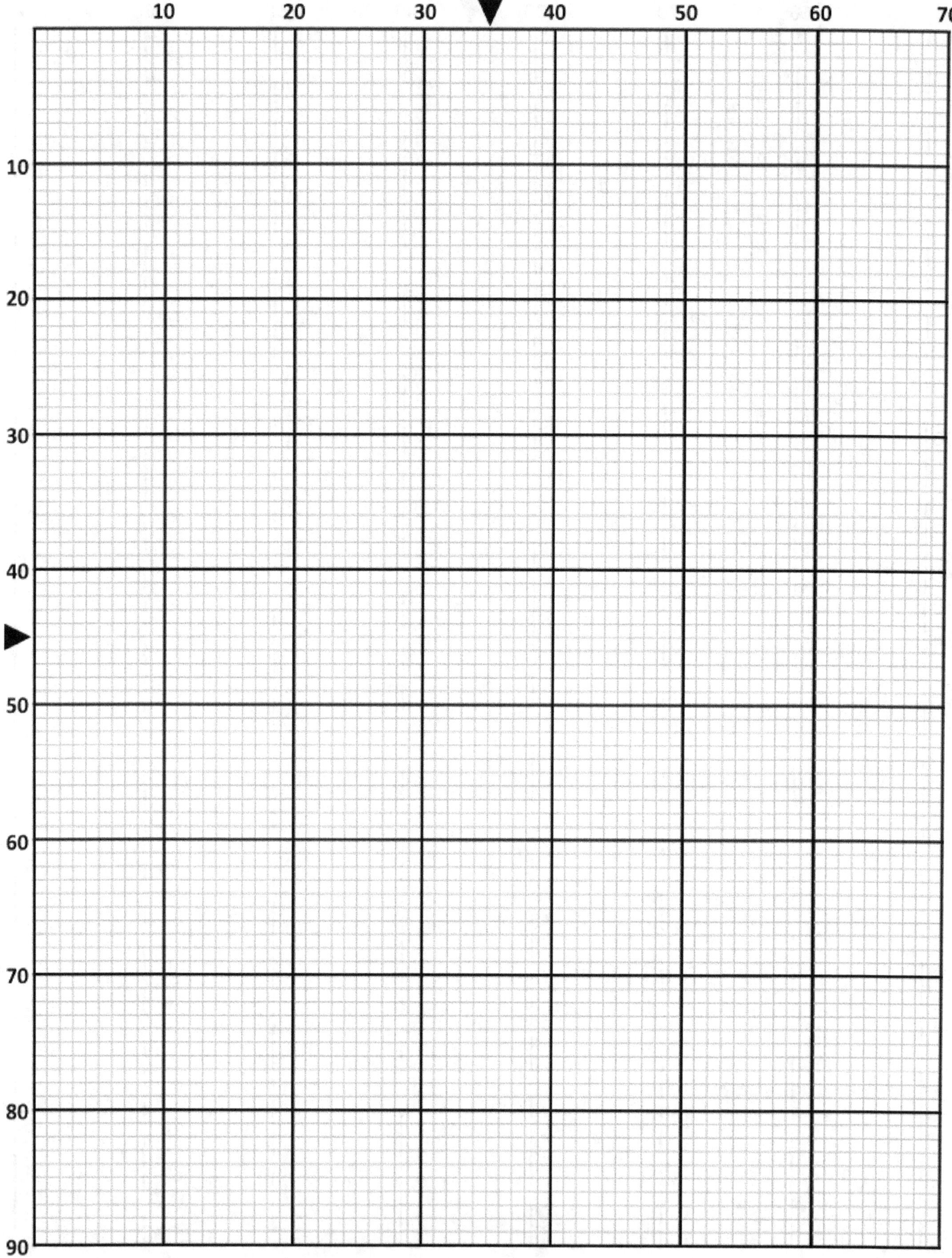

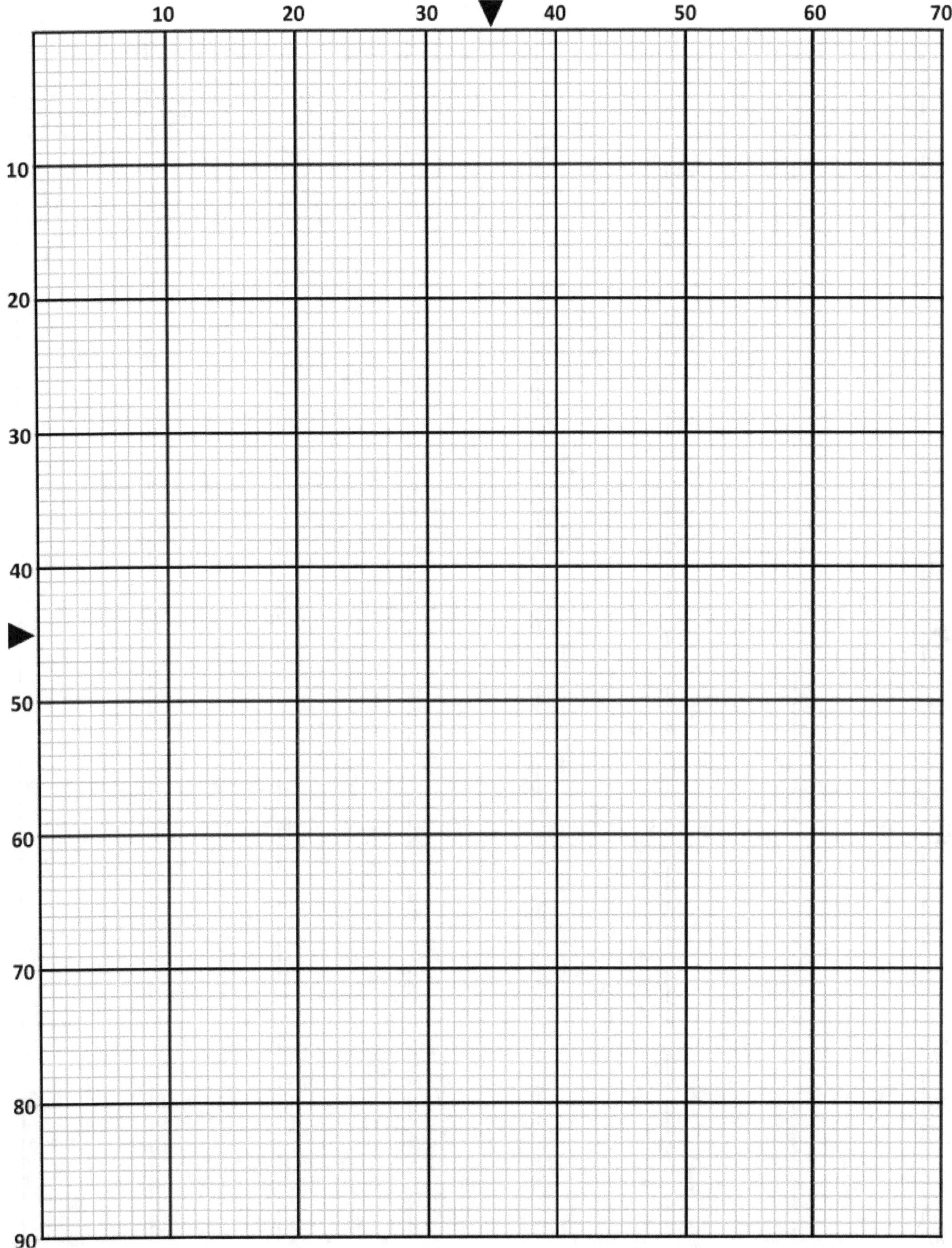

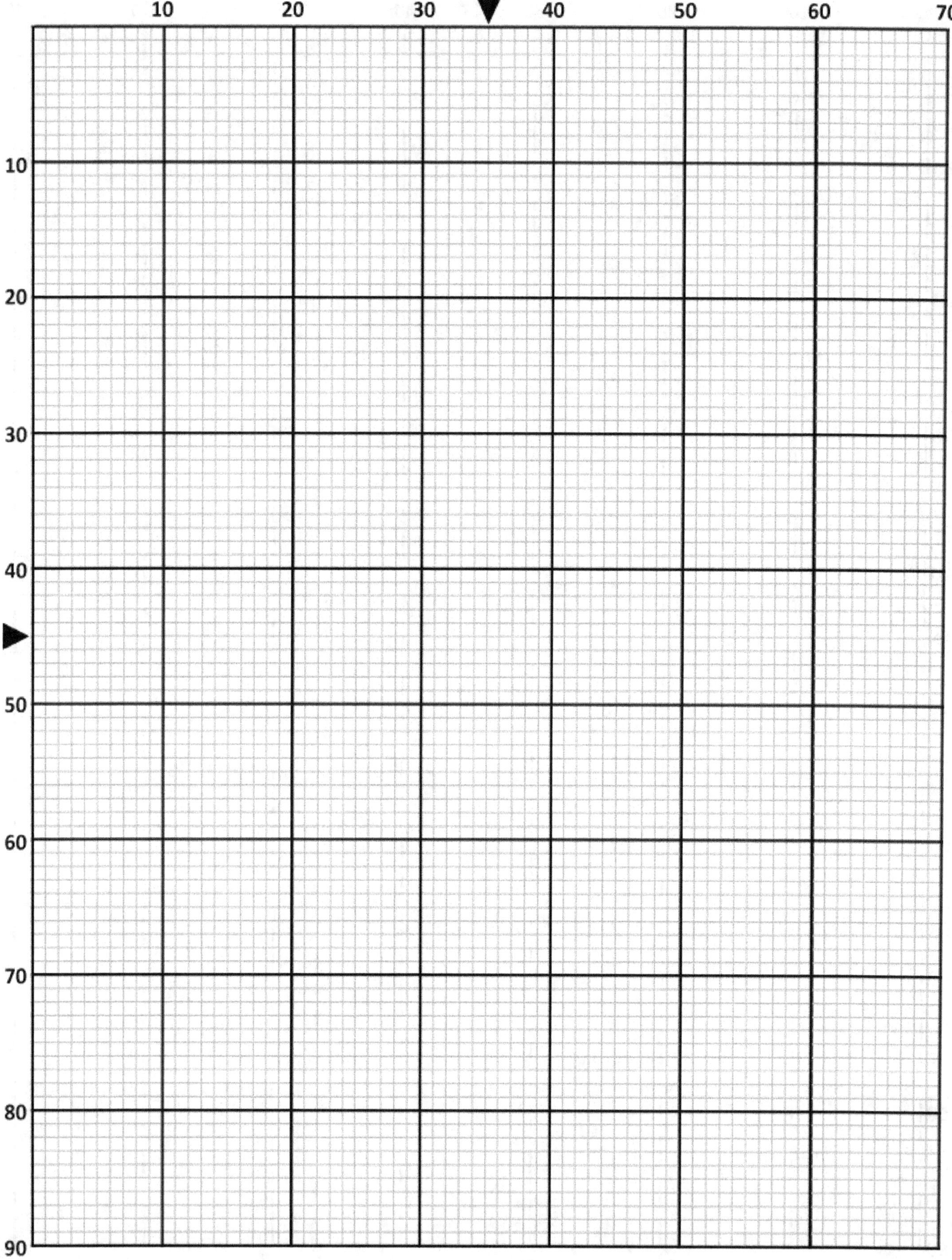

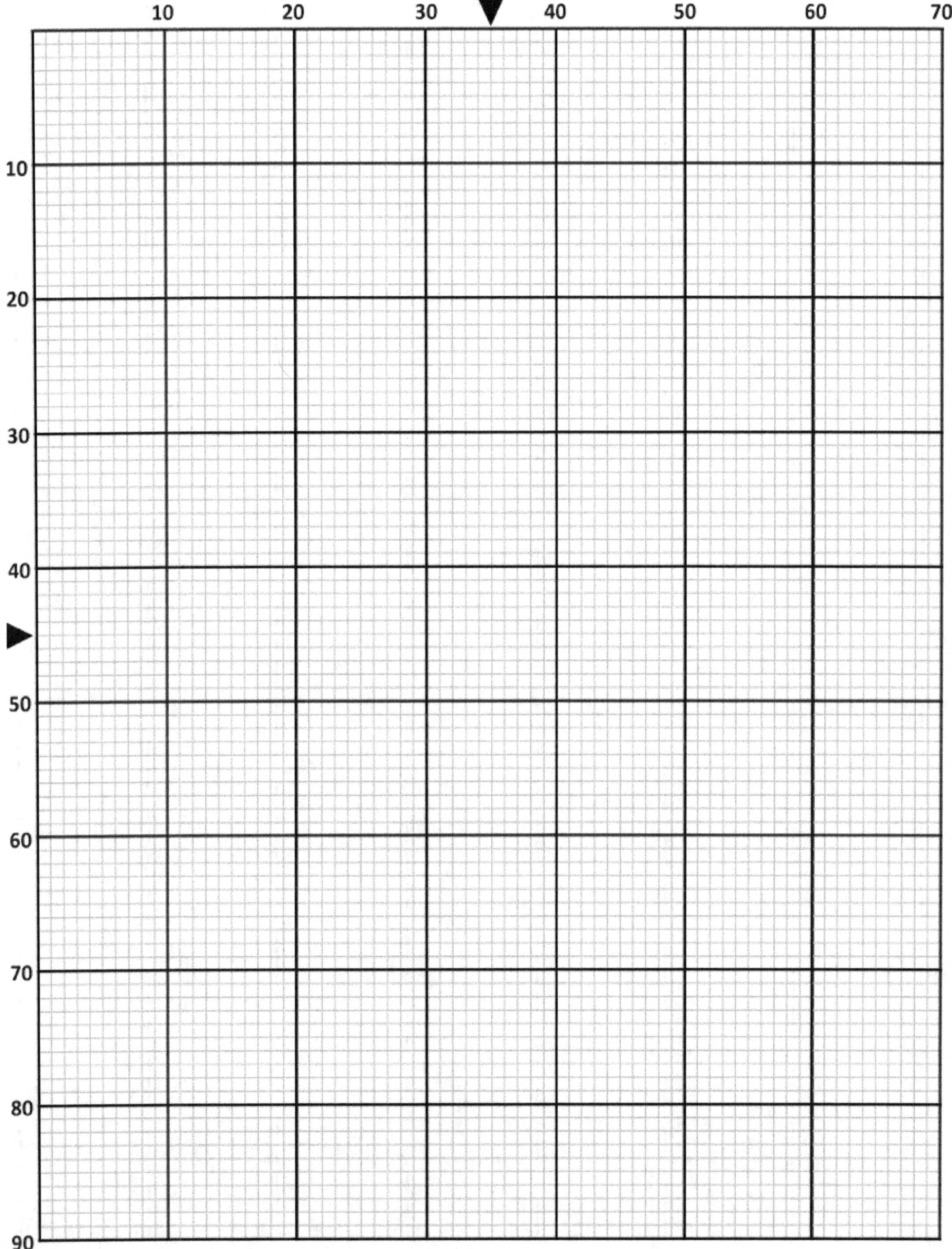

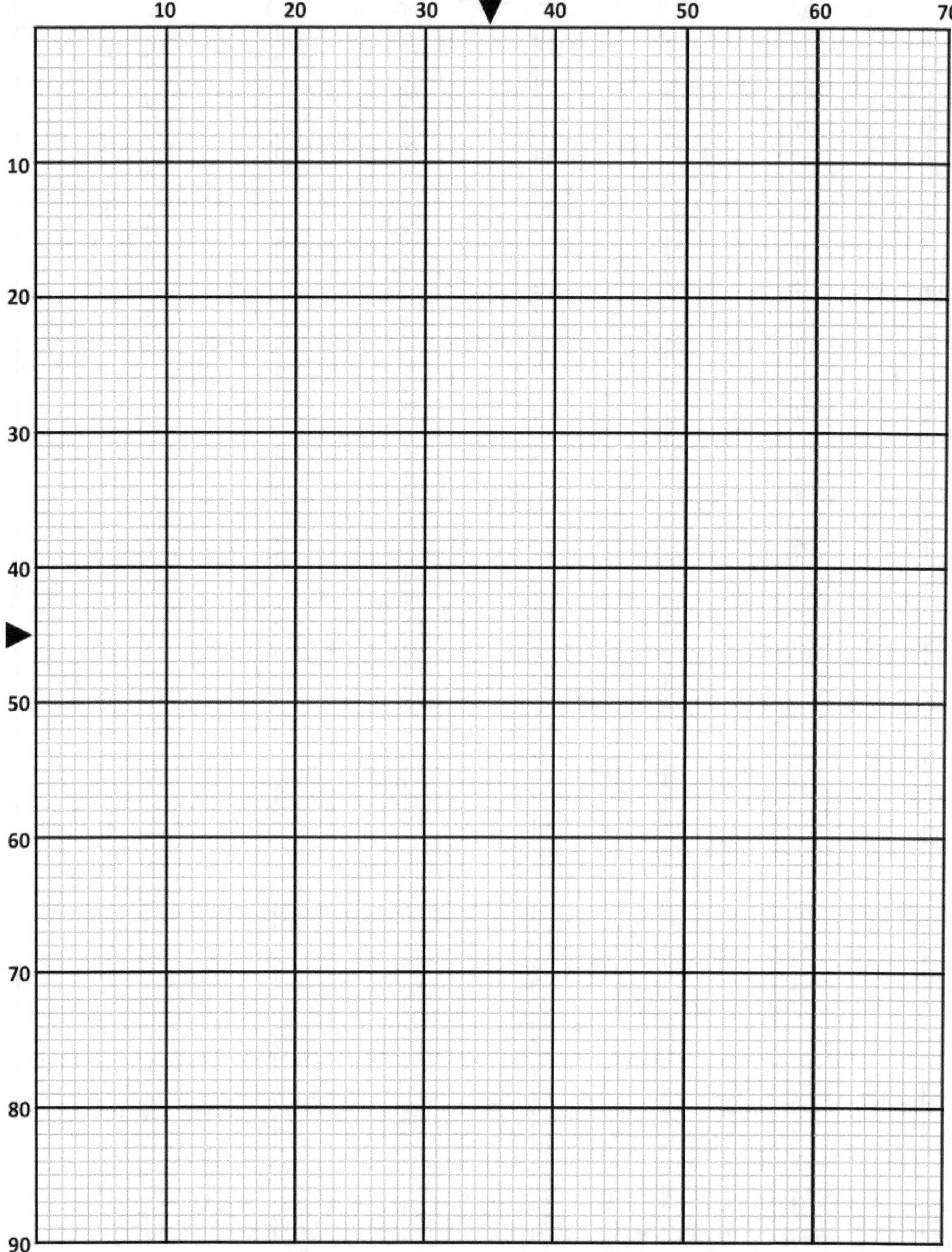

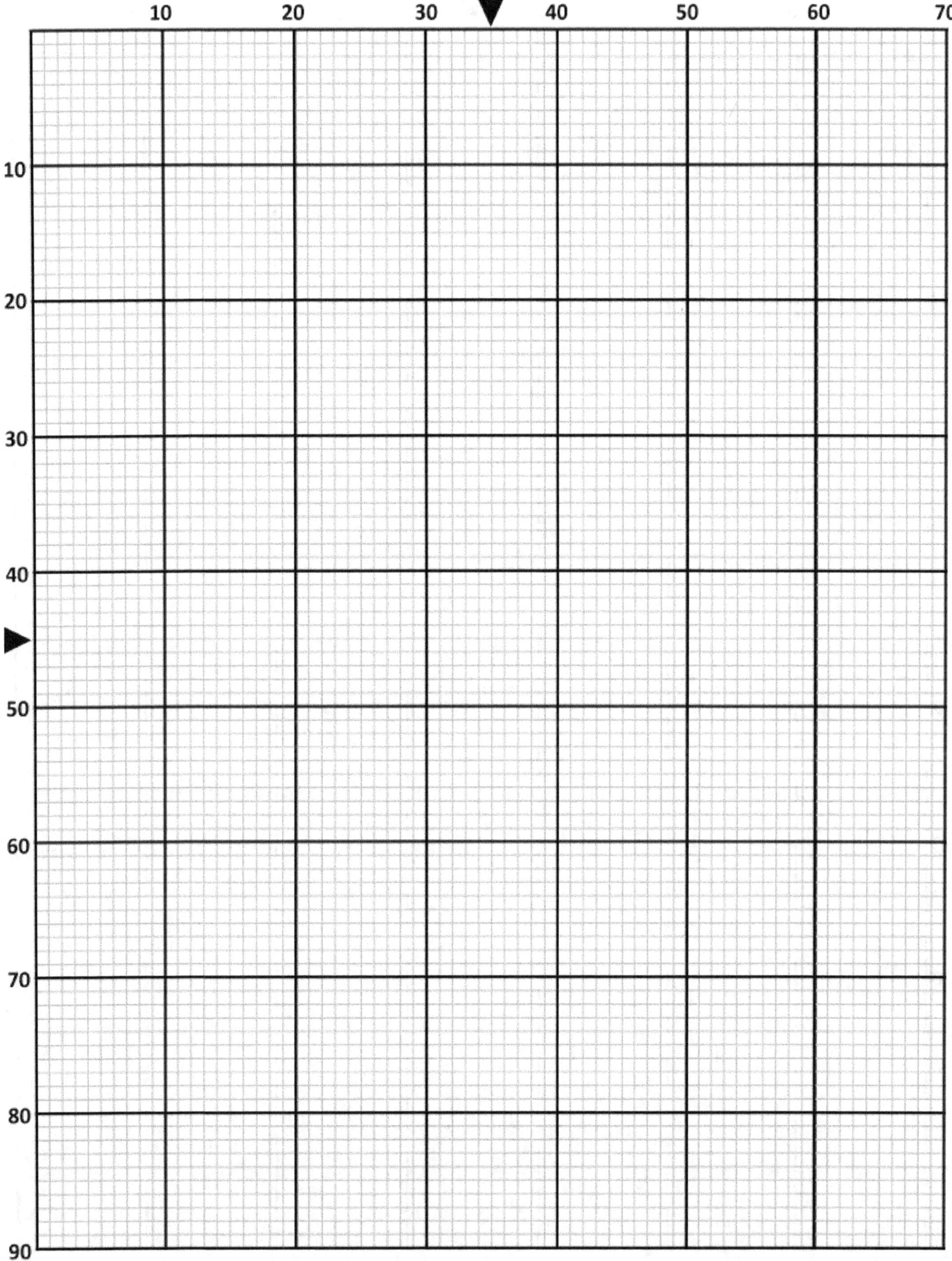

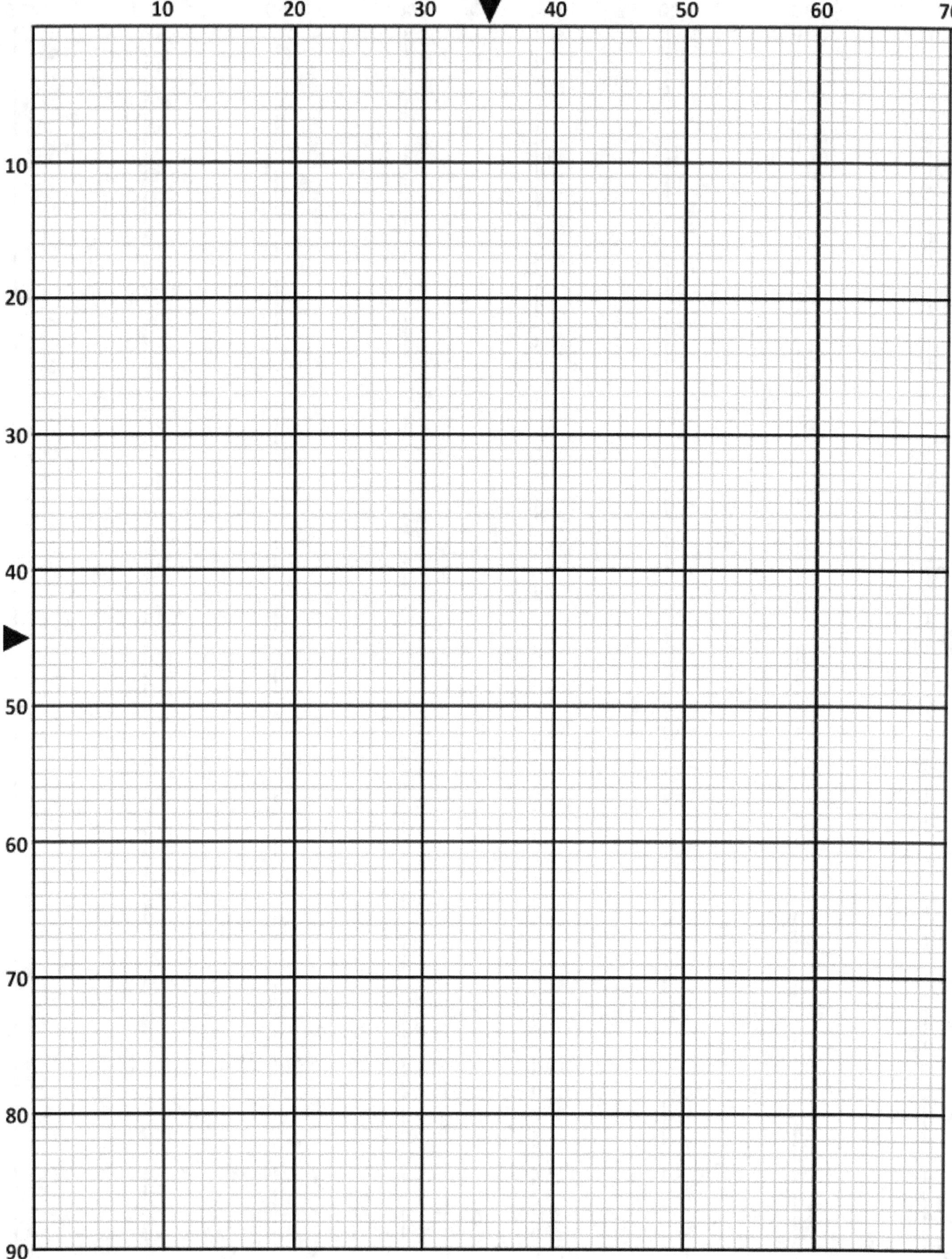

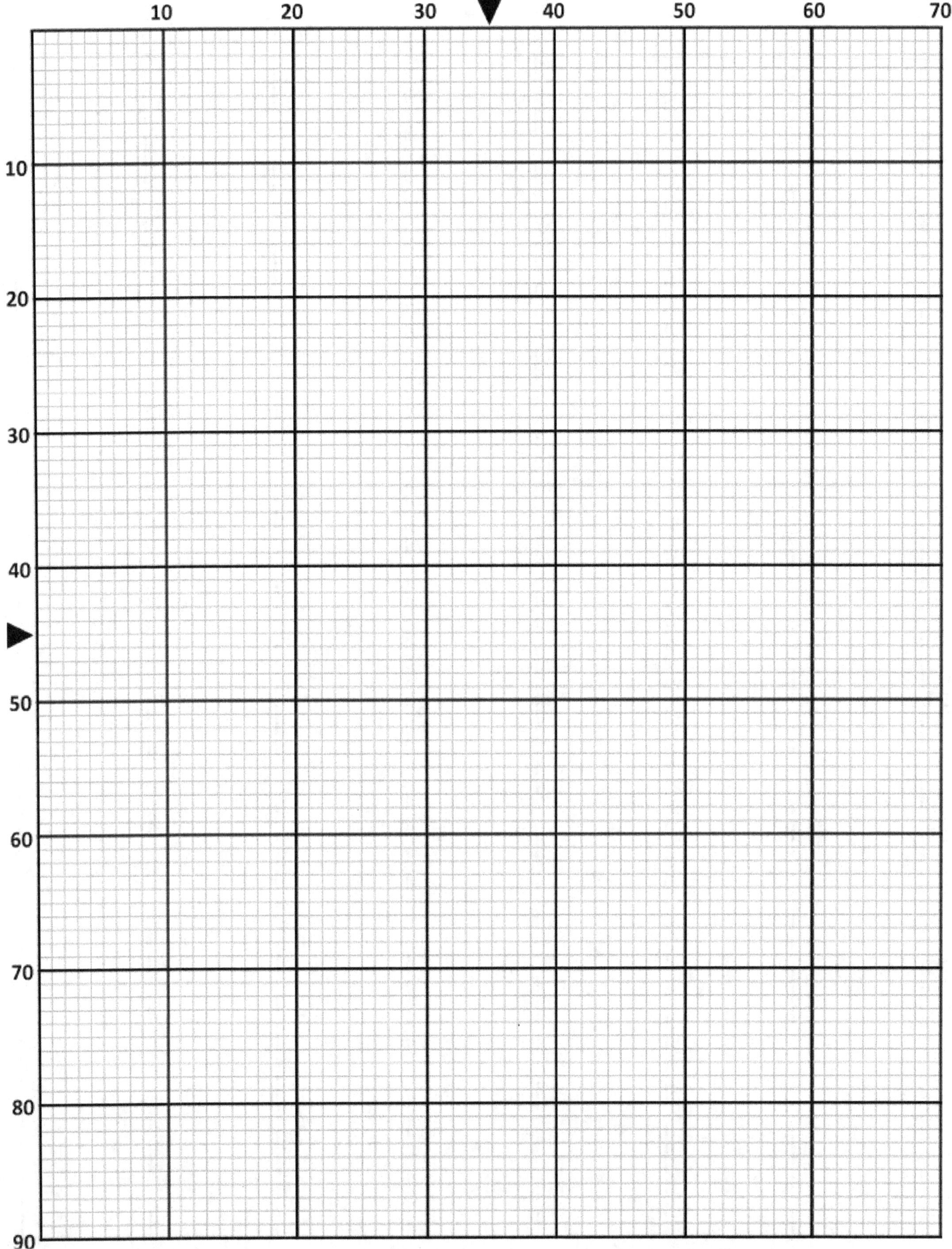

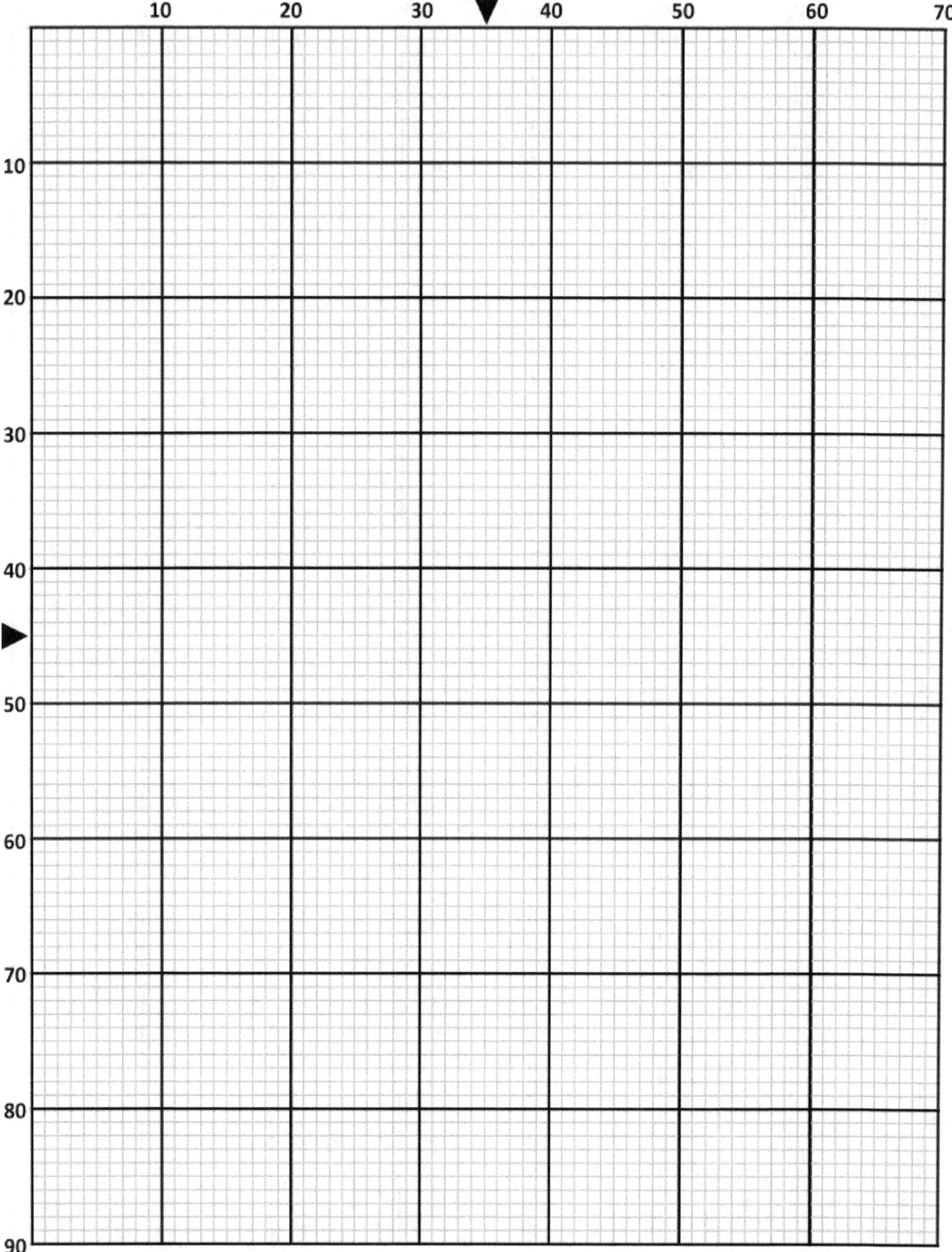

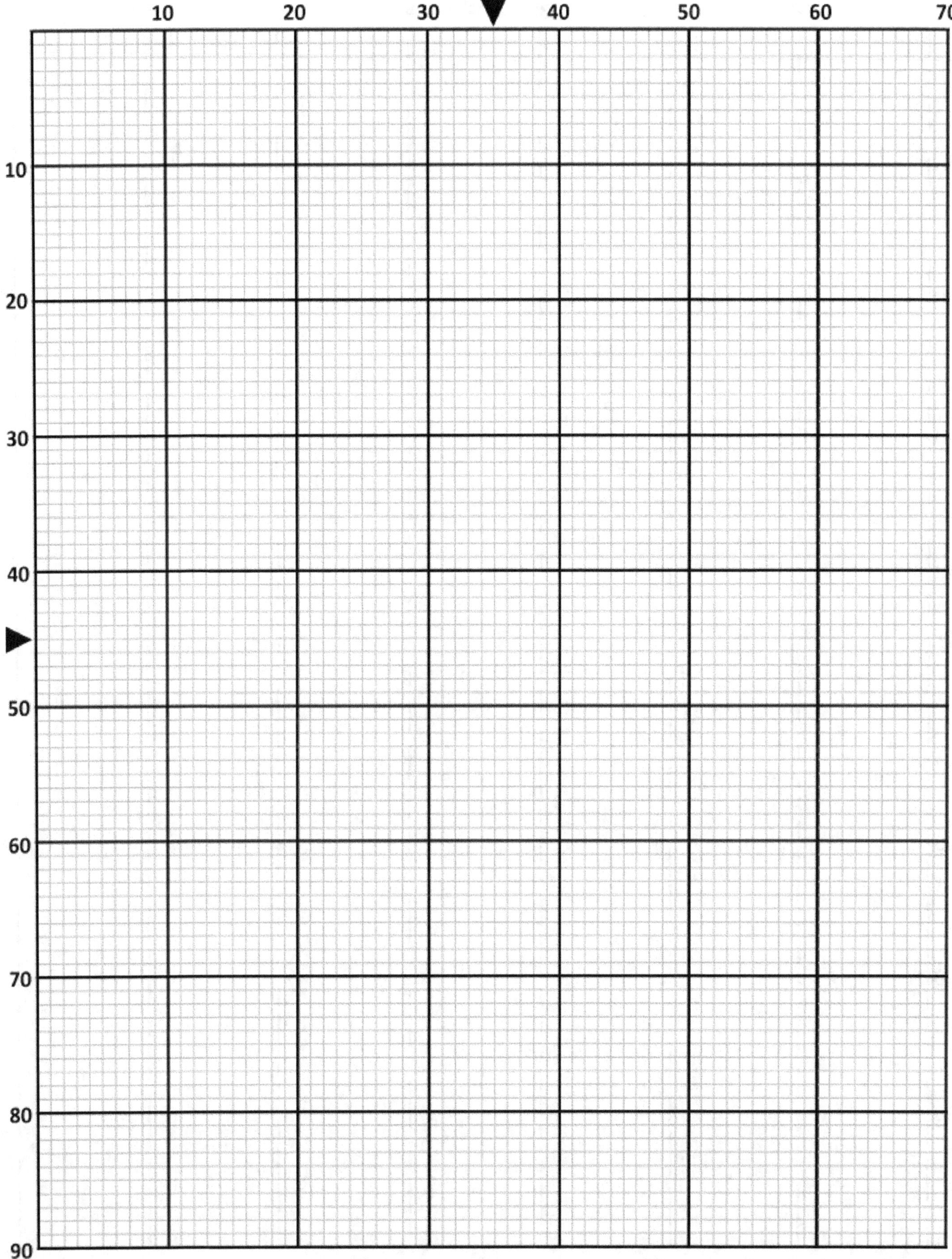

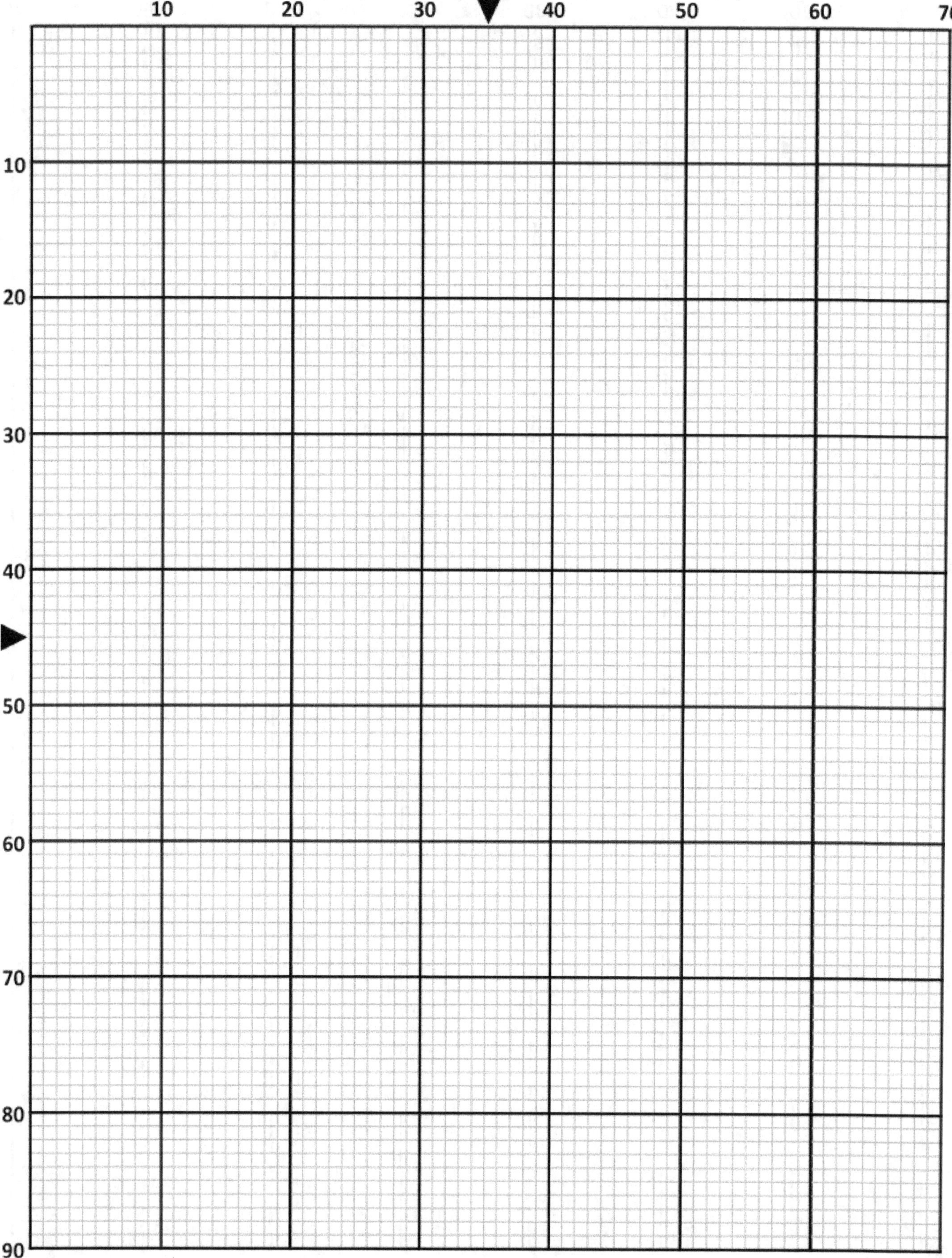

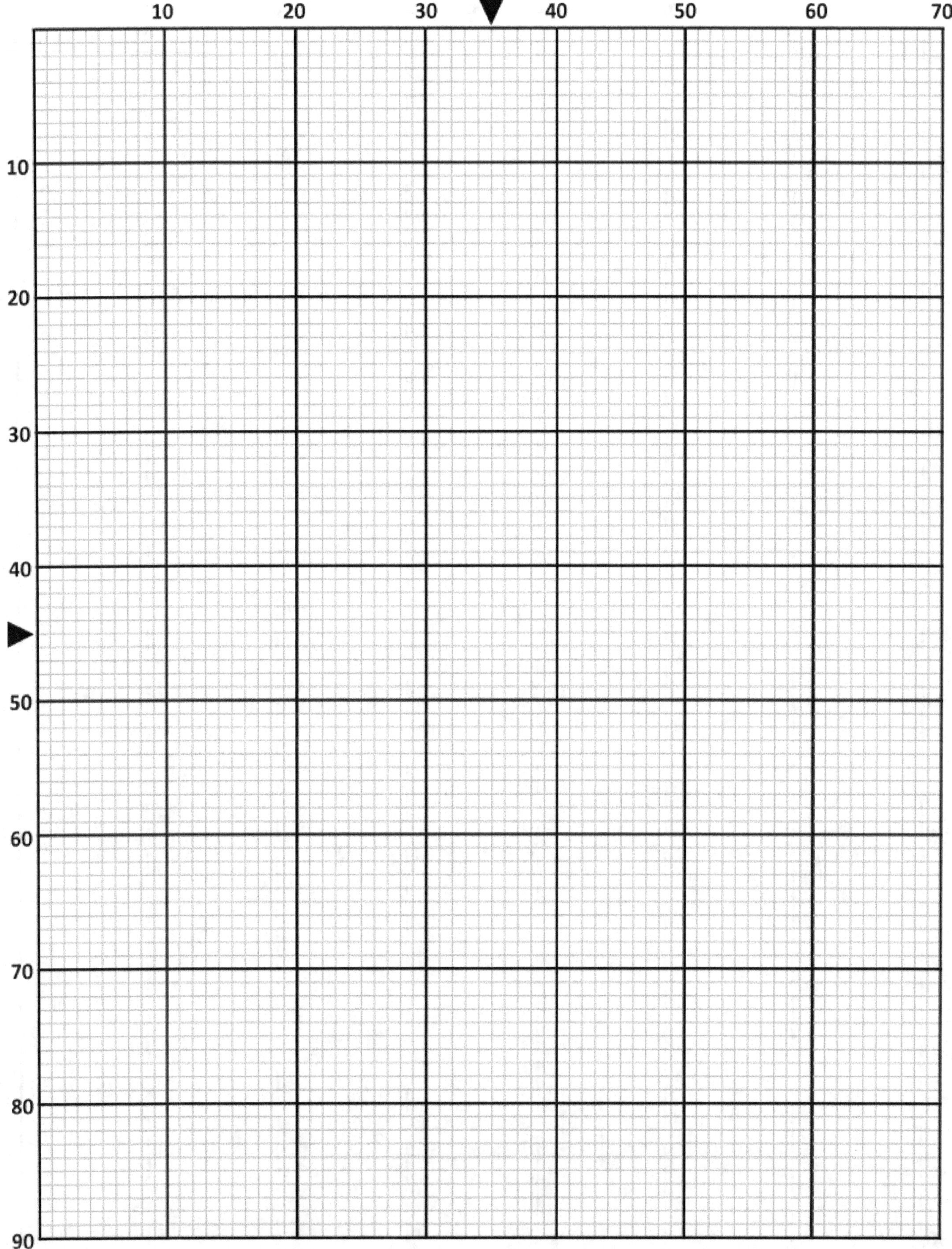

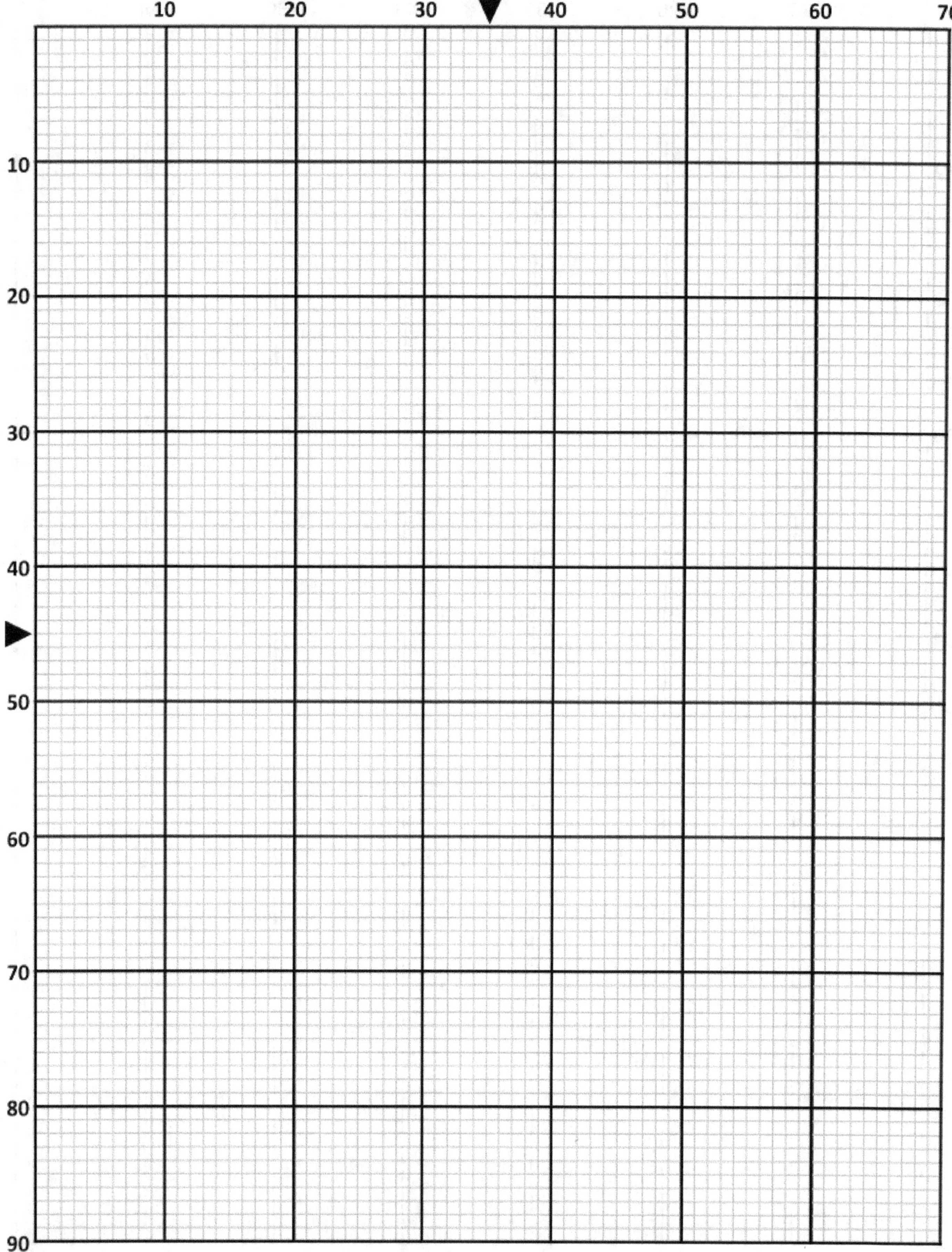

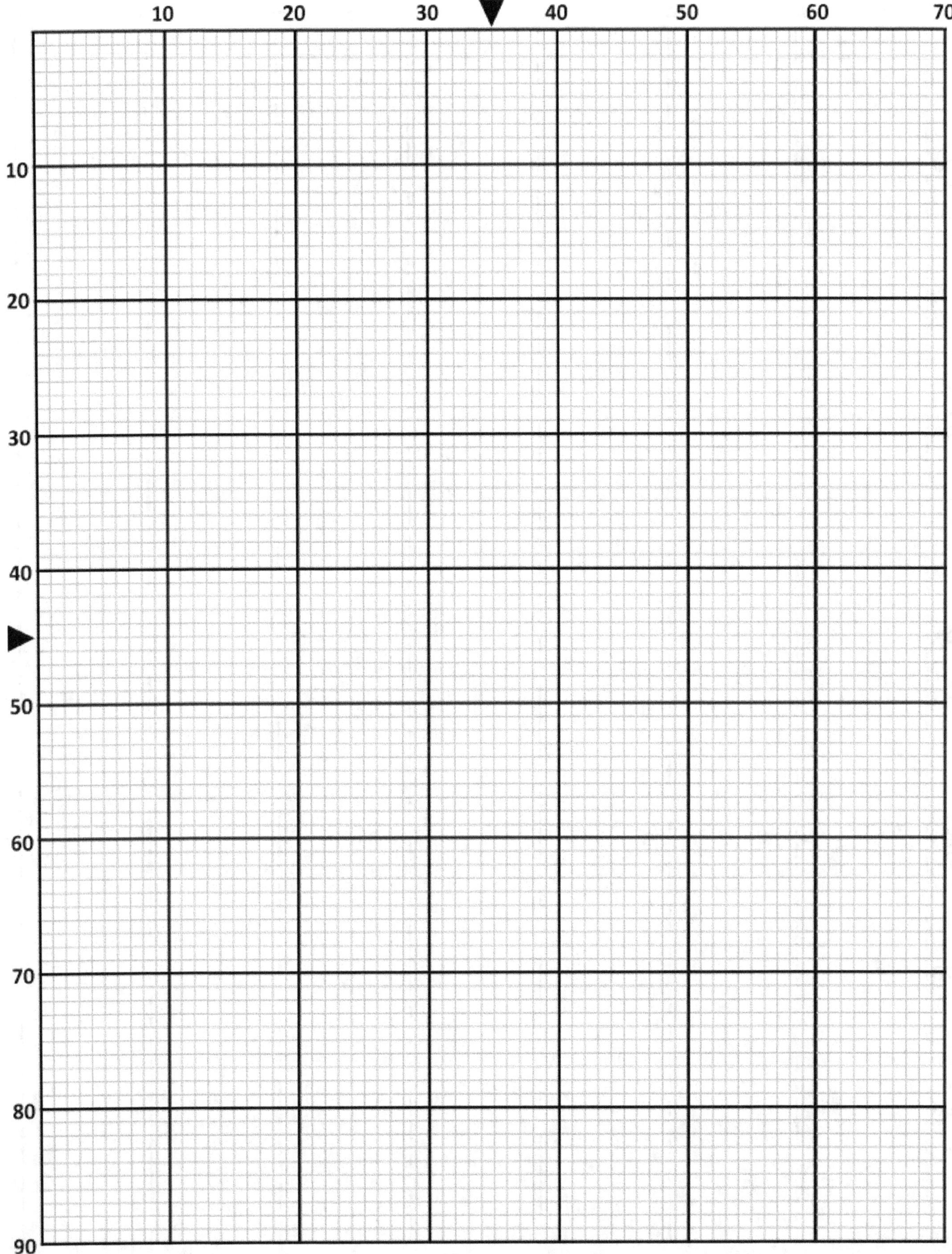

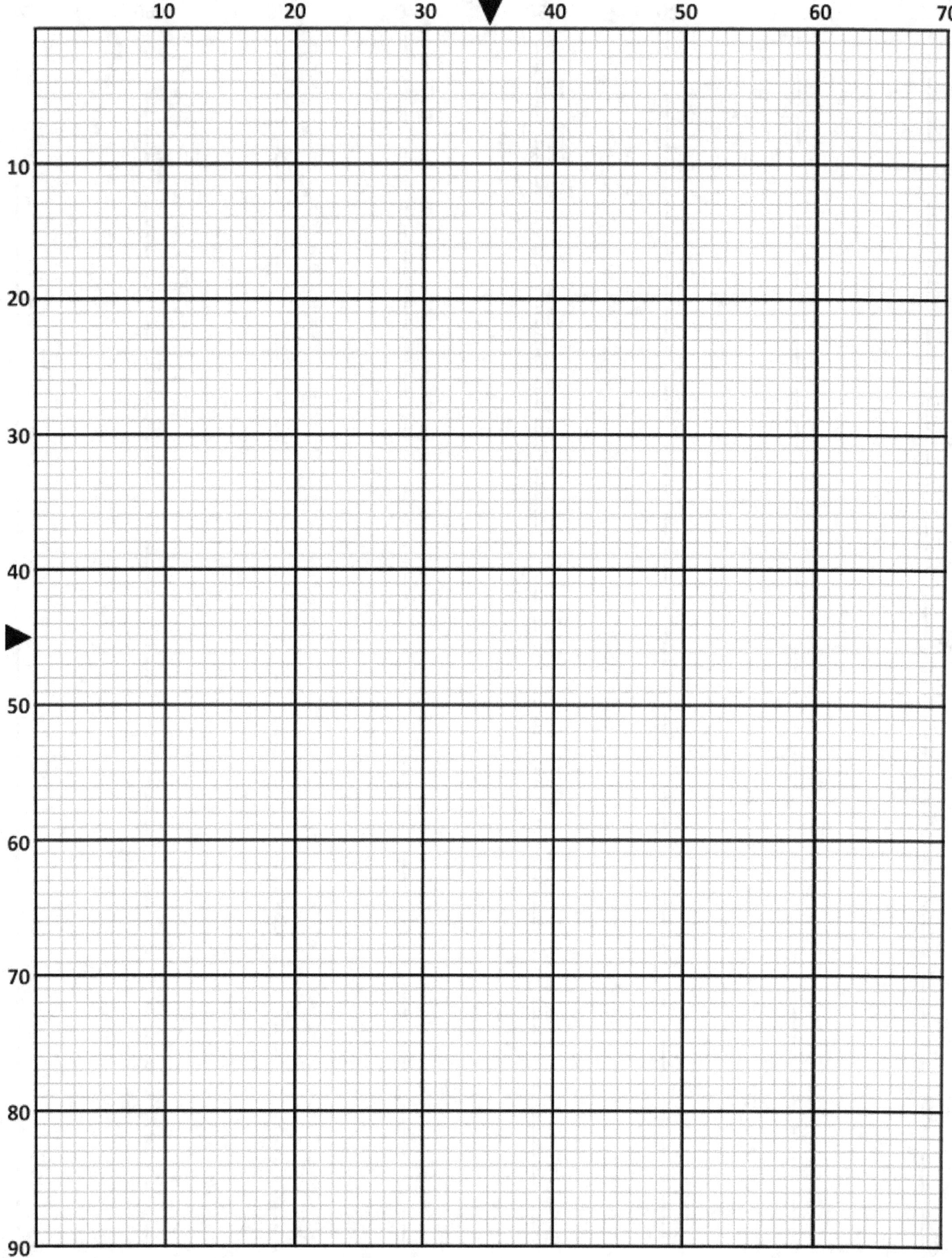

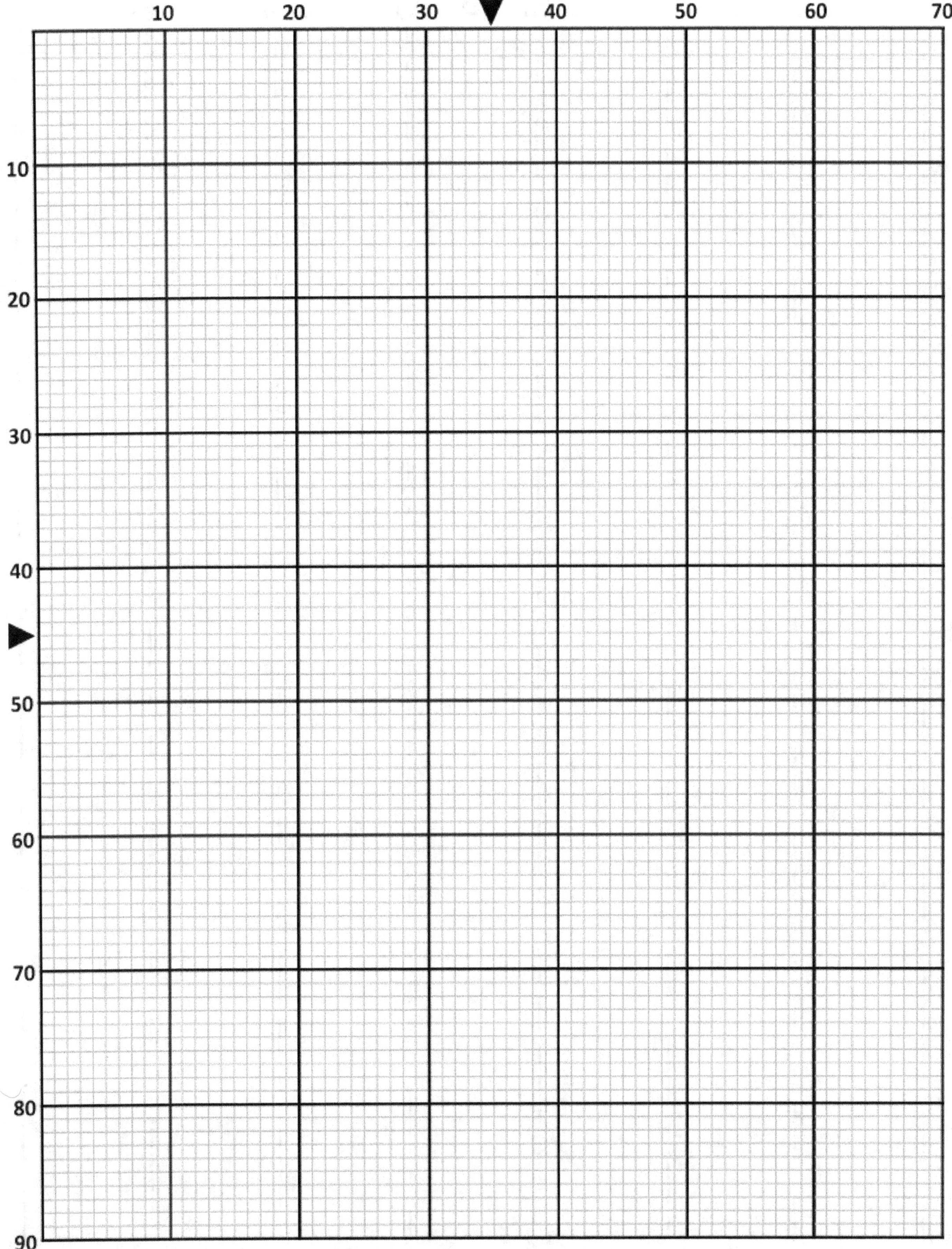

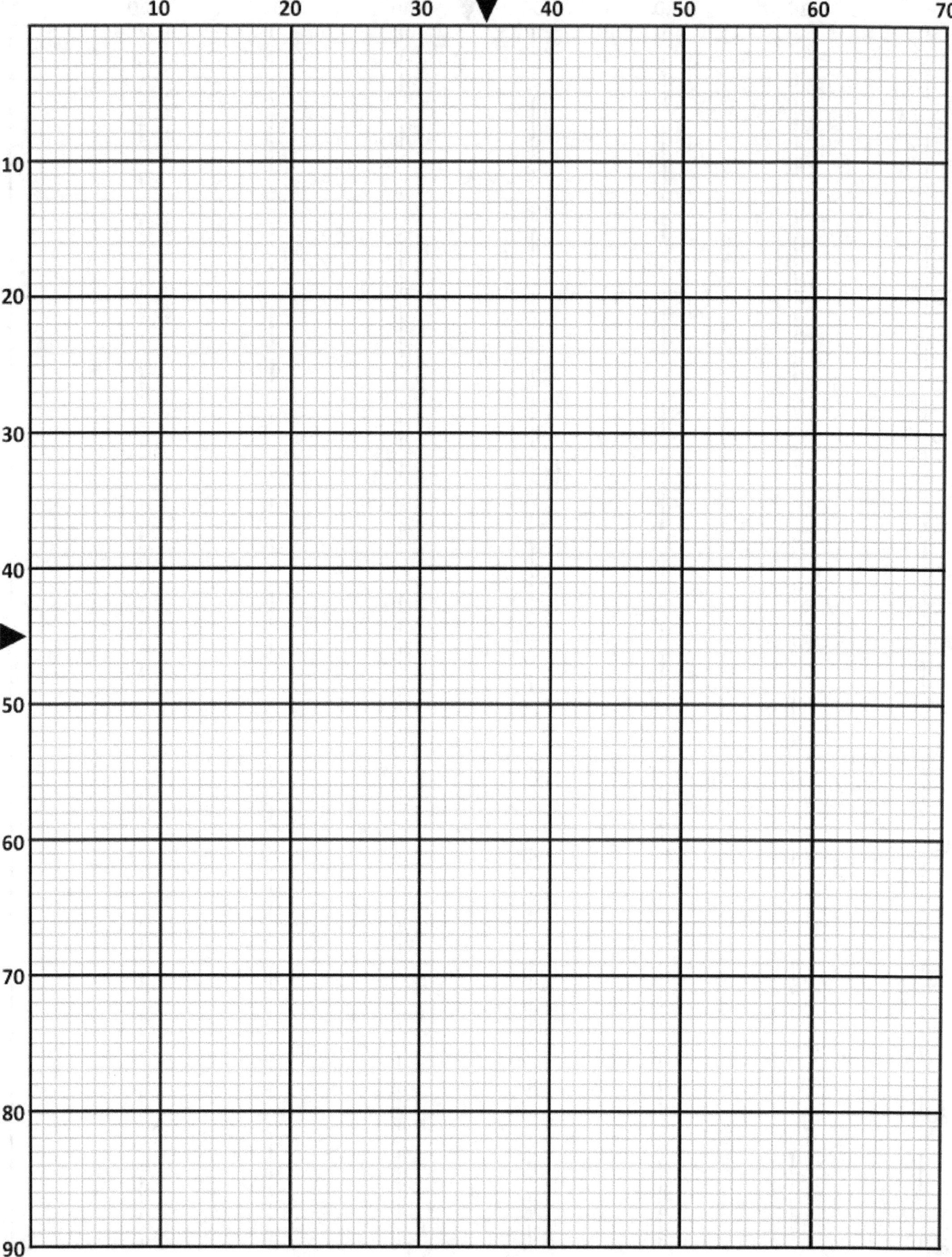

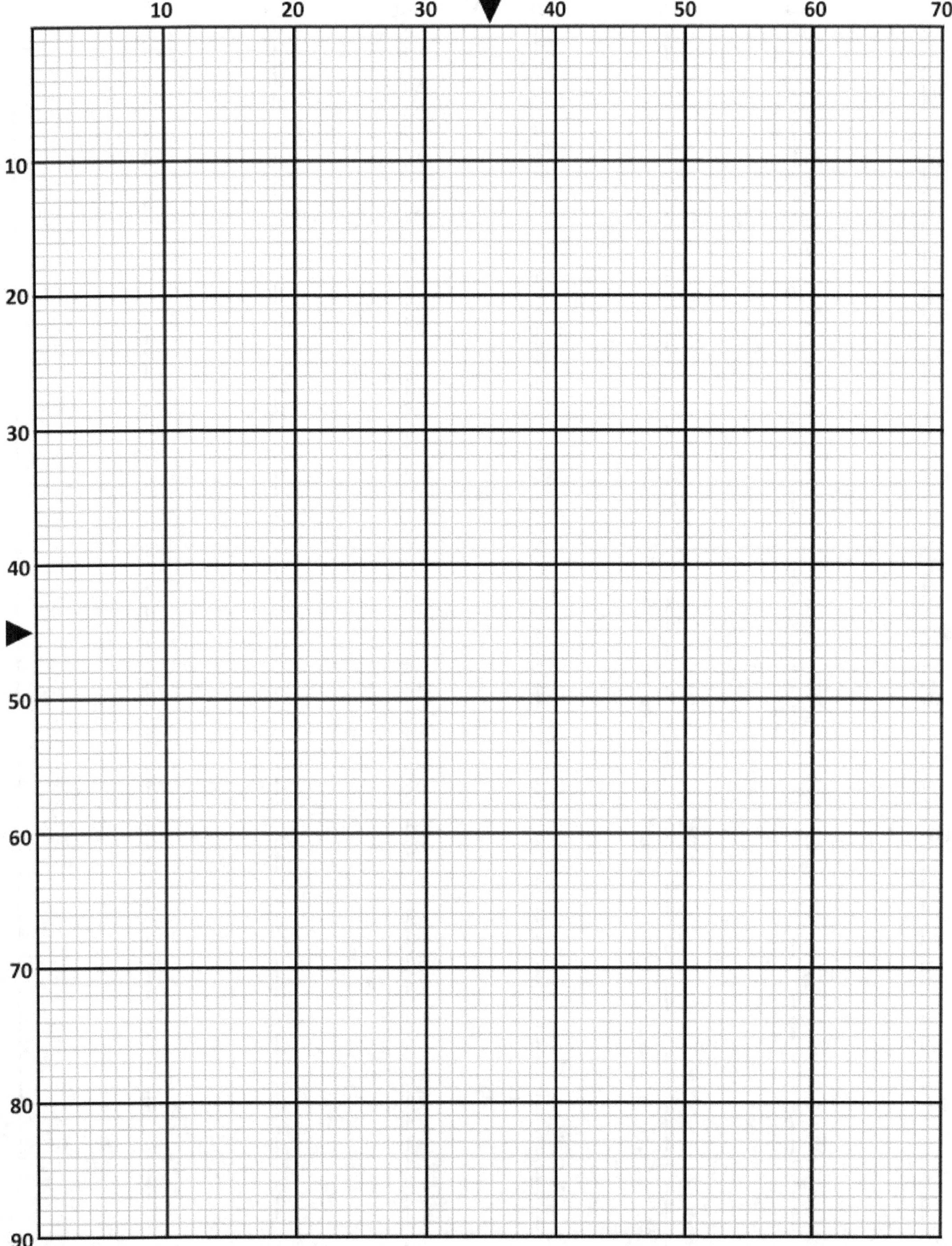

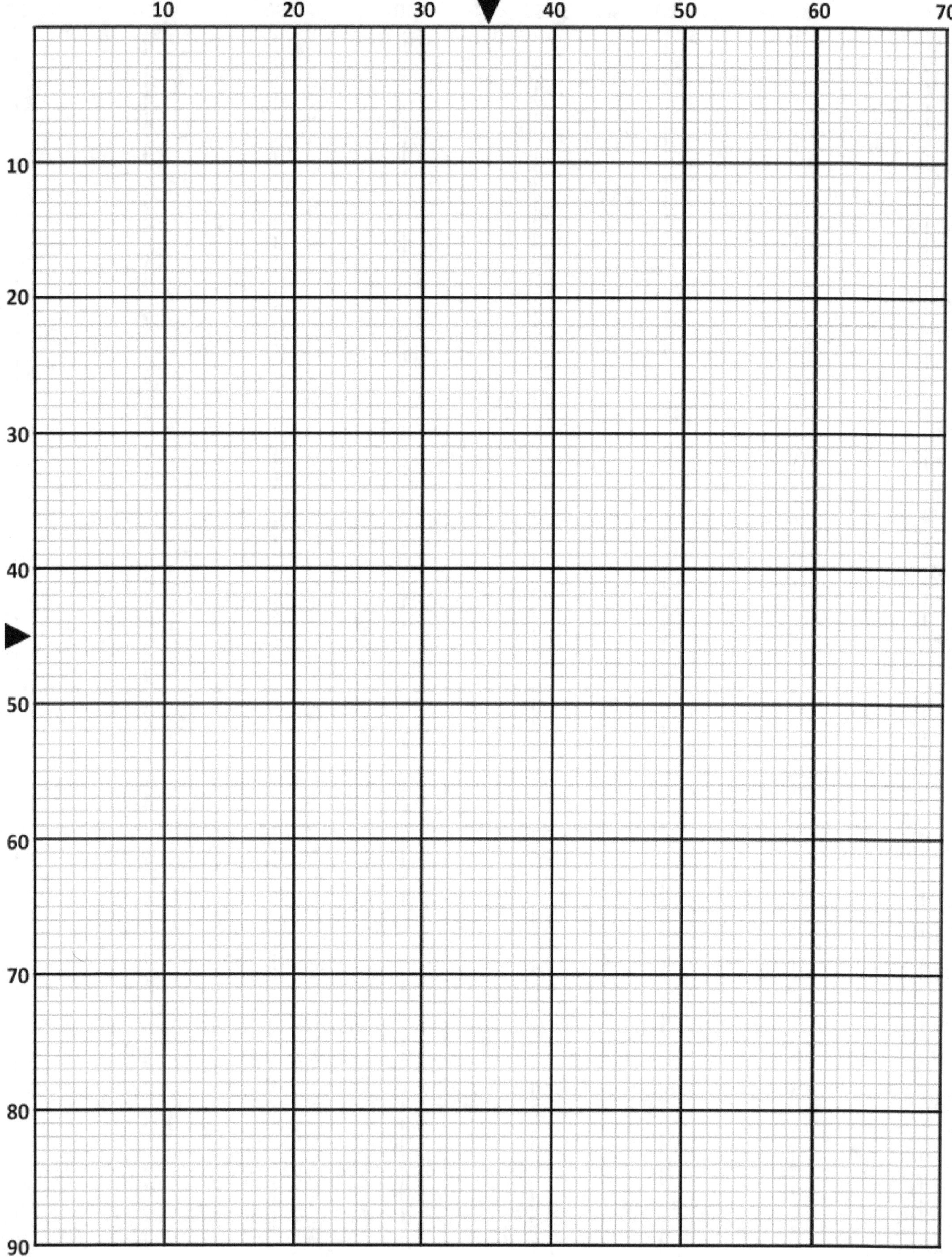

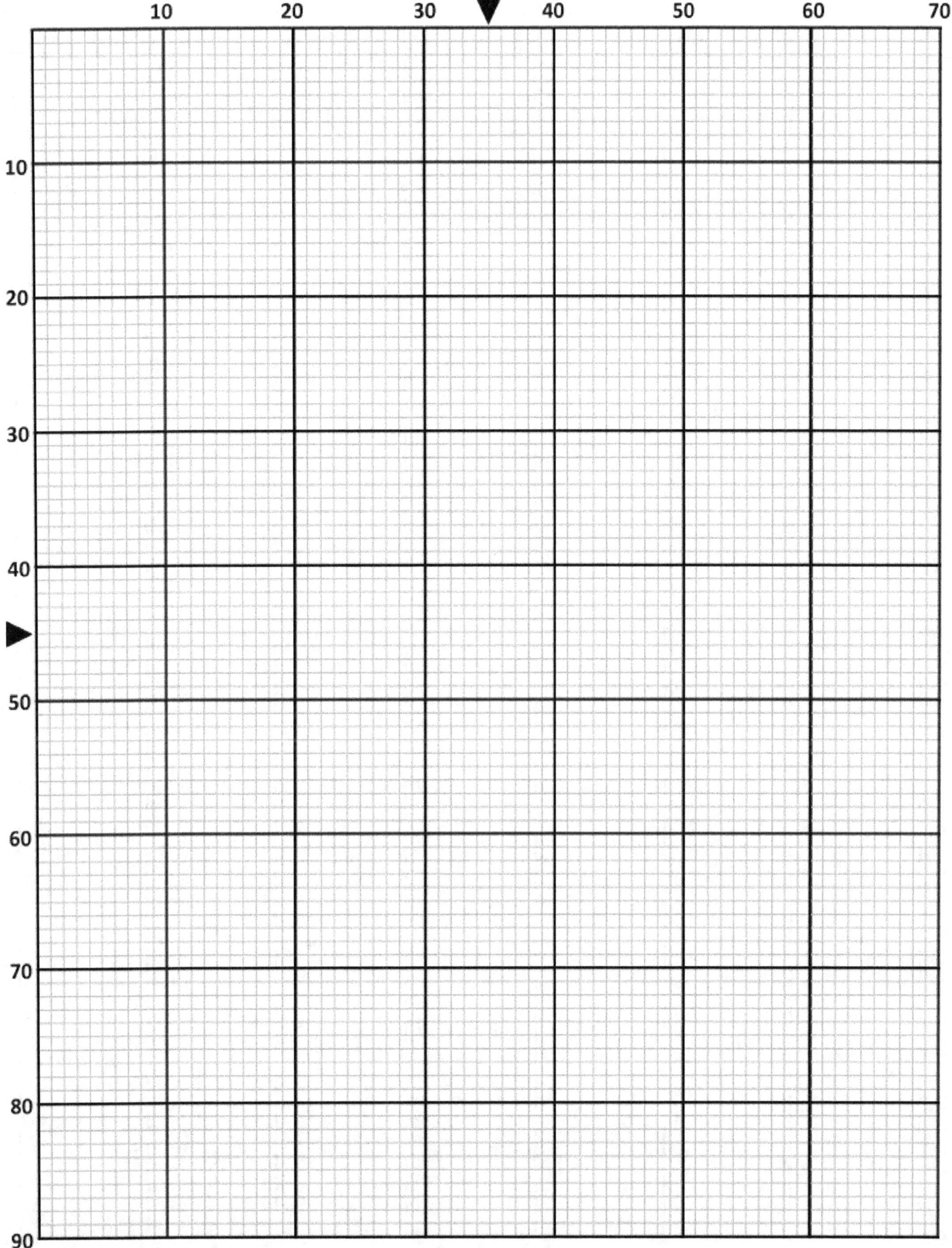

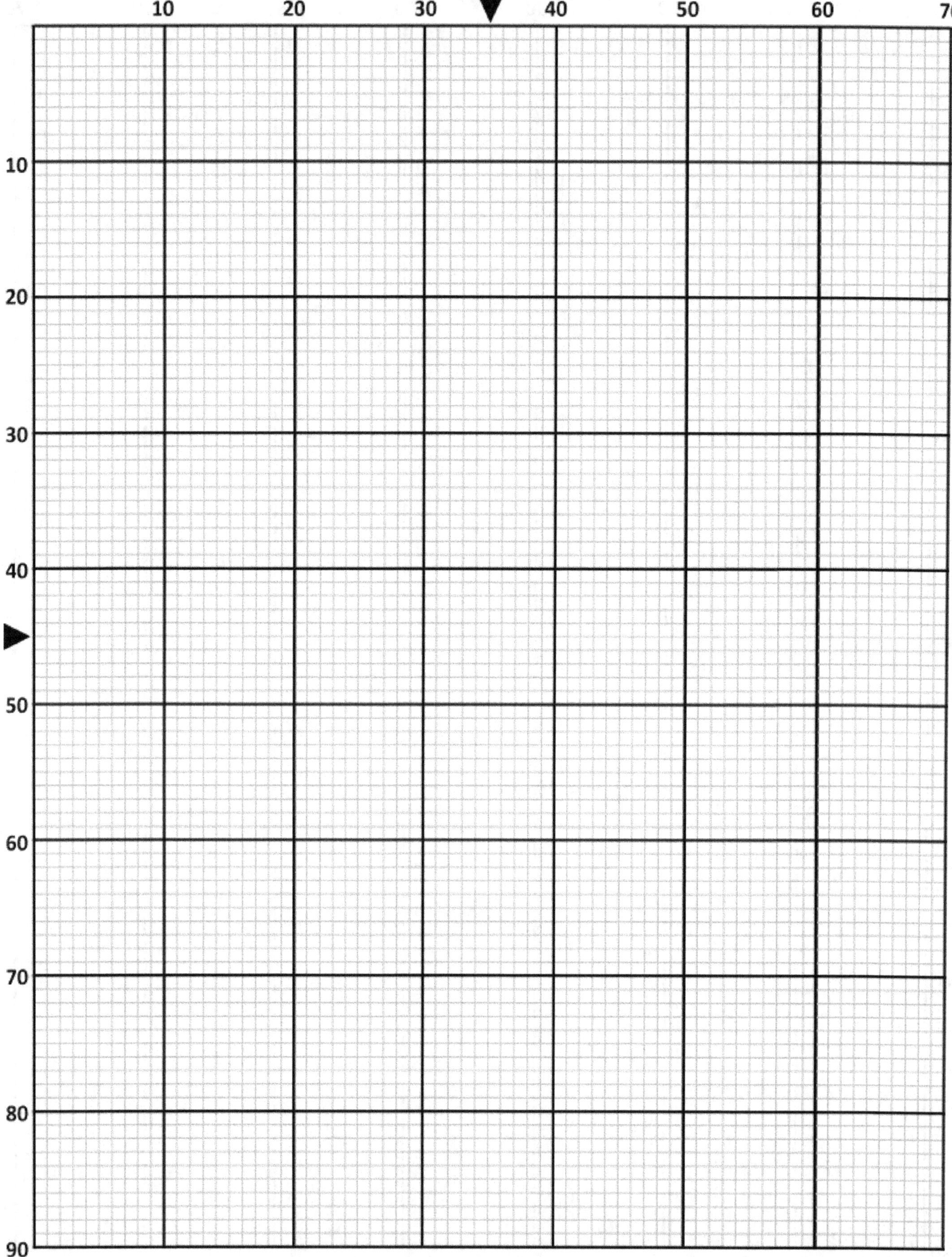

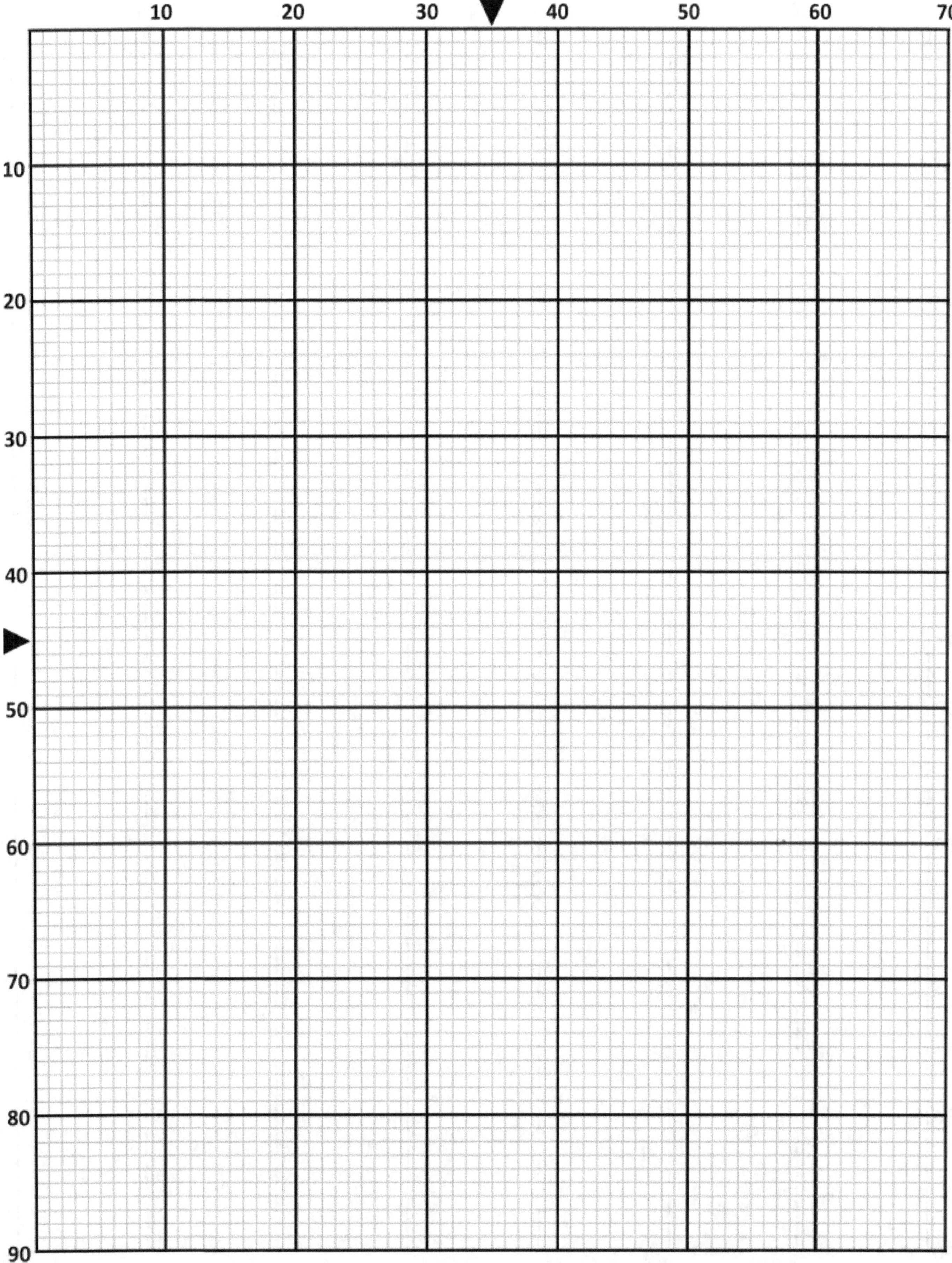

10
20
30
40
50
60
70
10
20
30
40
50
60
70
80
90

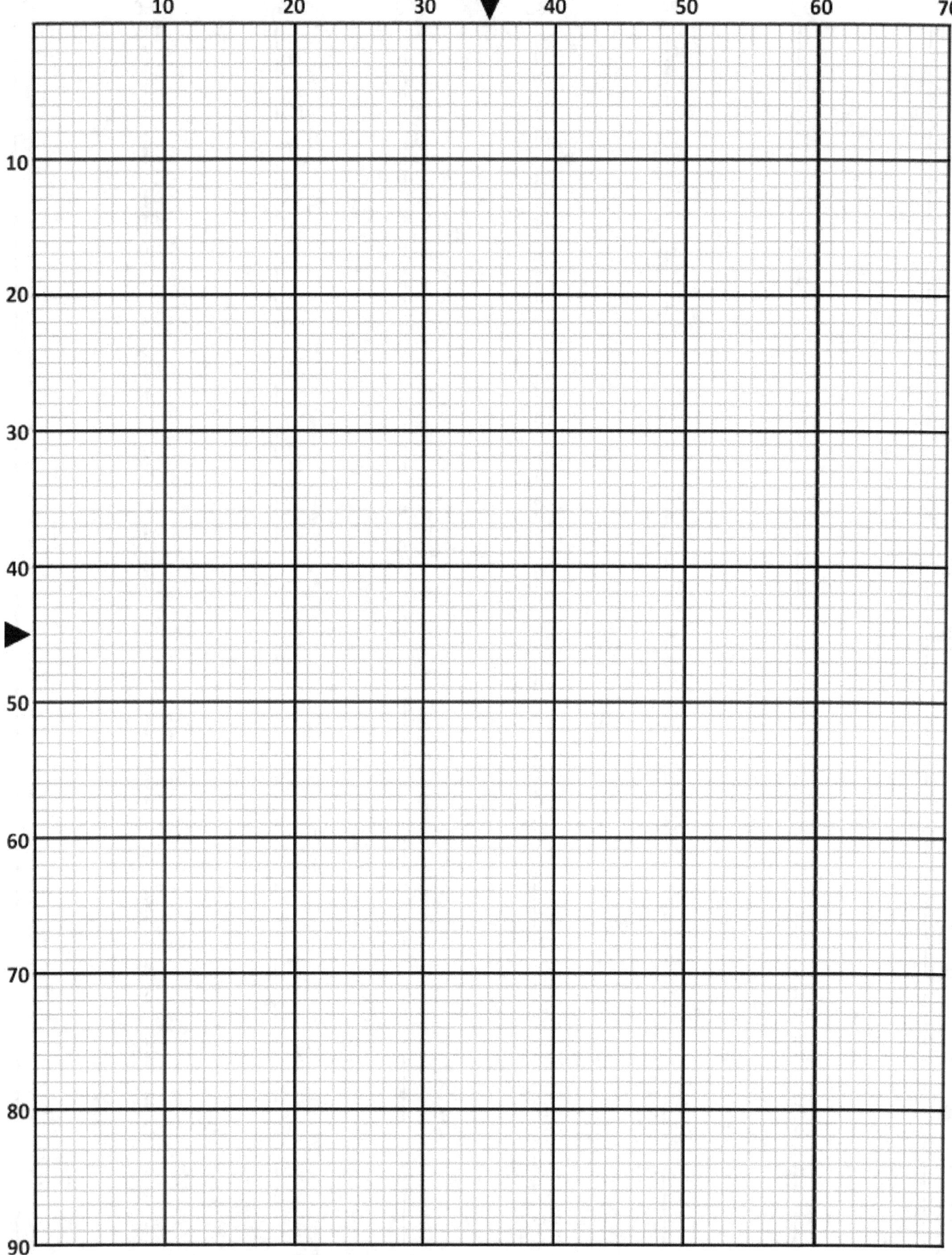

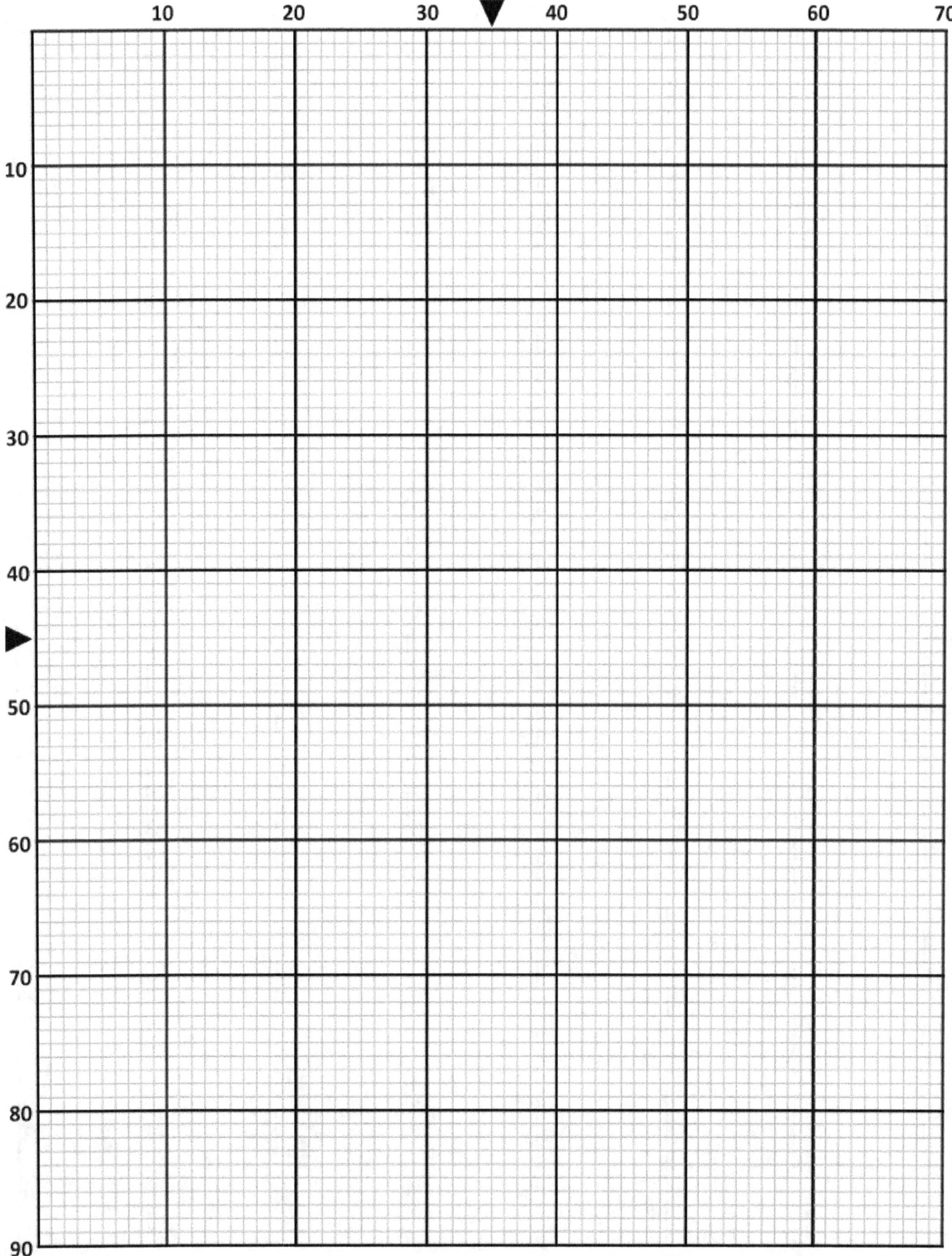

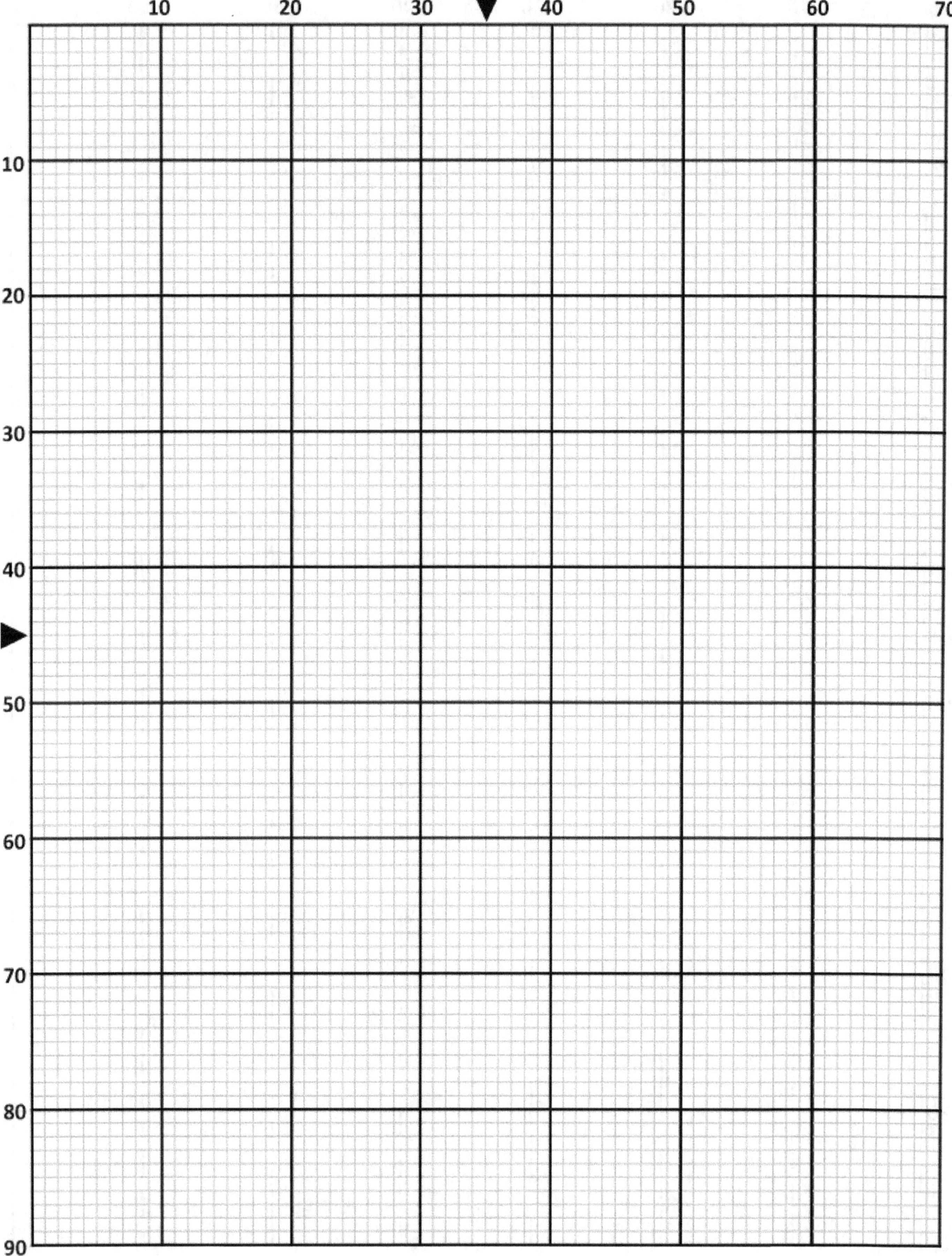

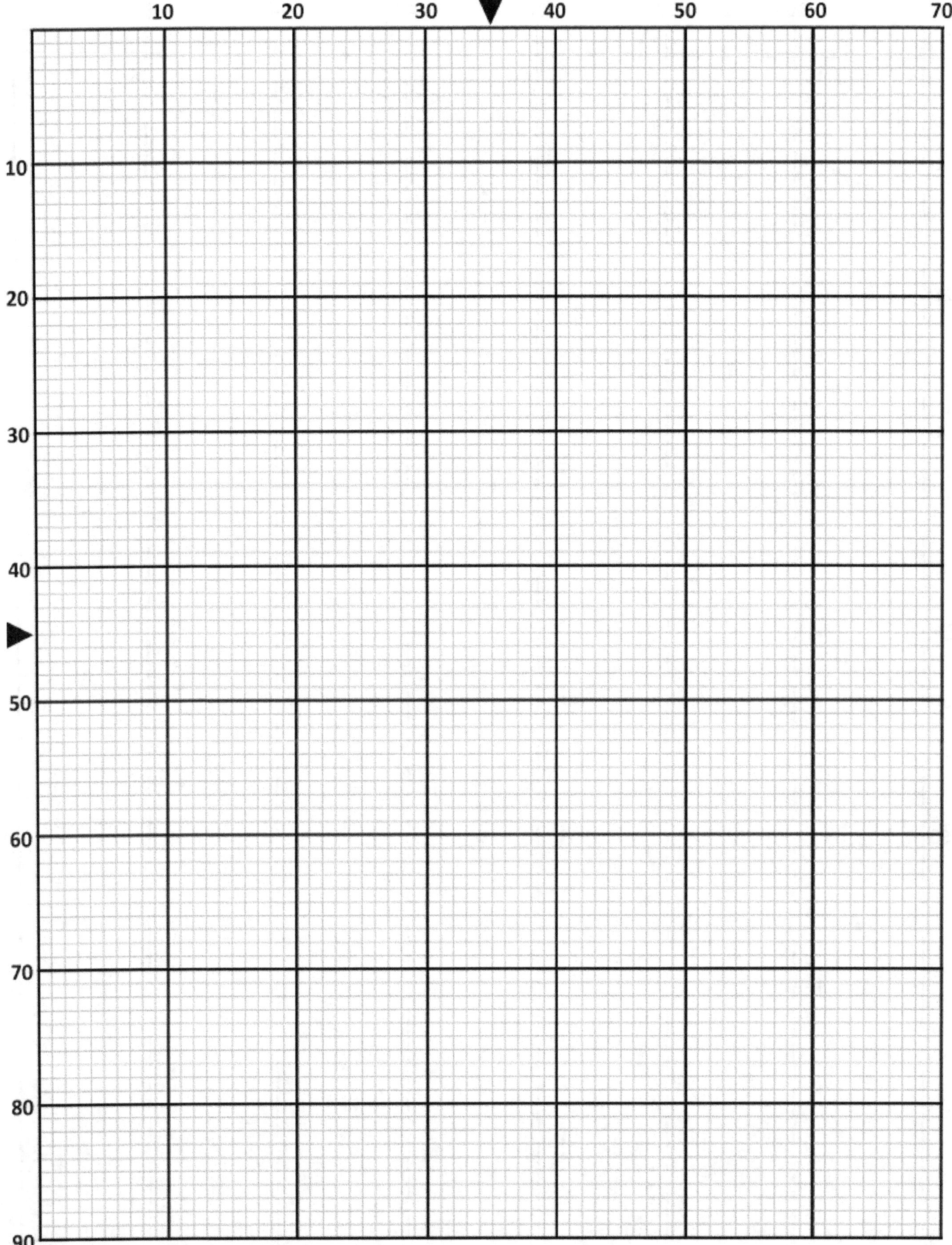

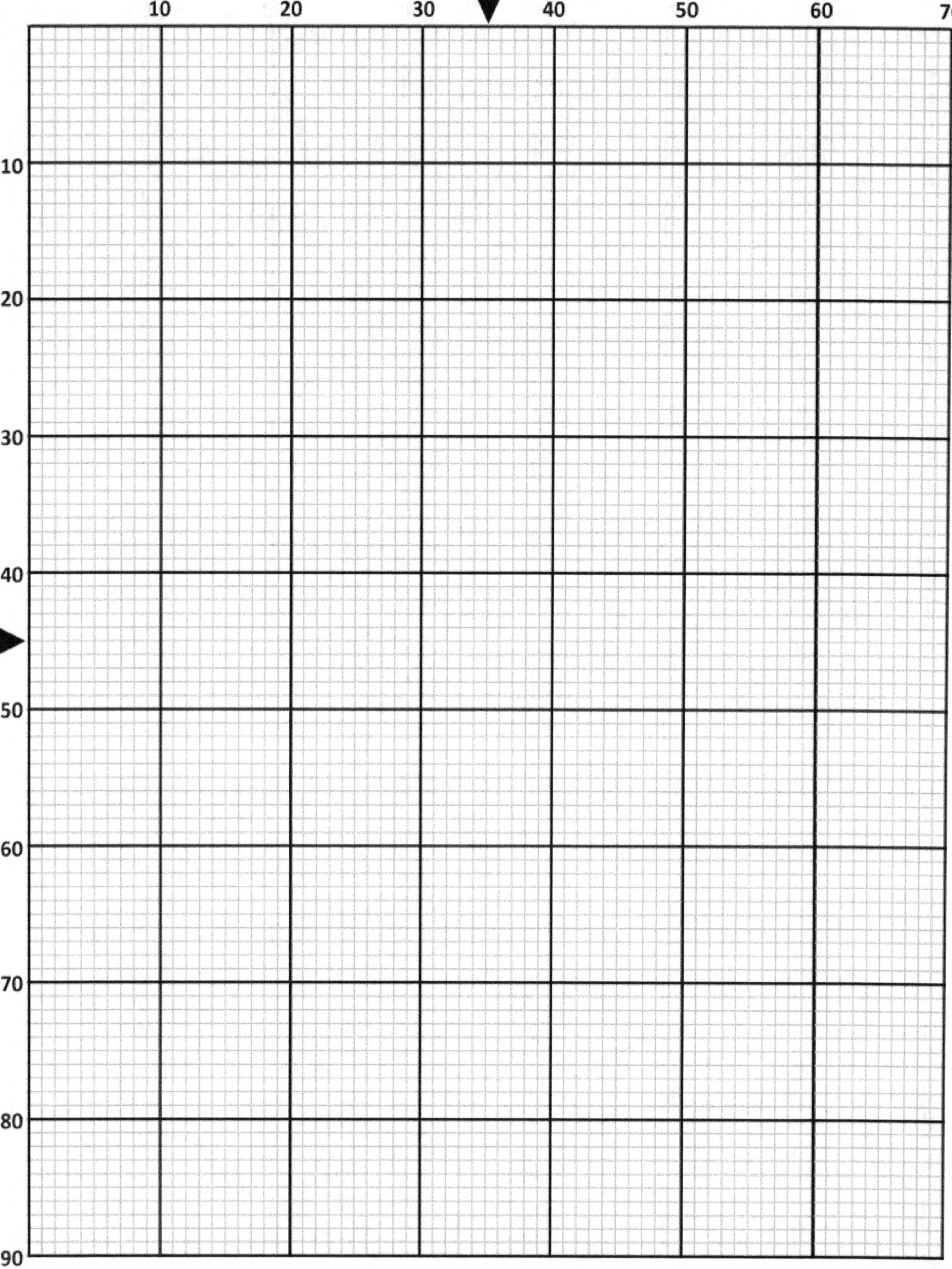

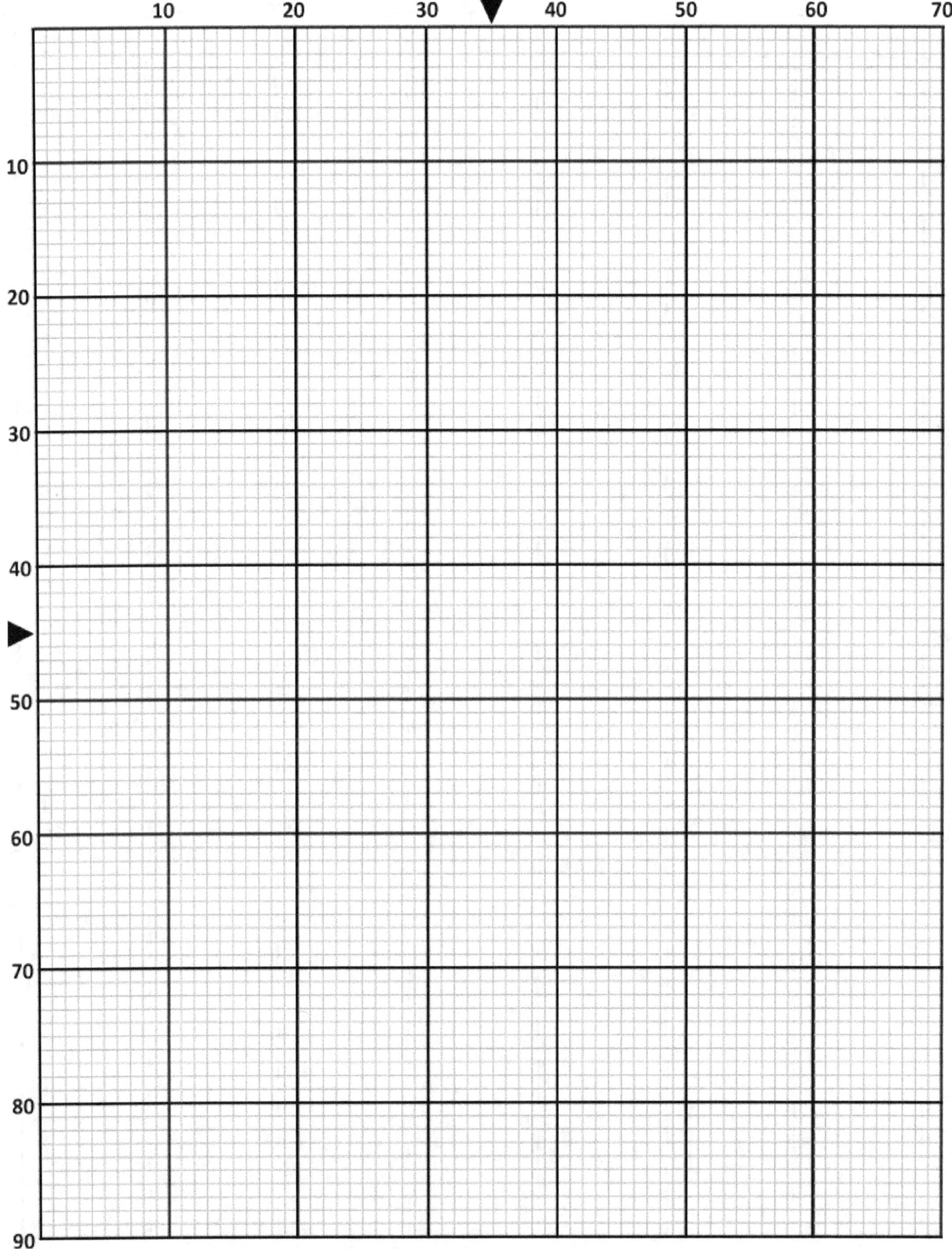

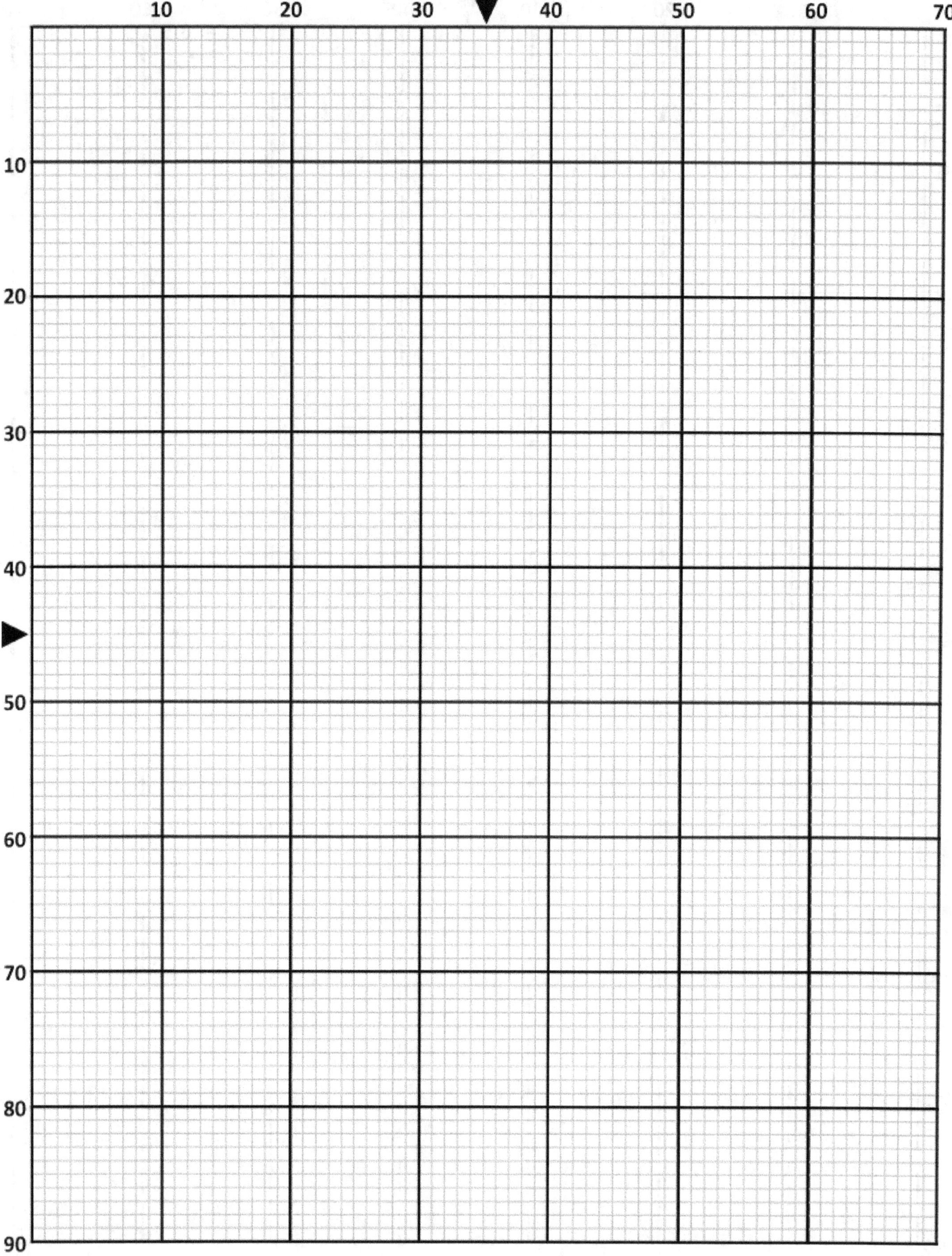

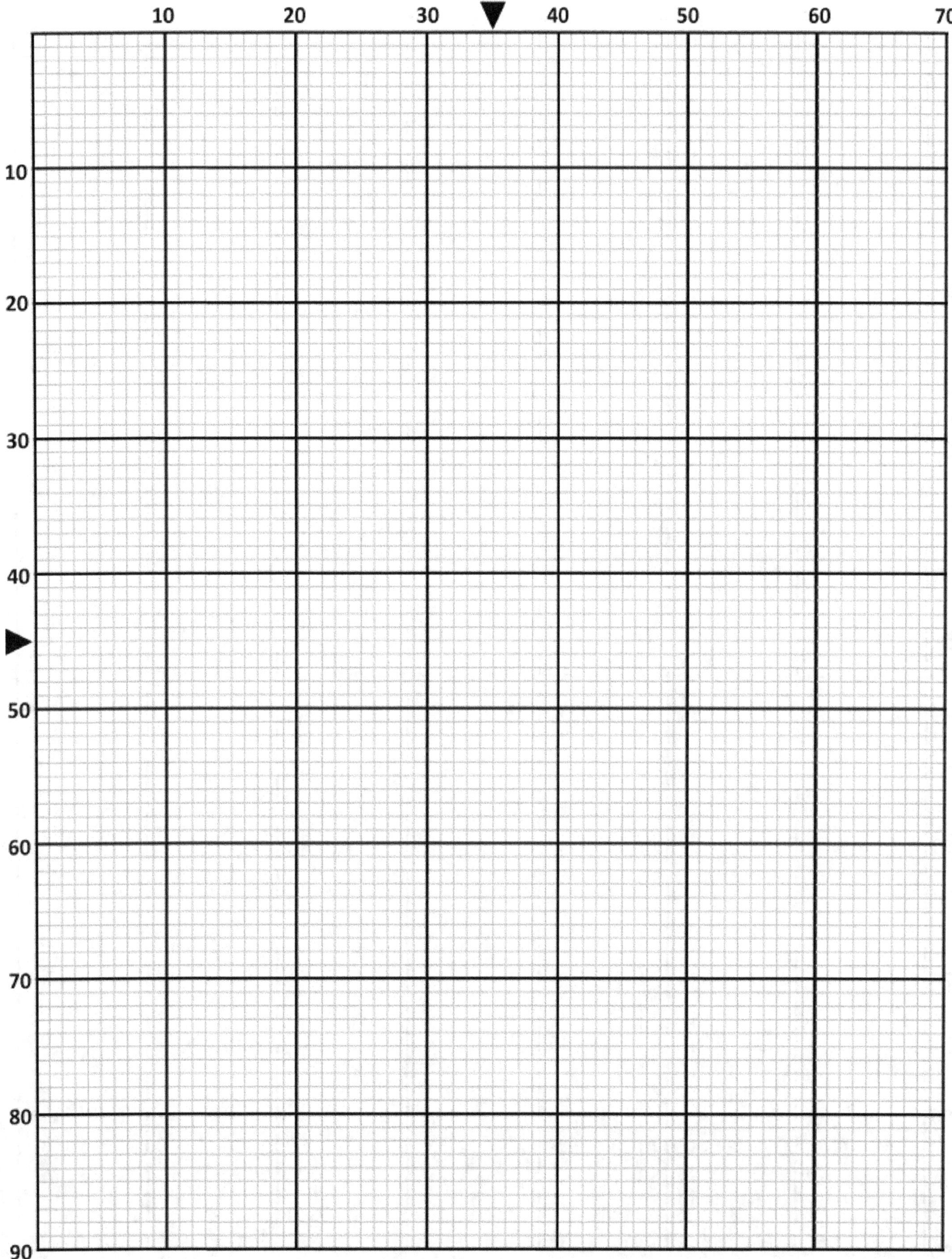

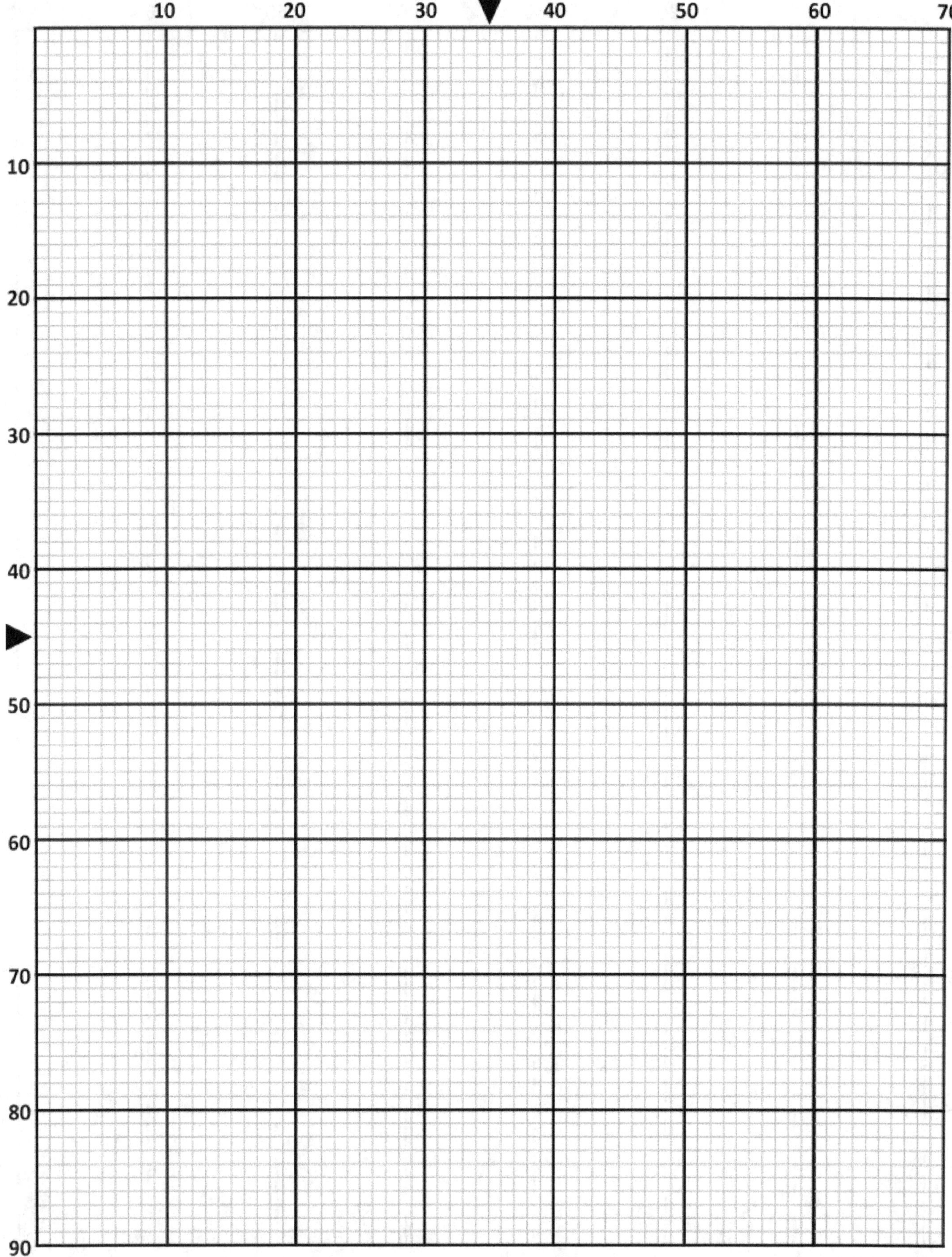

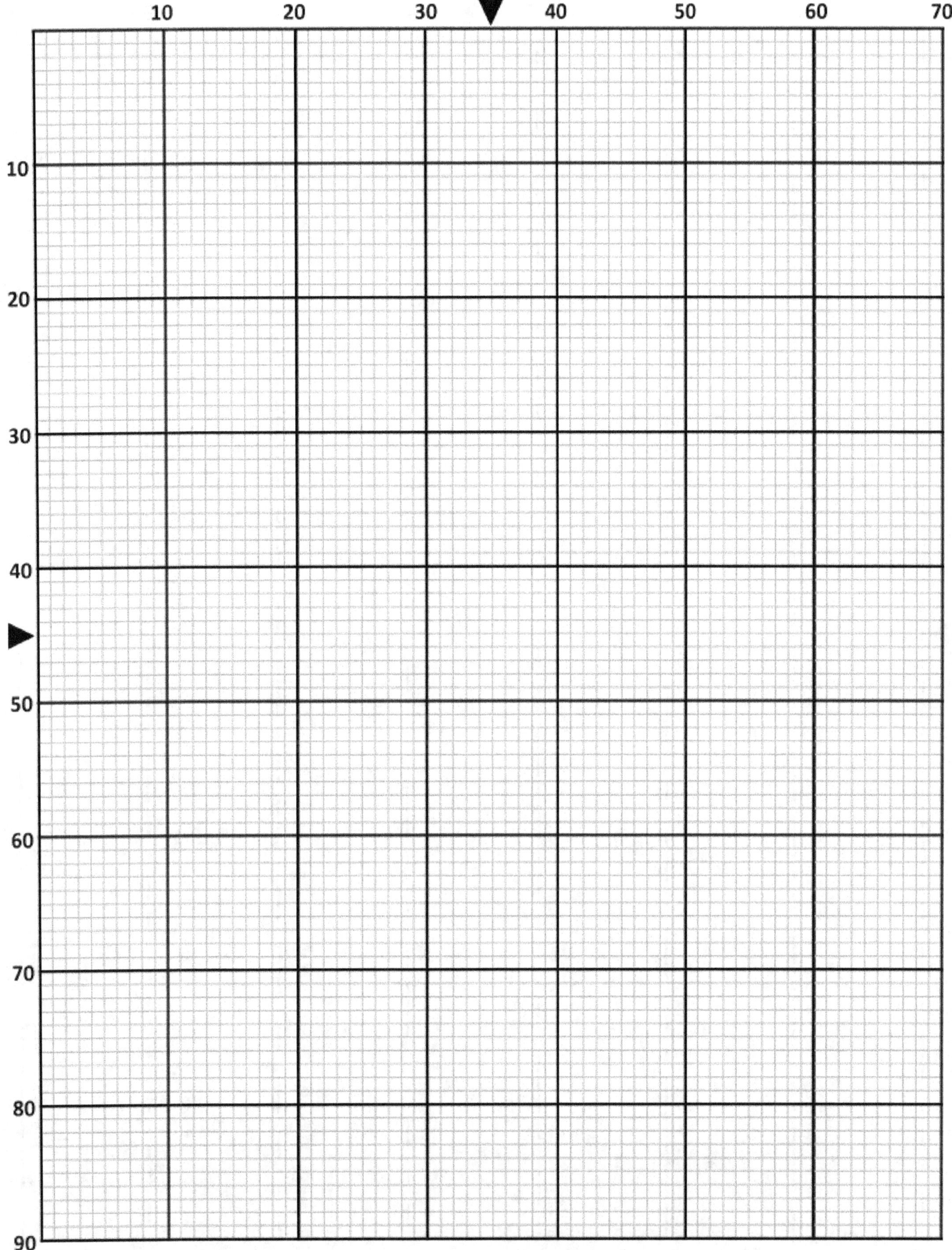

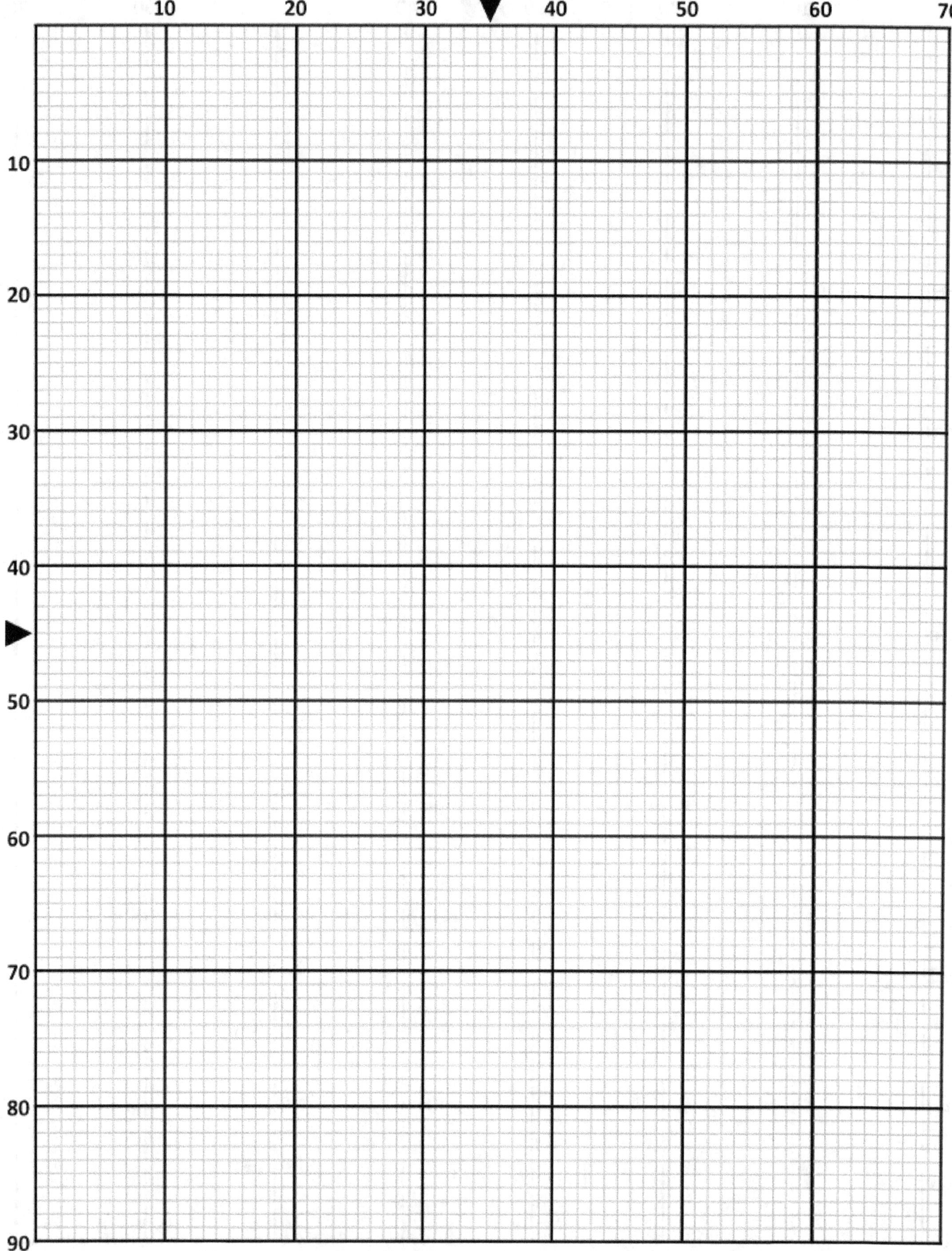

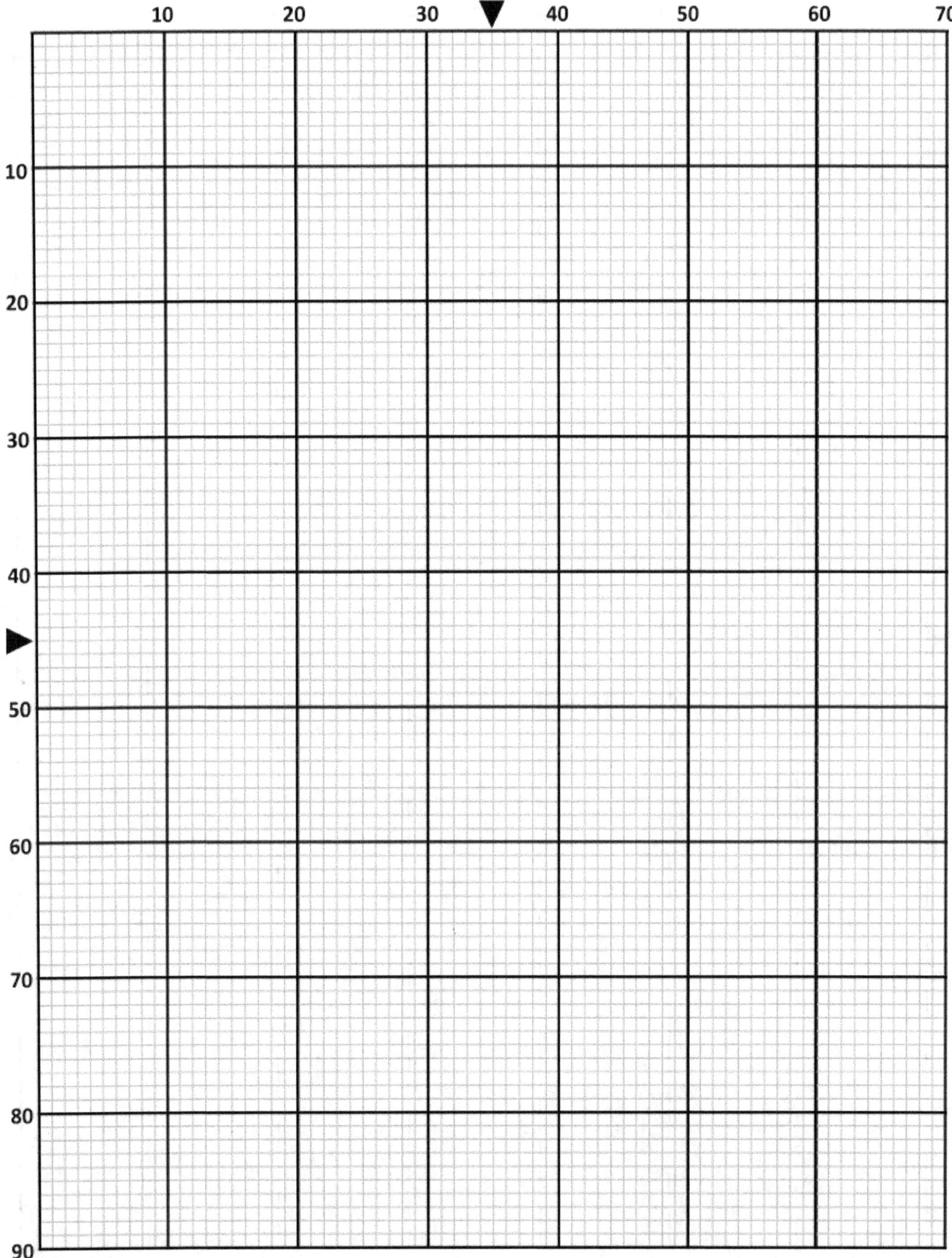

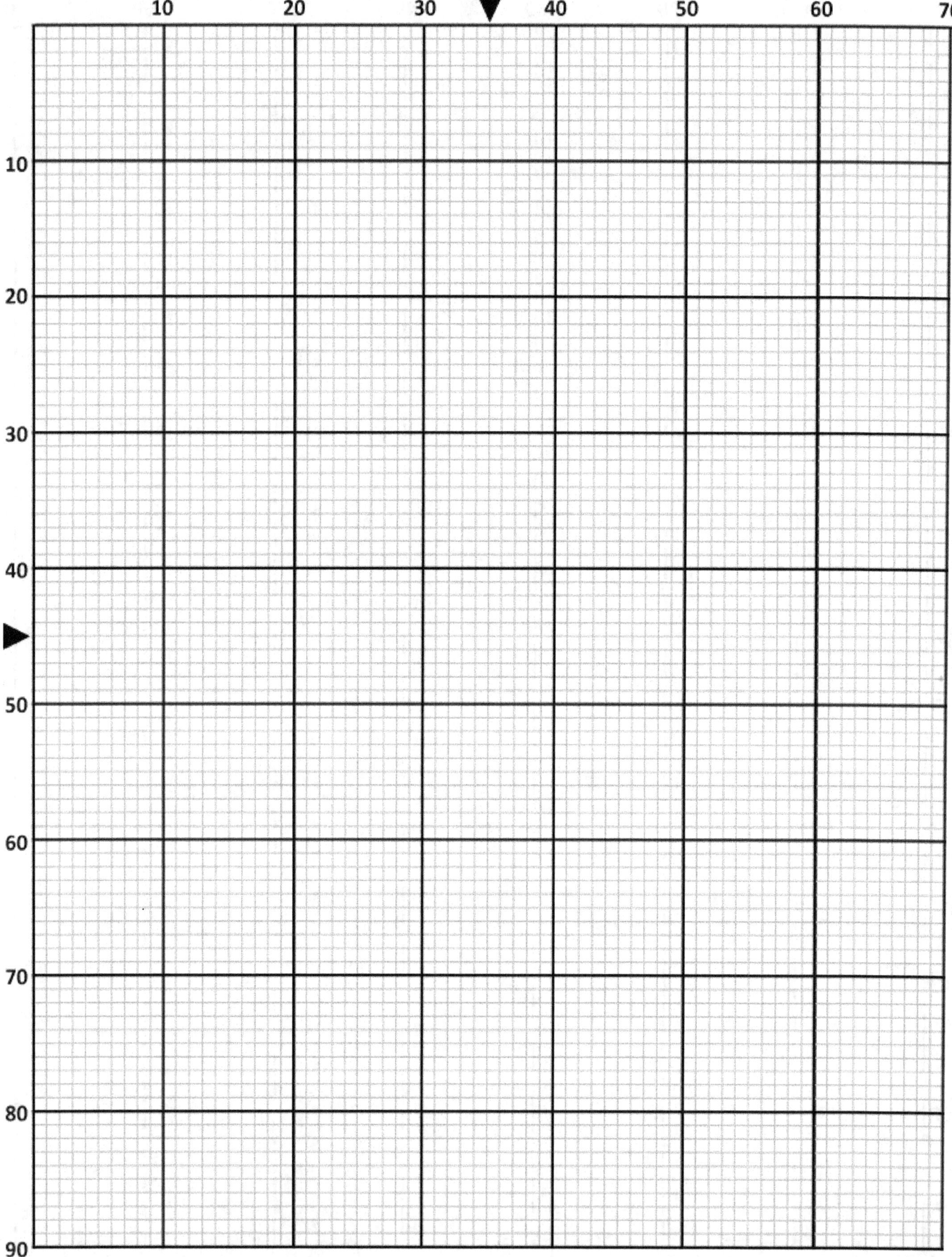

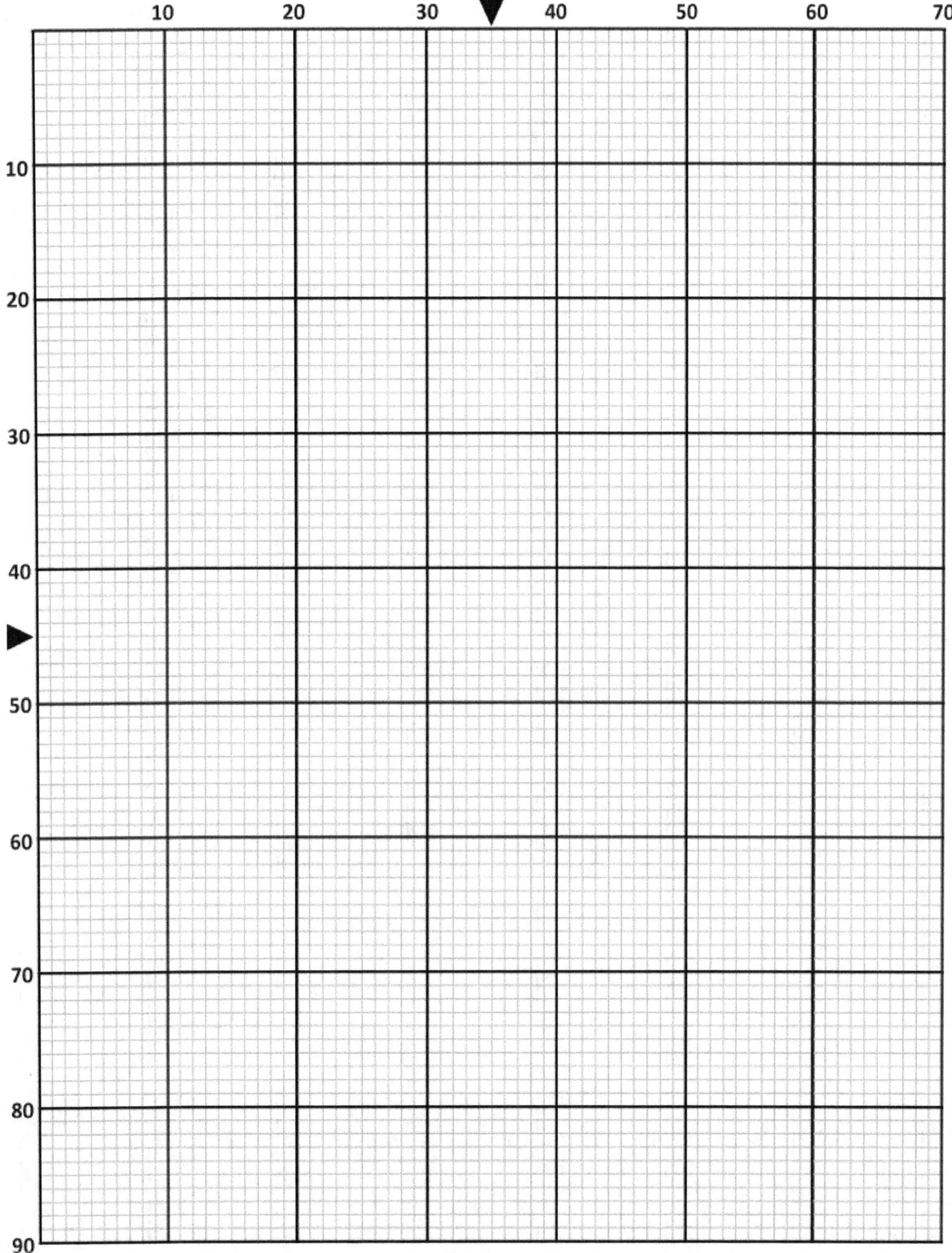

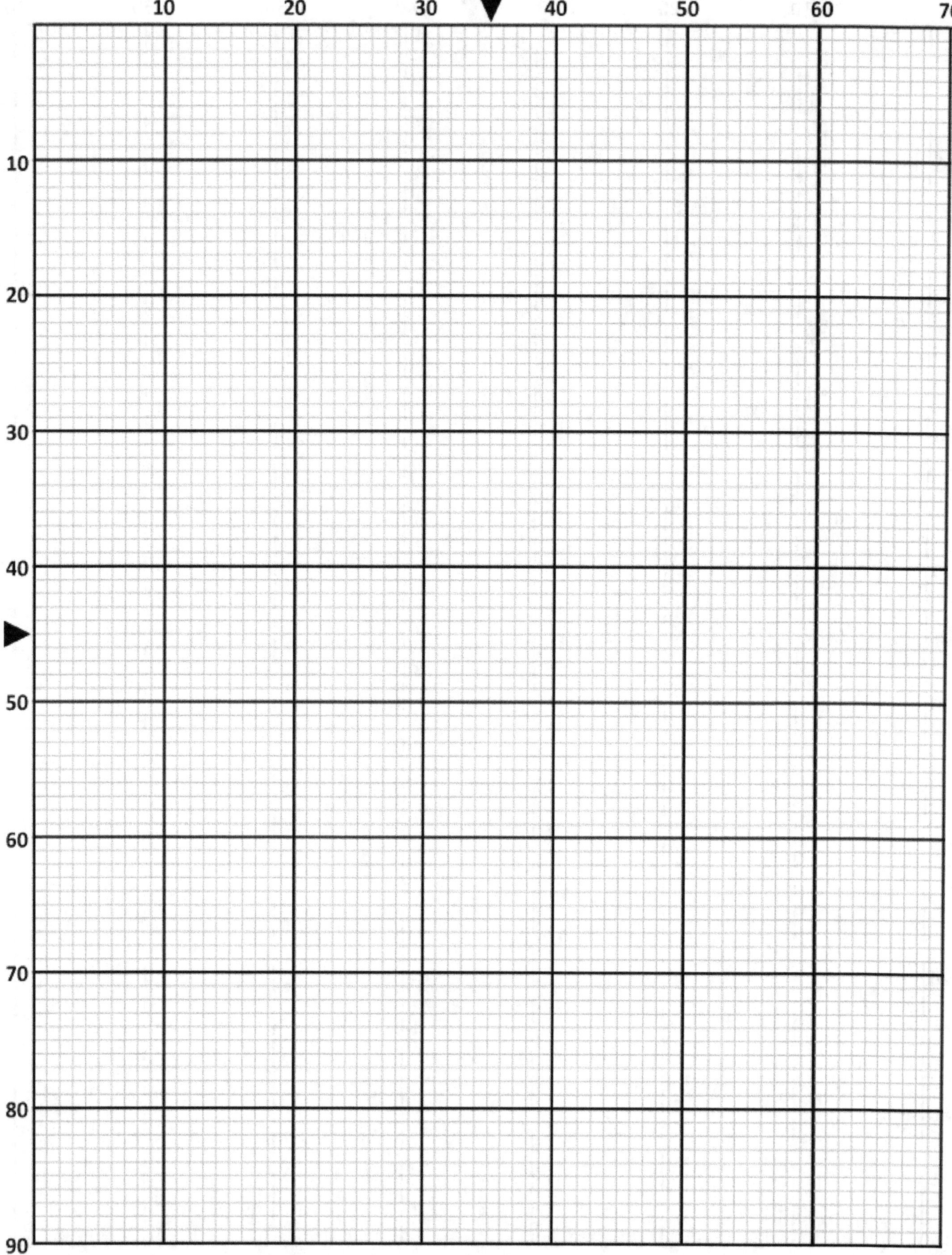

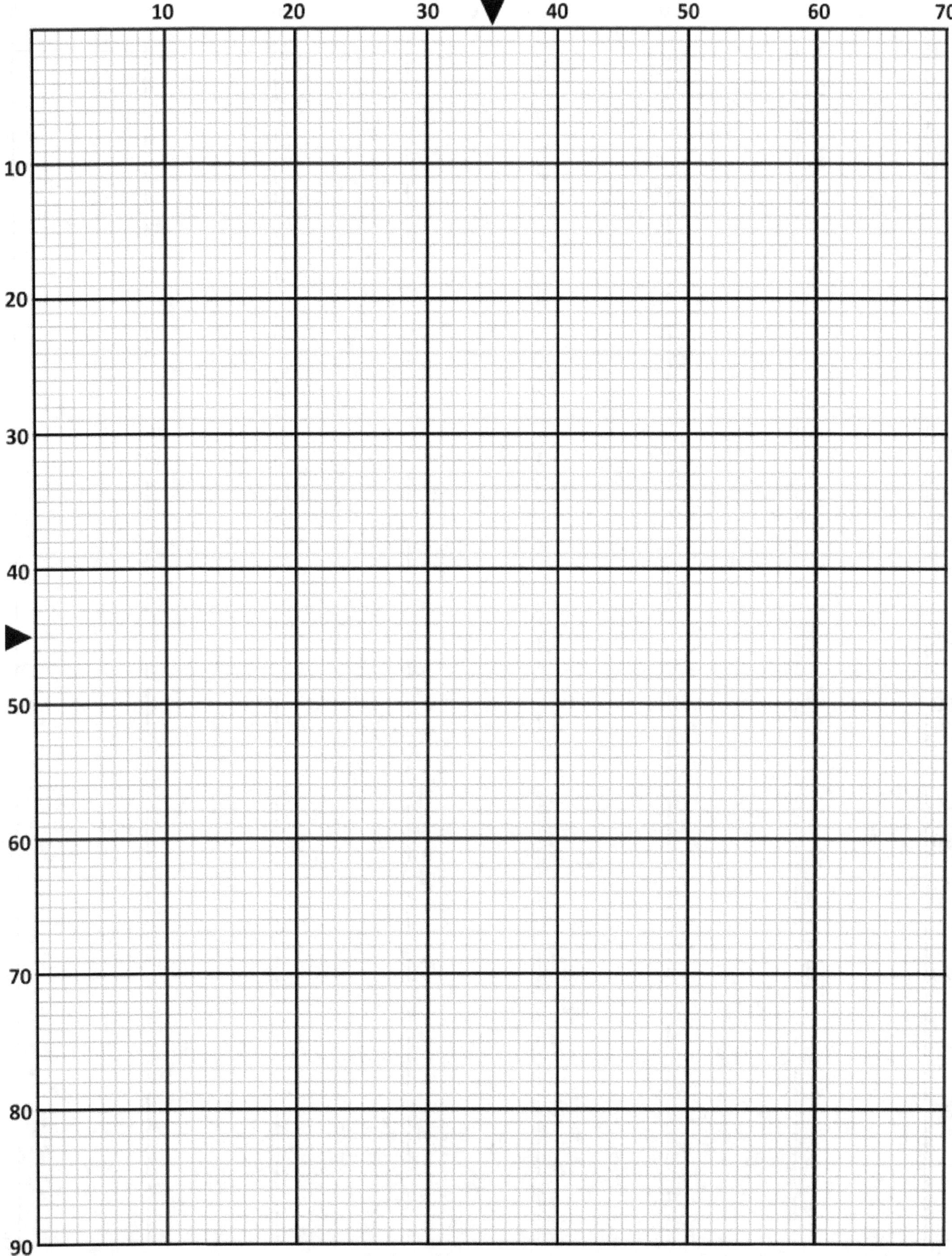

10
20
30
40
50
60
70
10
20
30
40
50
60
70
80
90

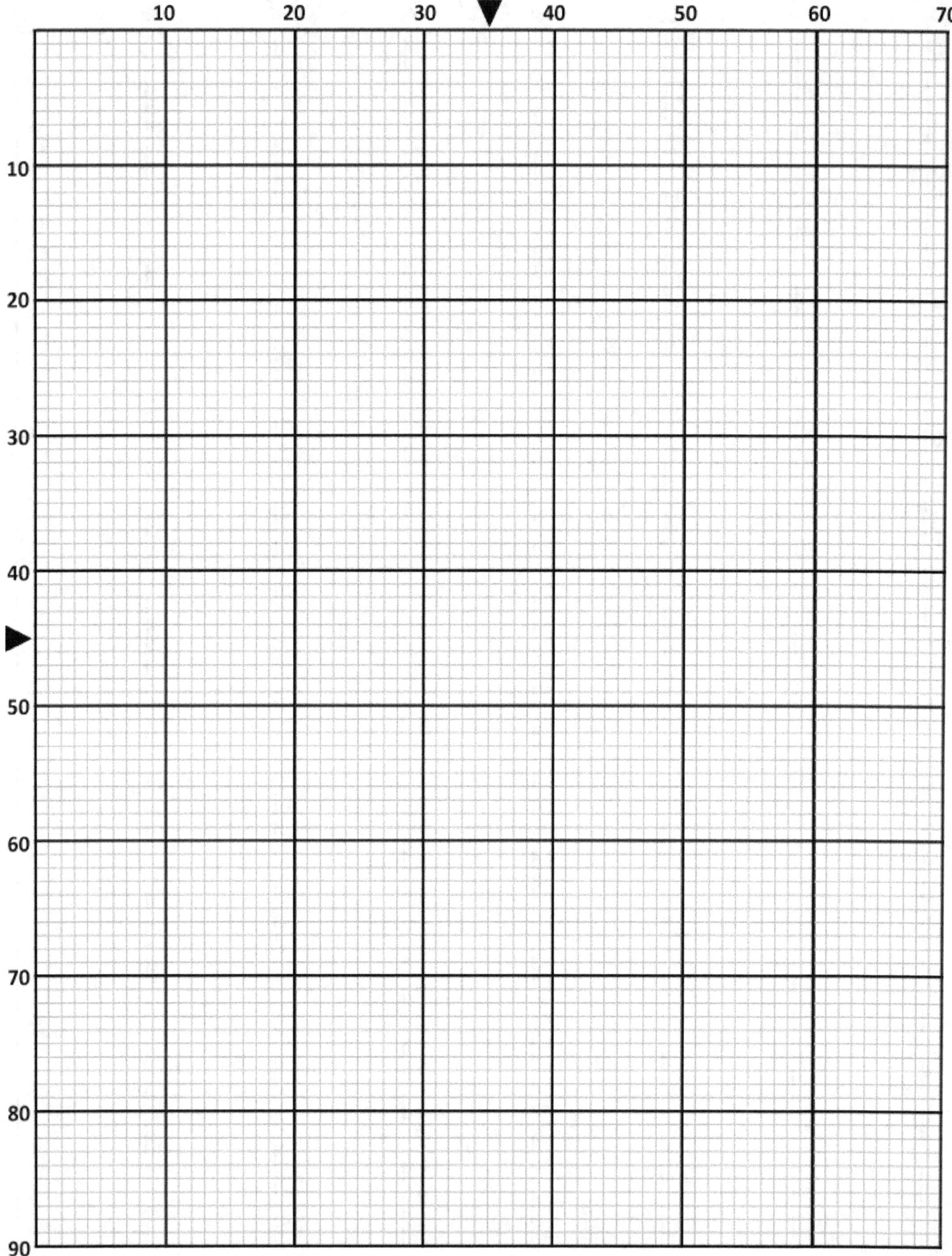

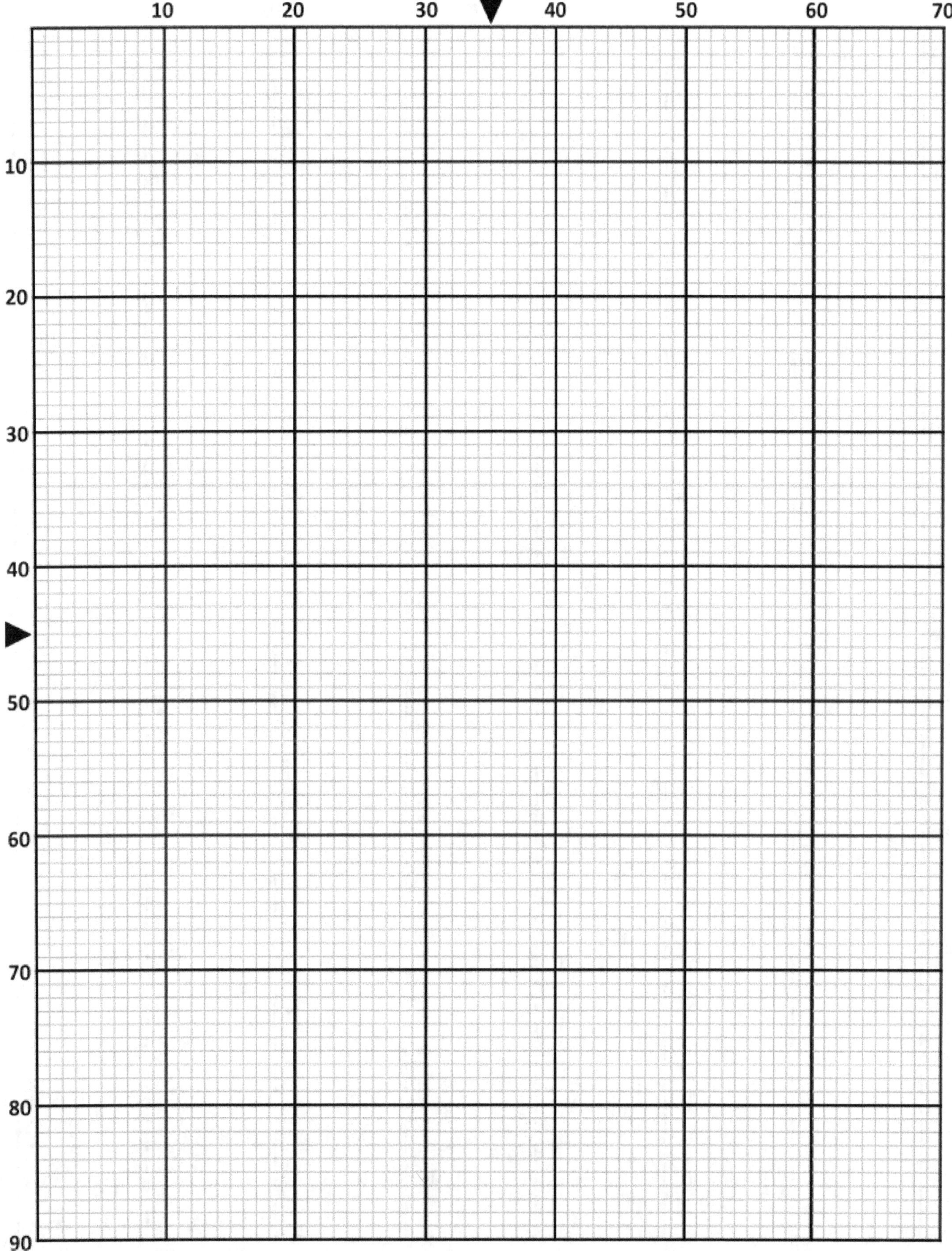

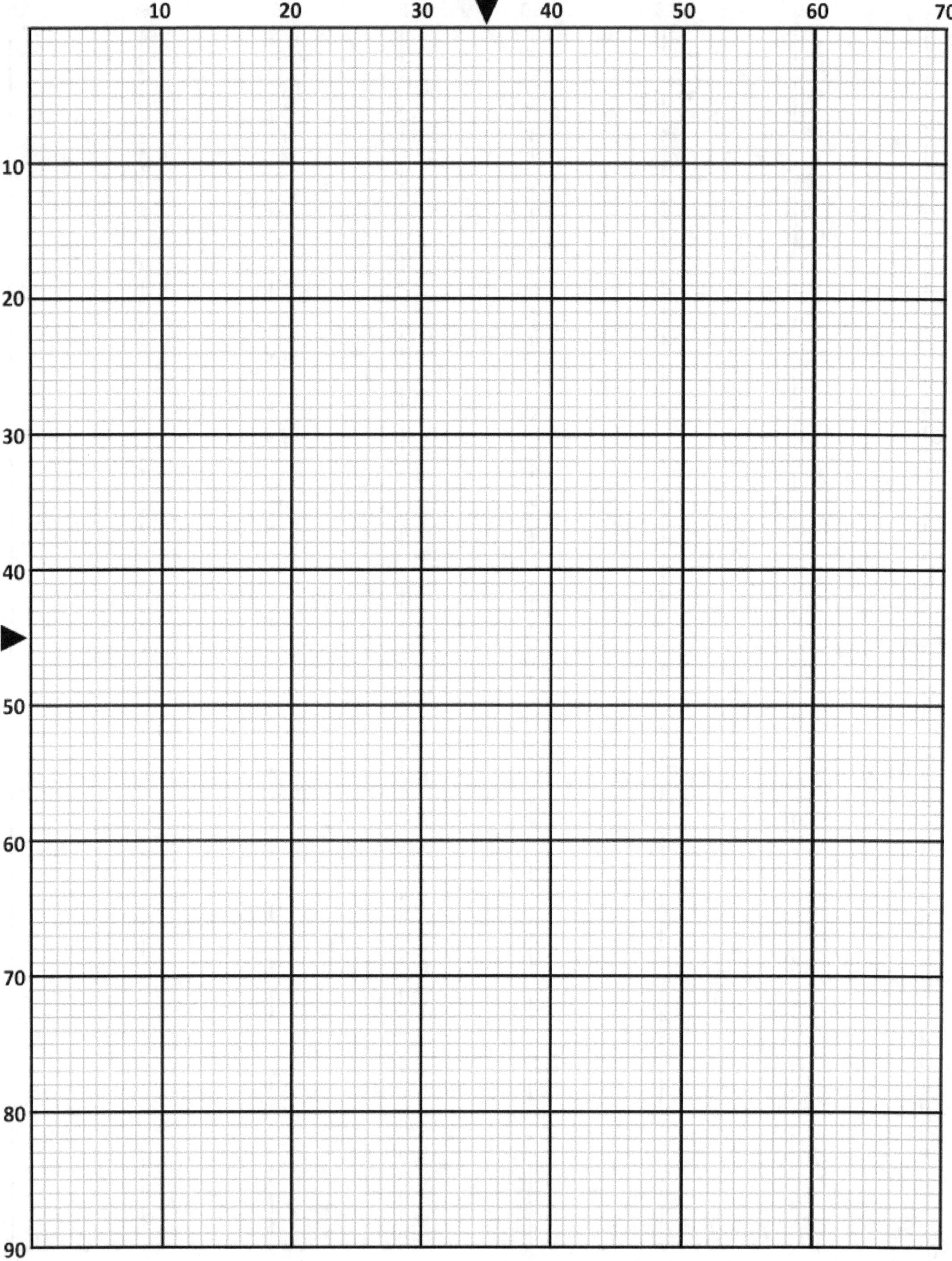

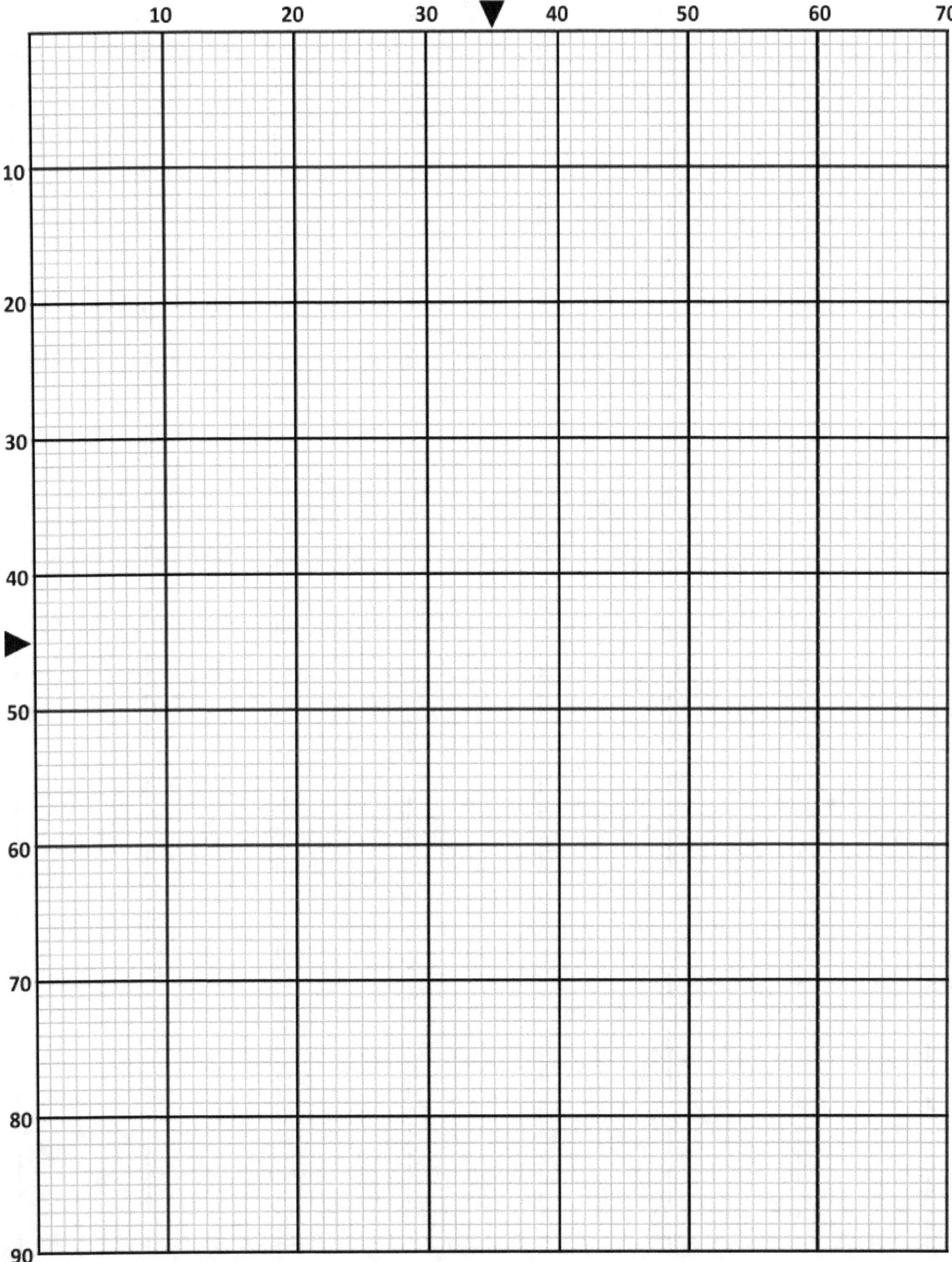

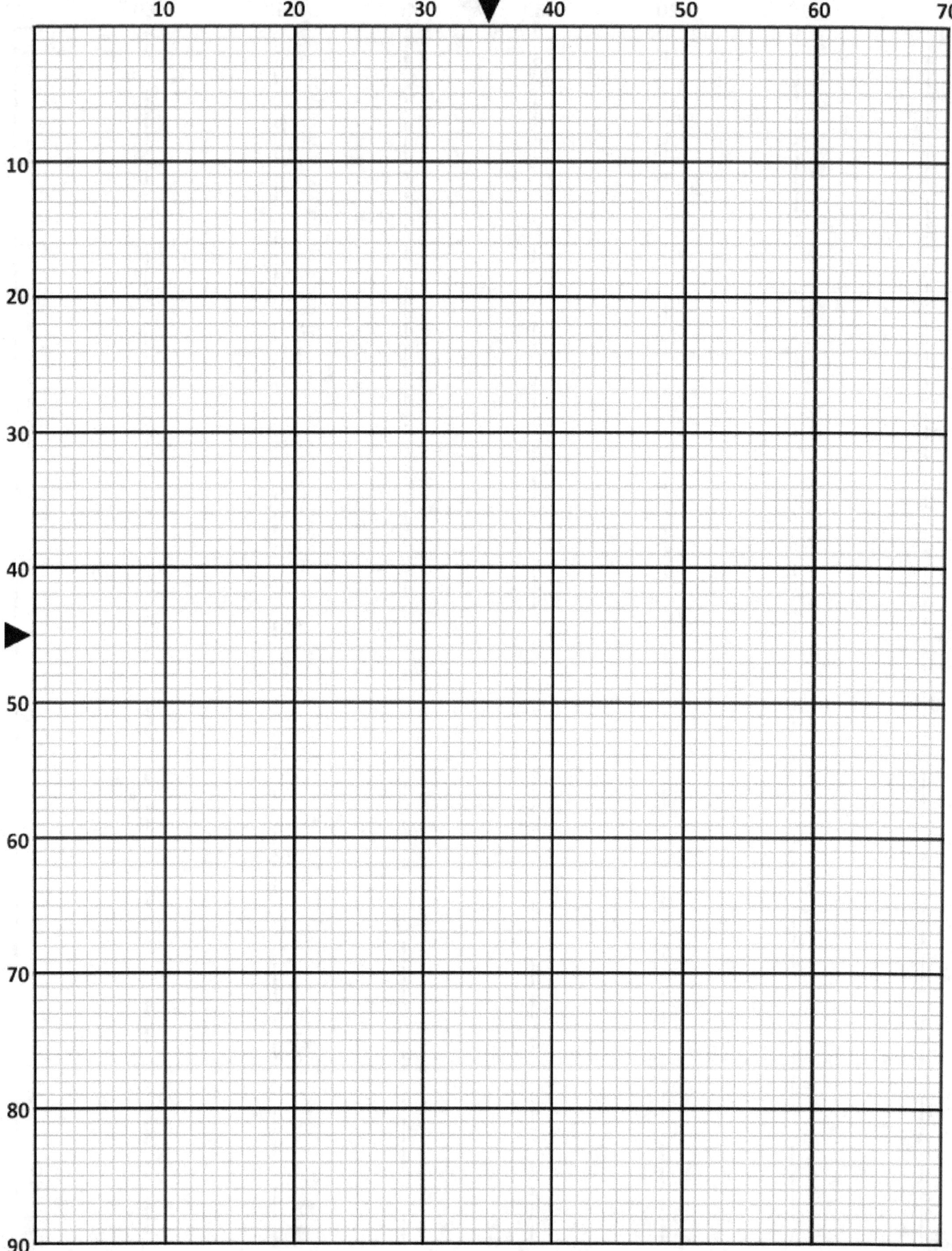

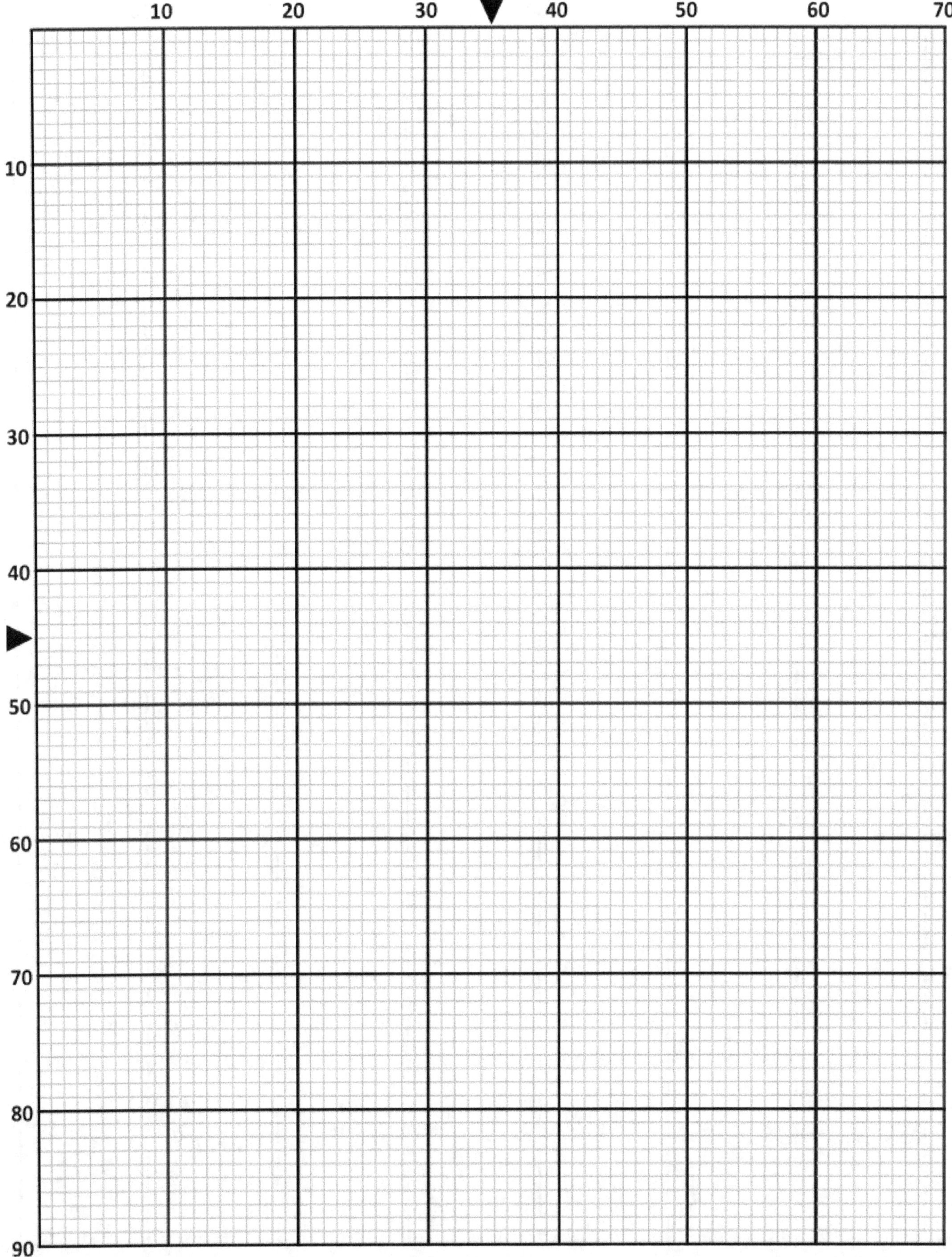

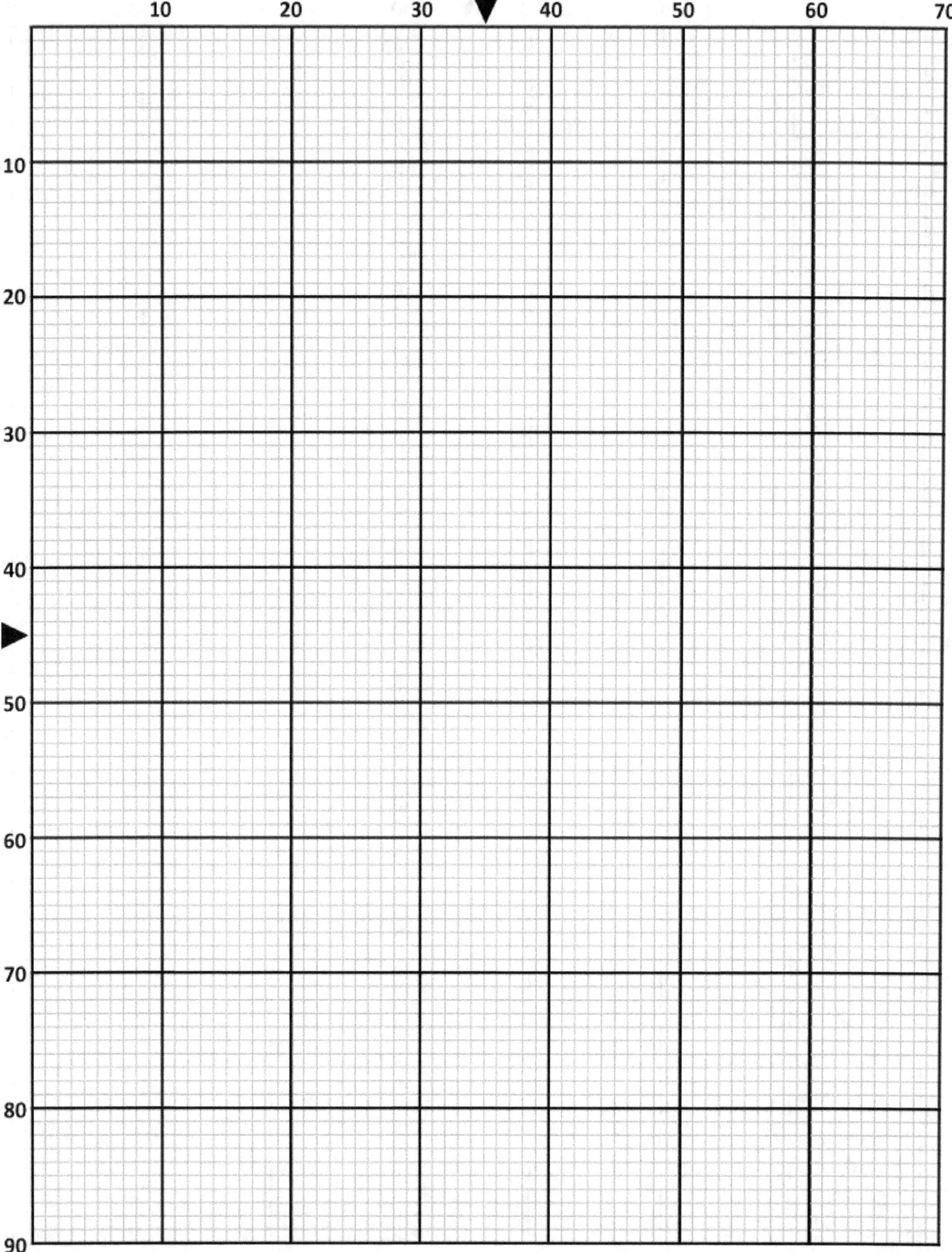

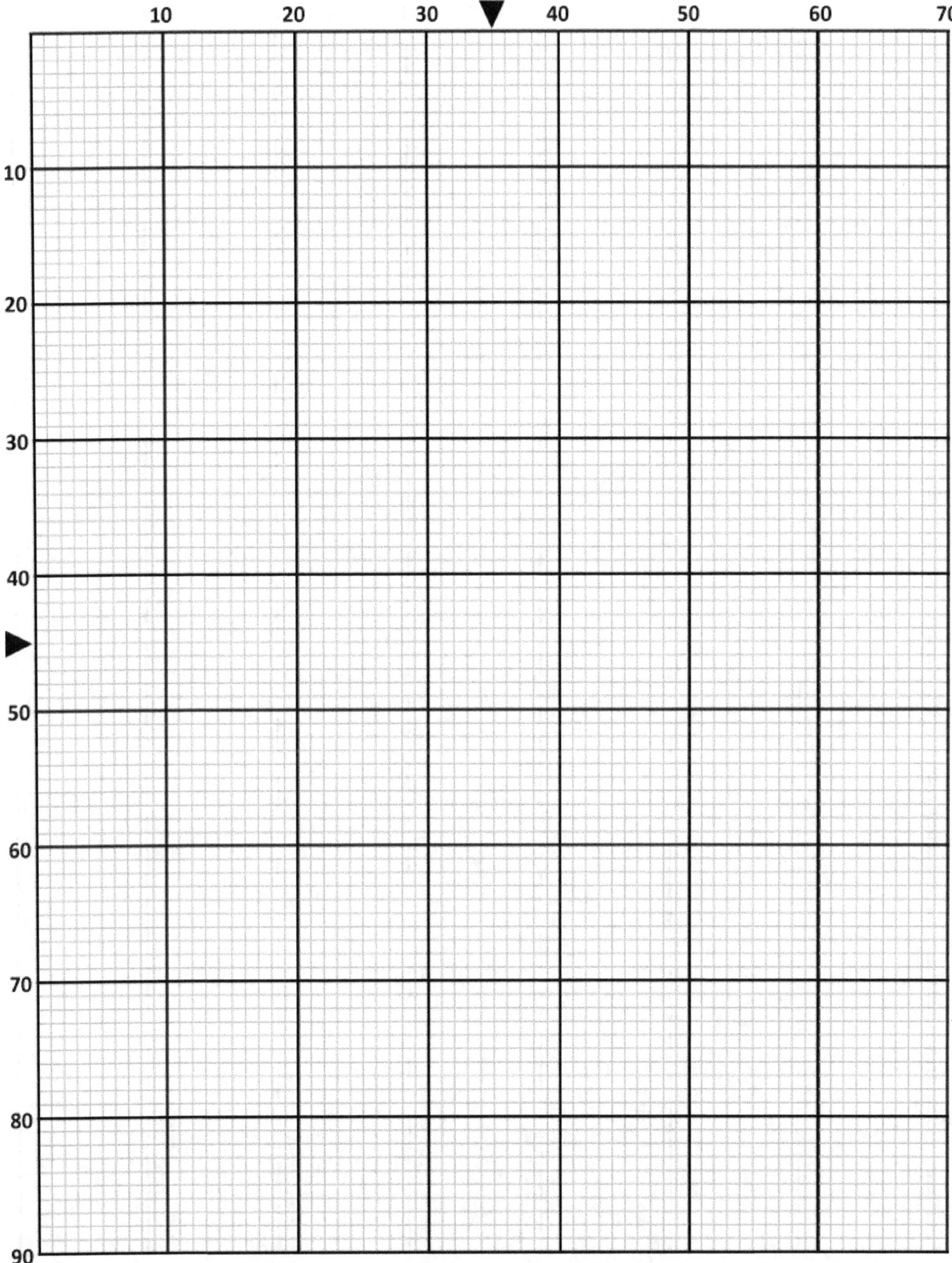

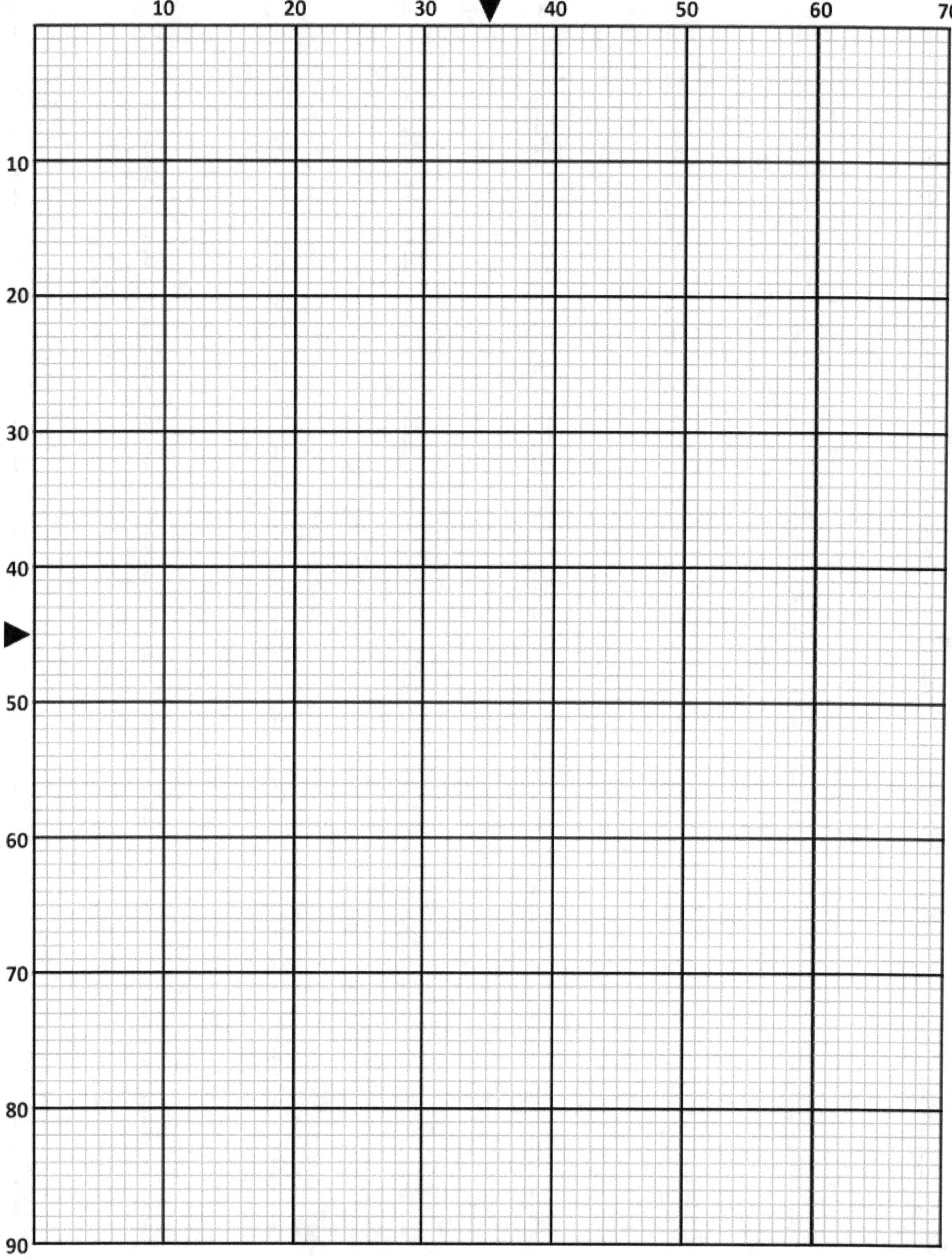

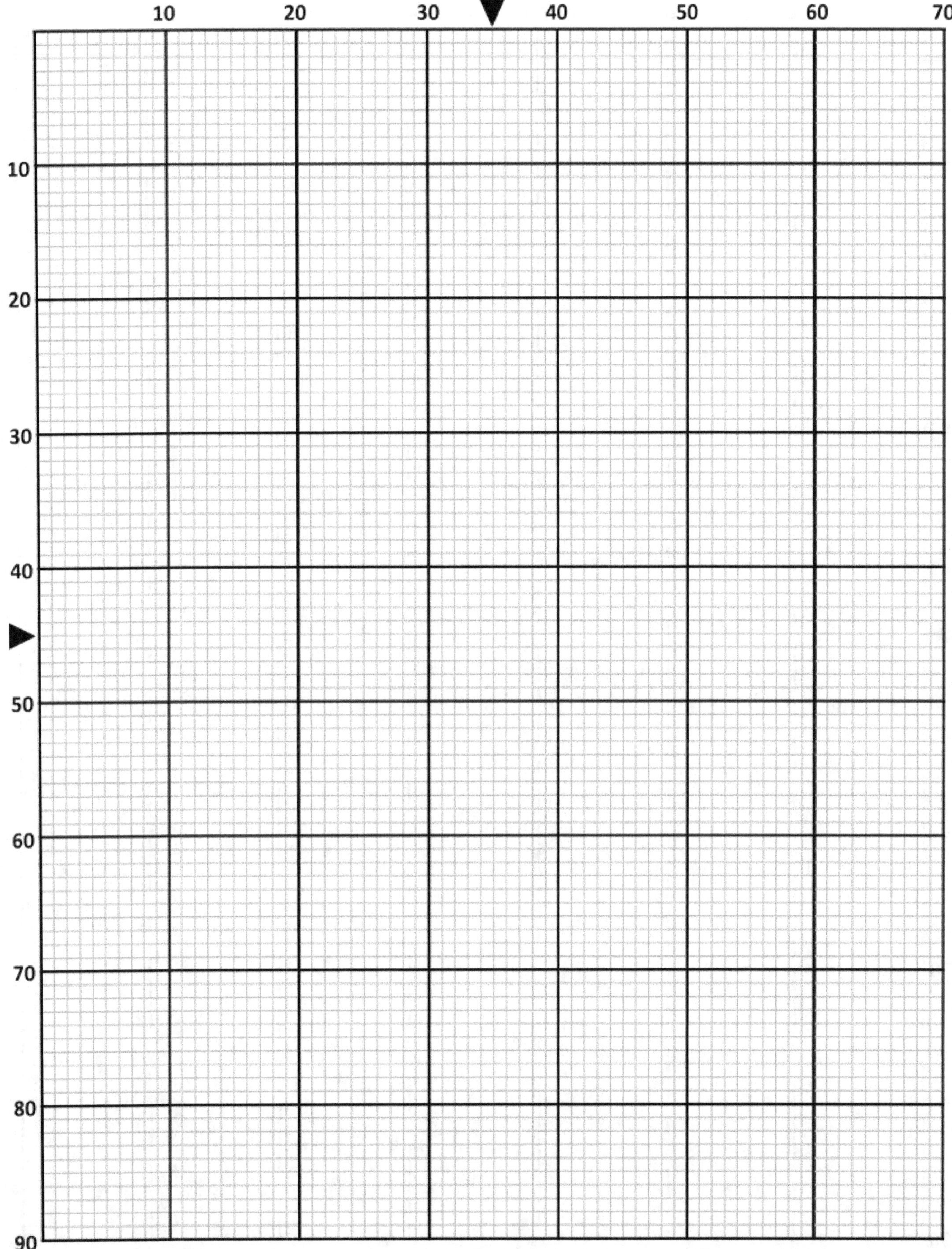

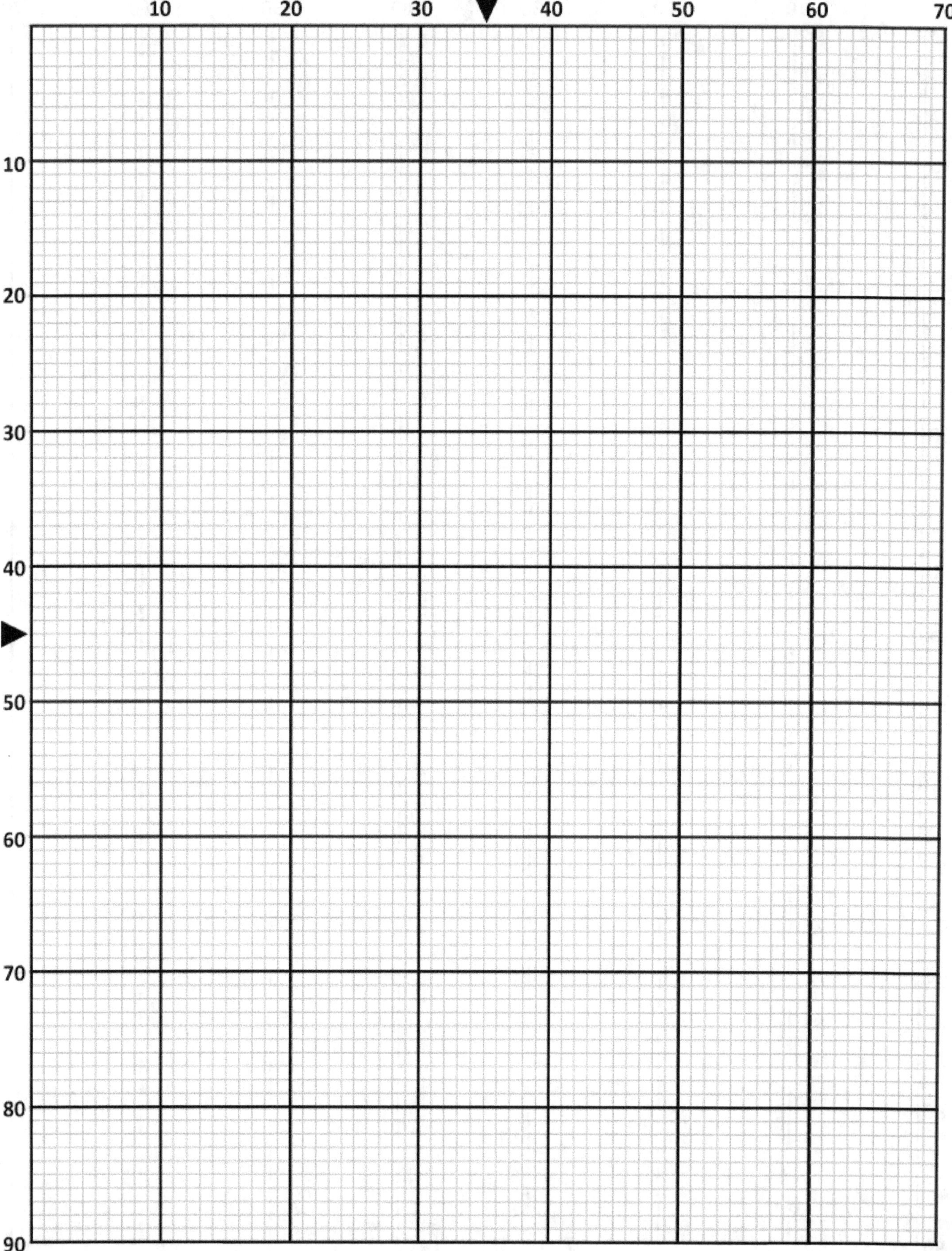

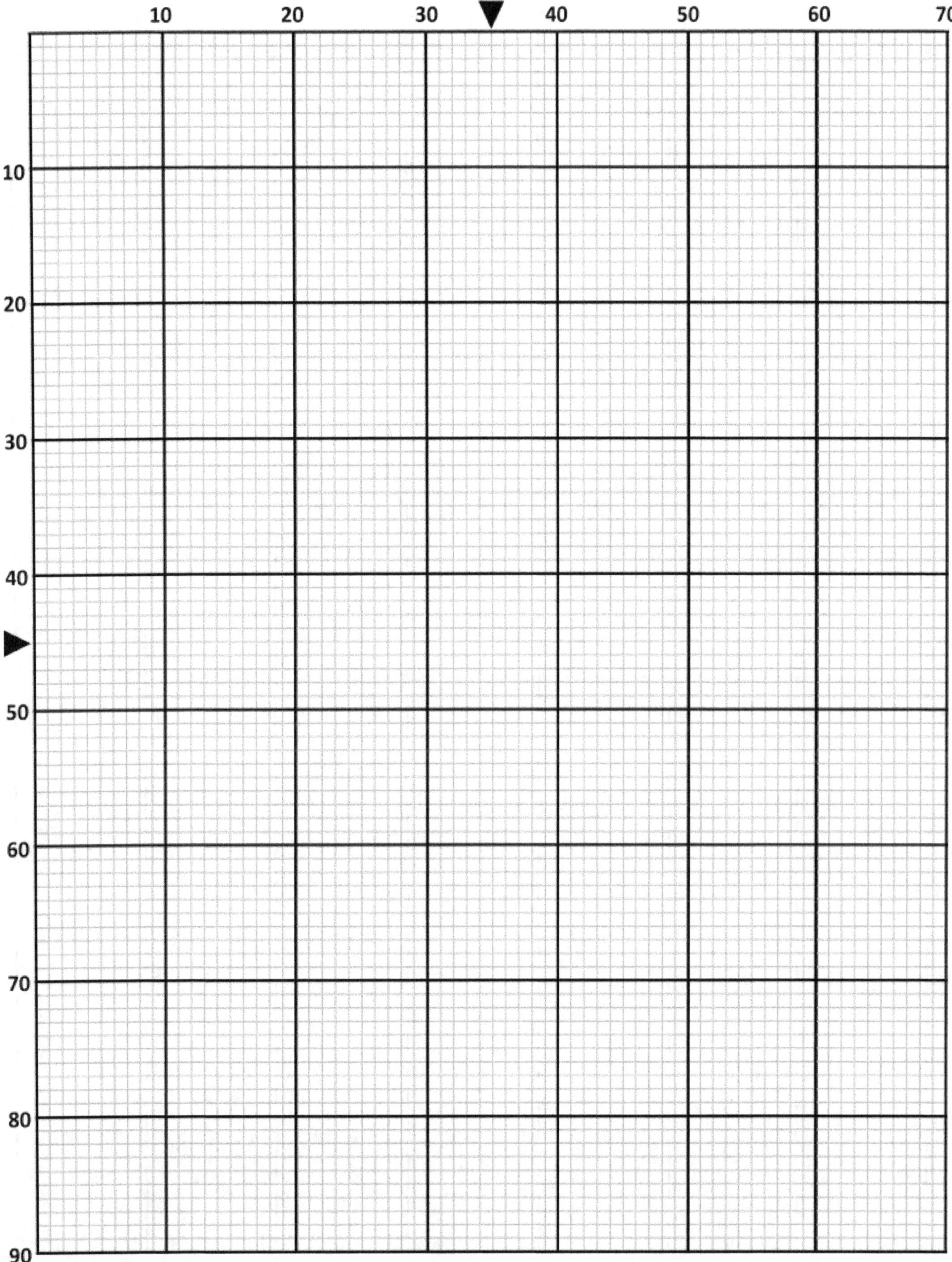

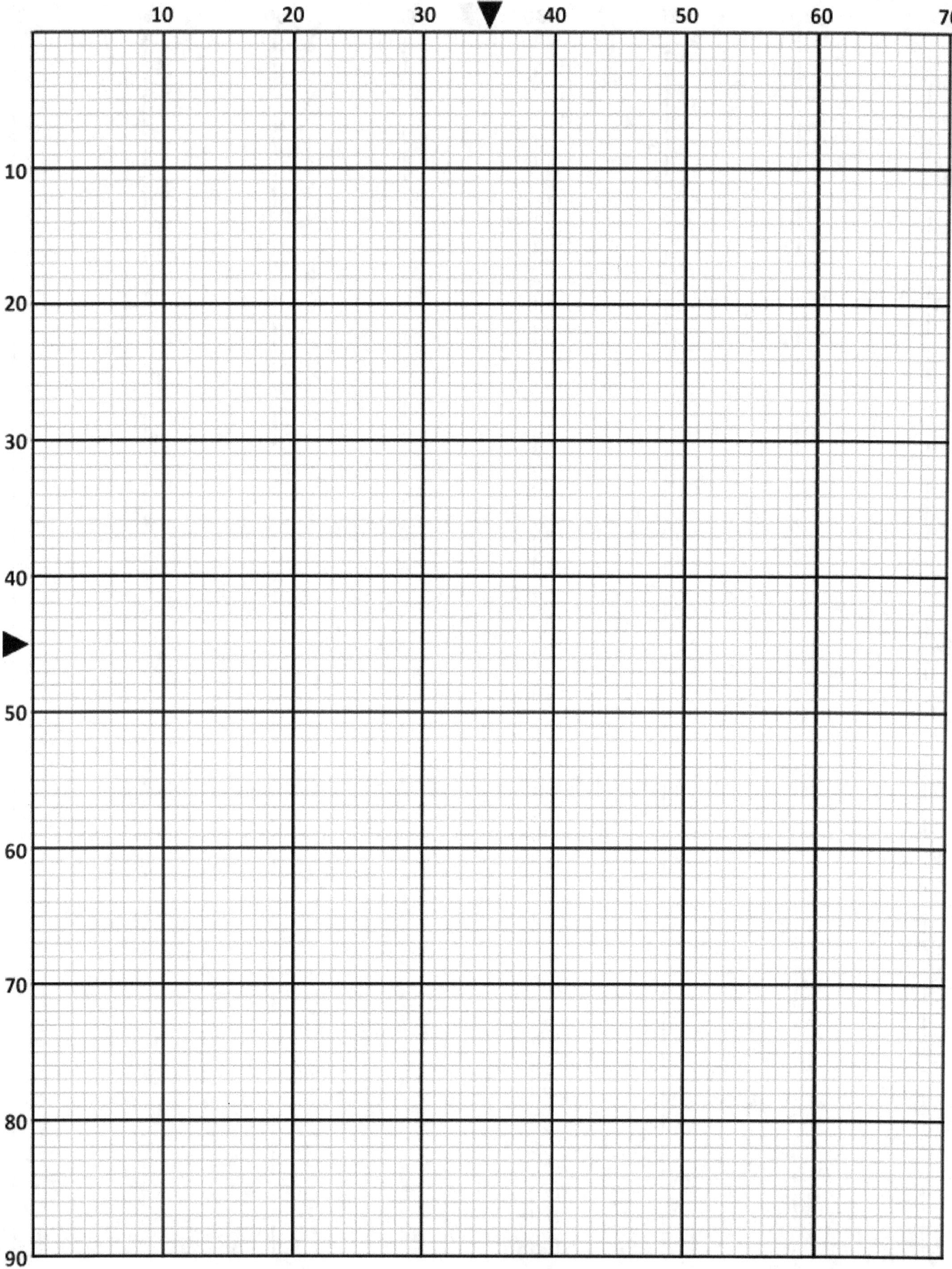

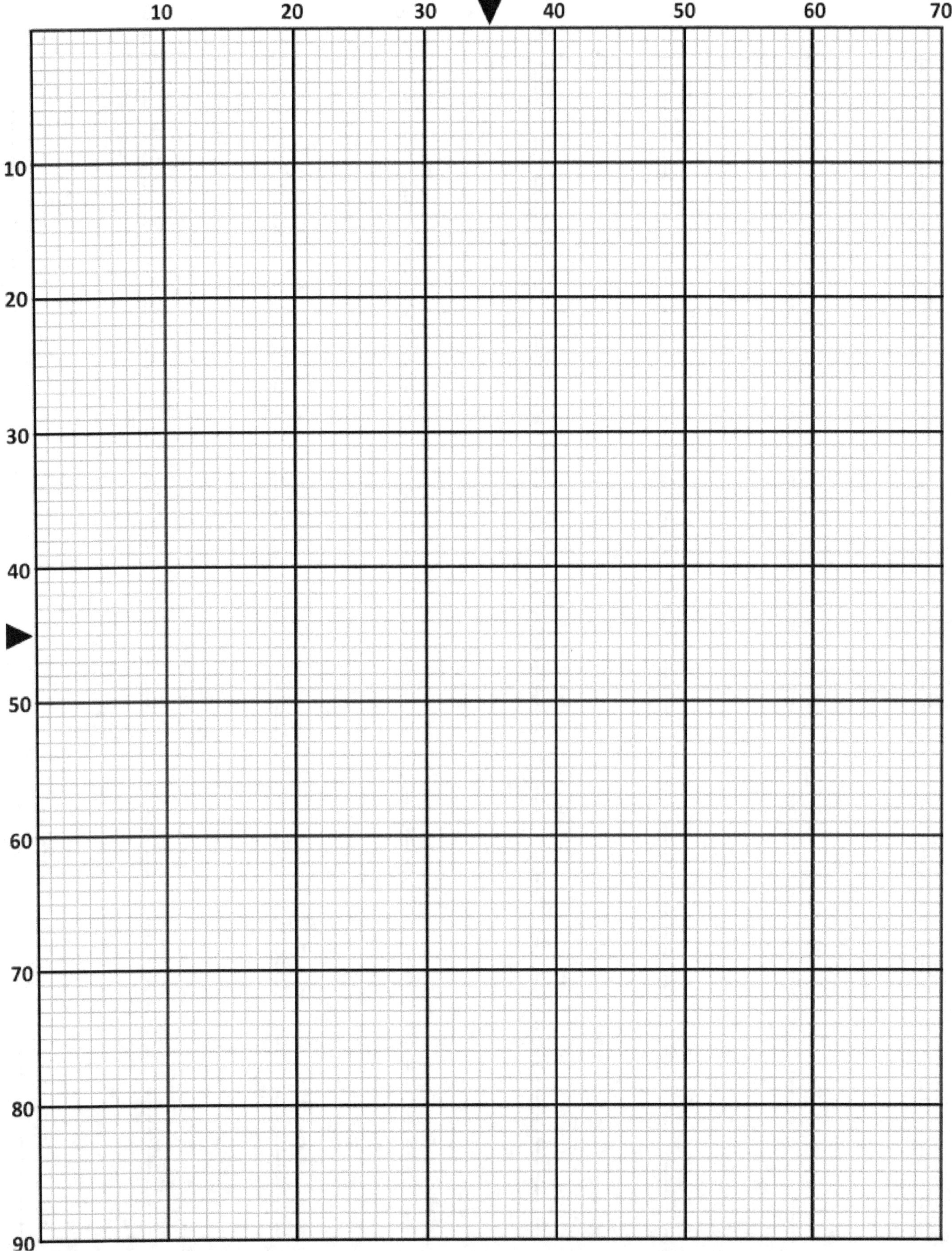

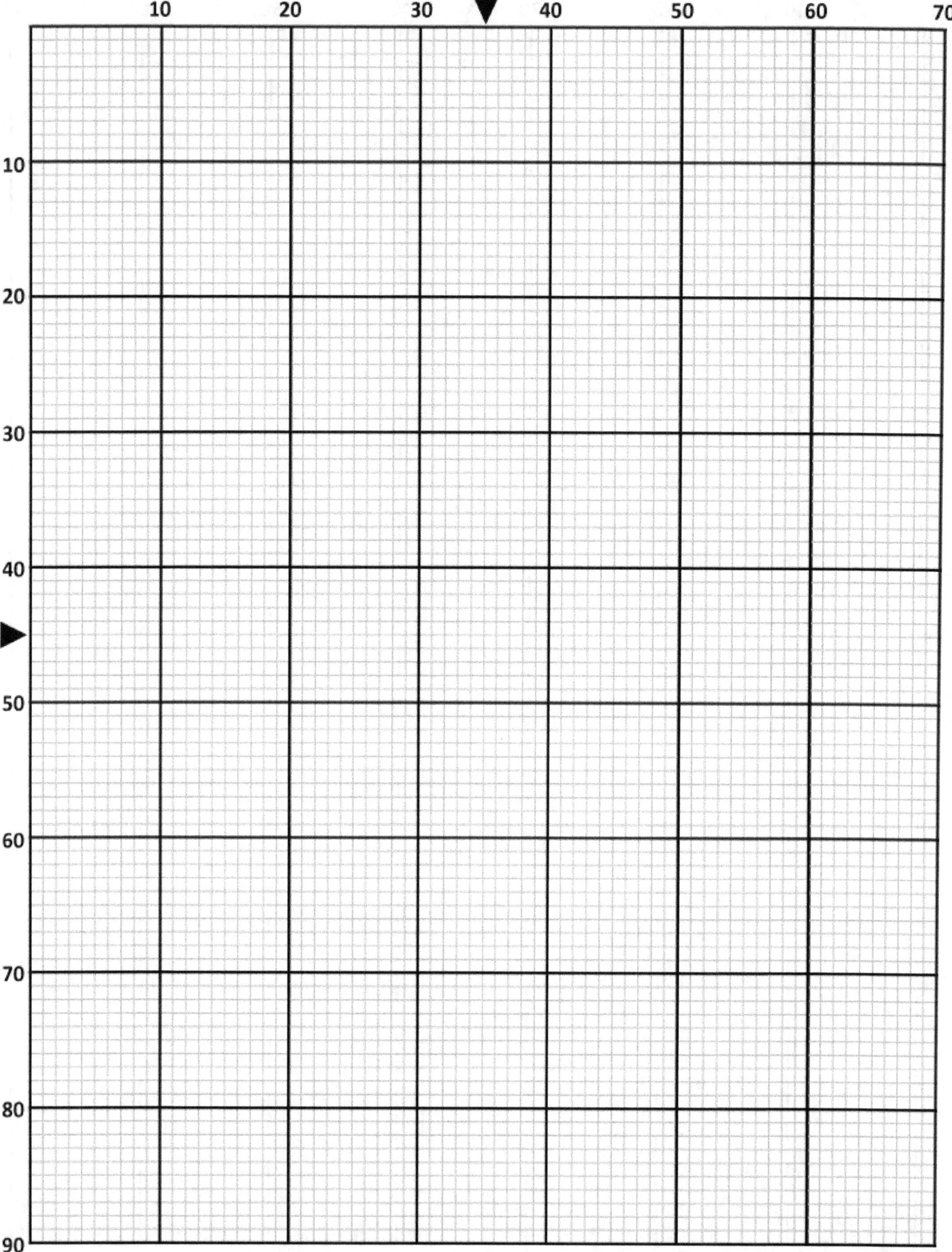

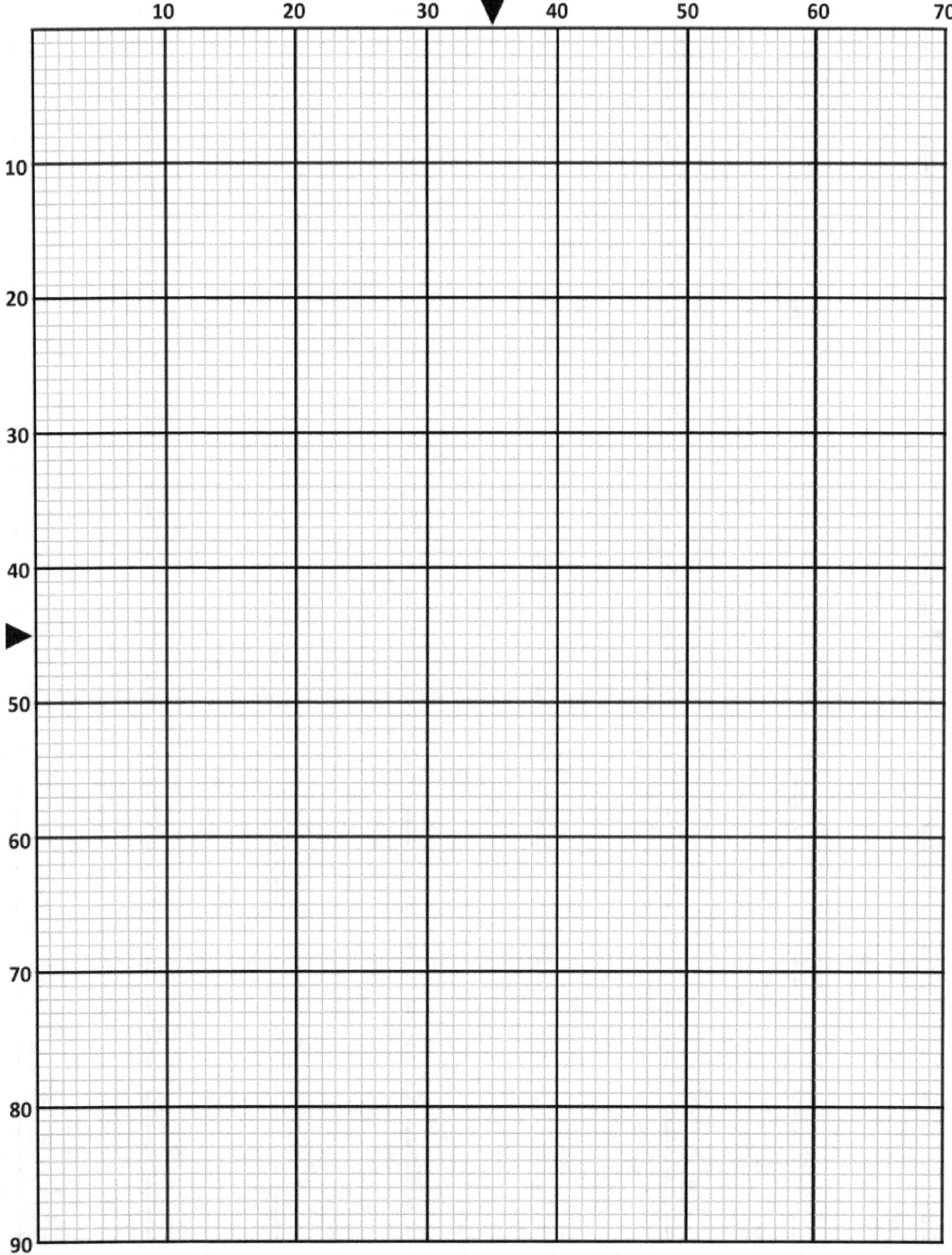

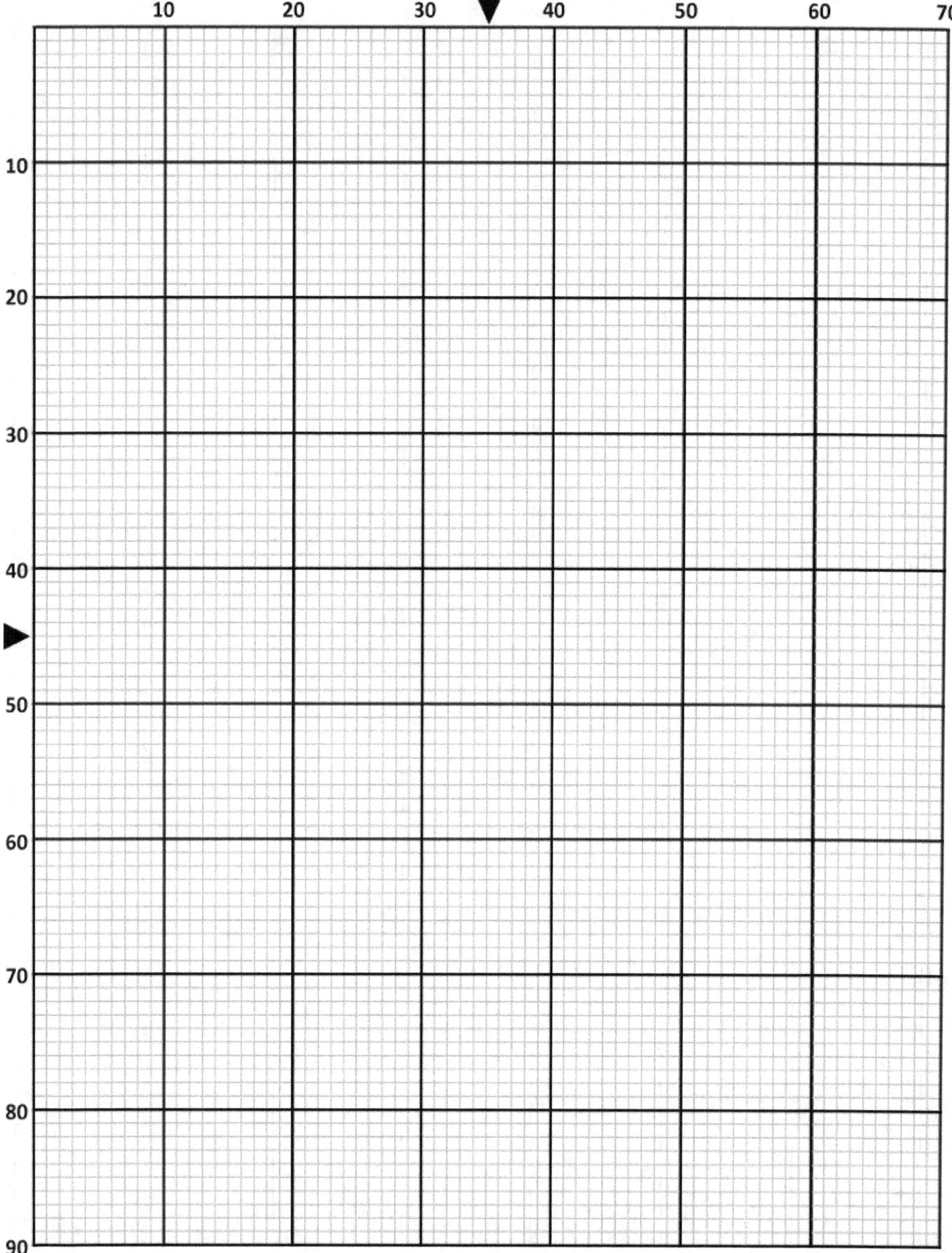

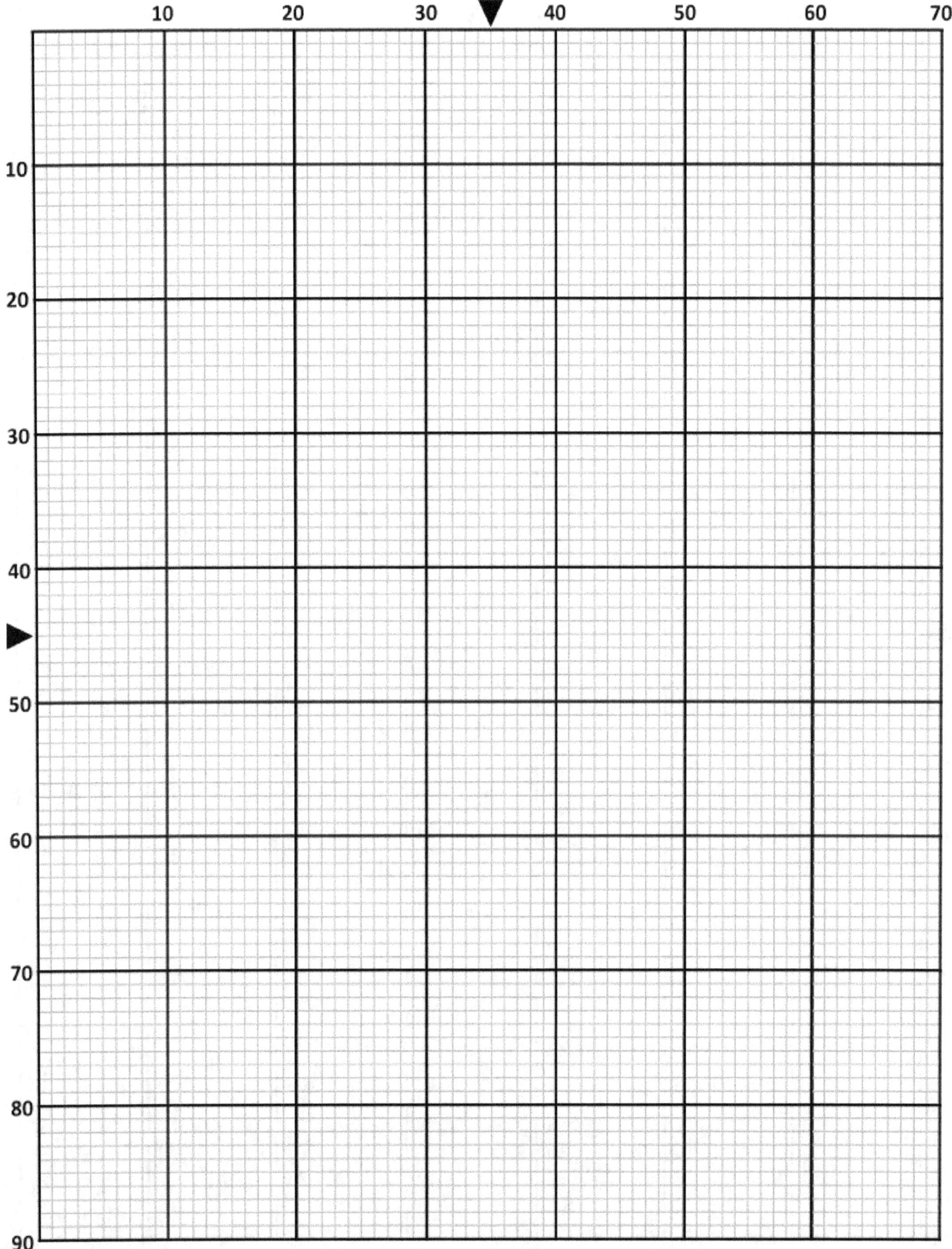

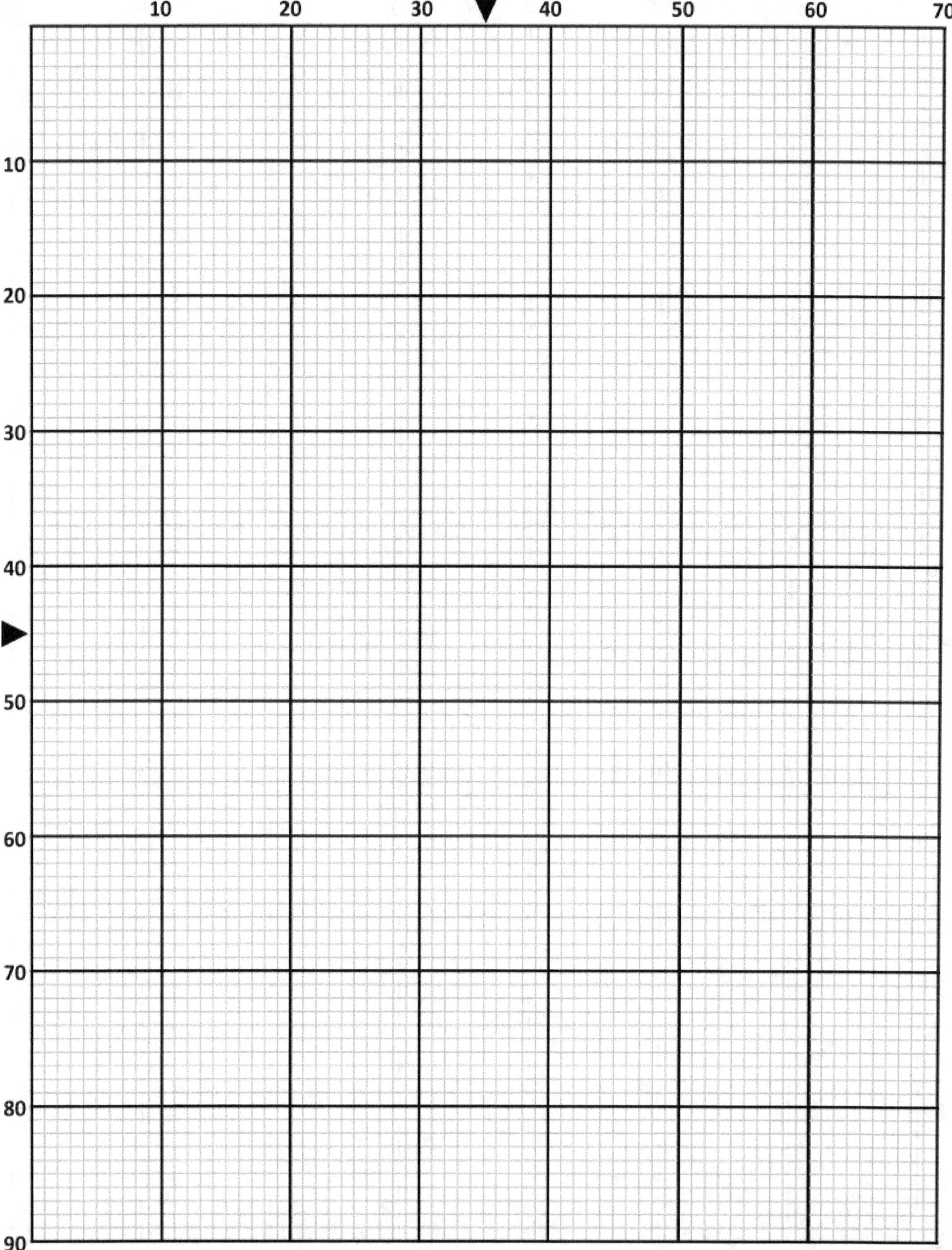

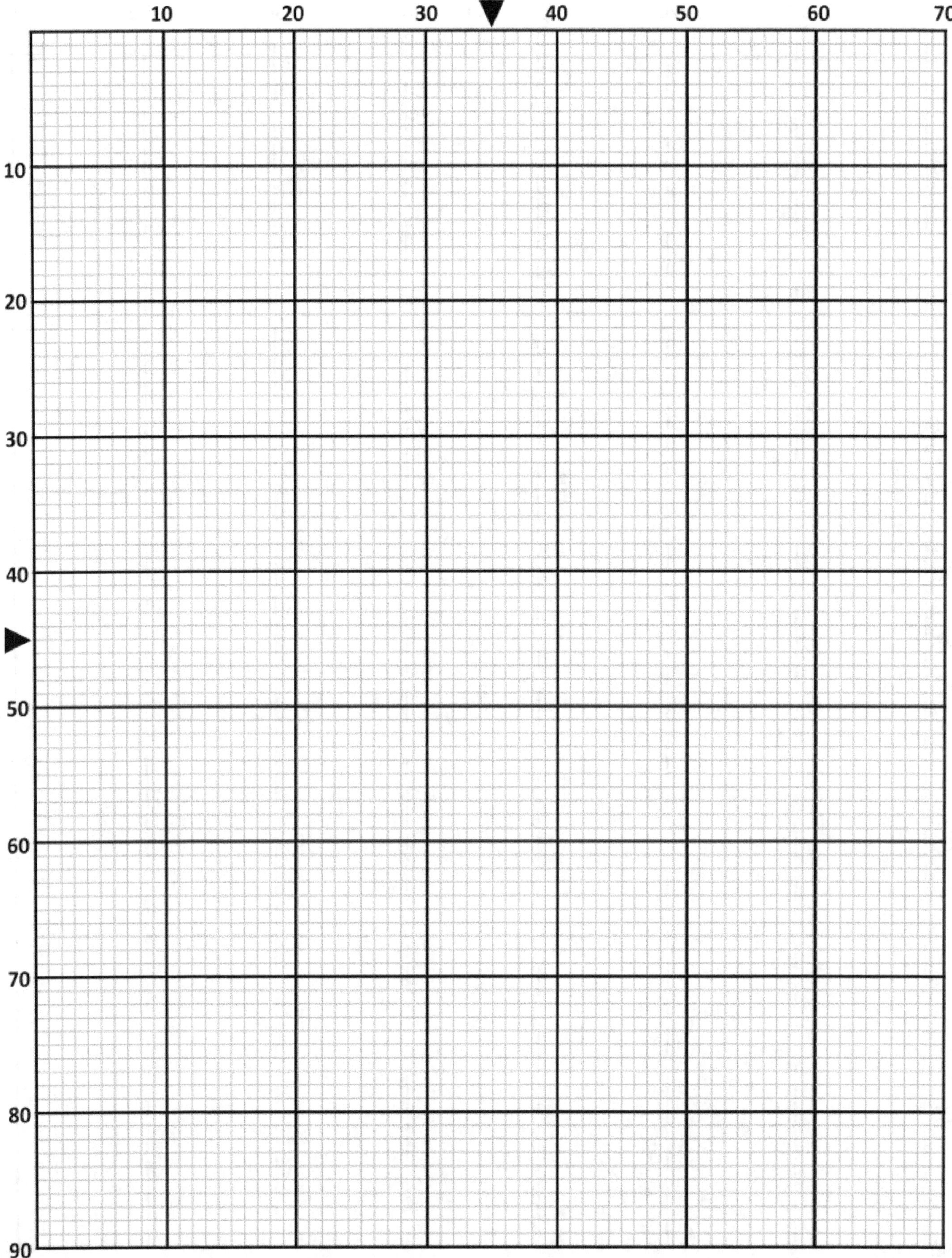

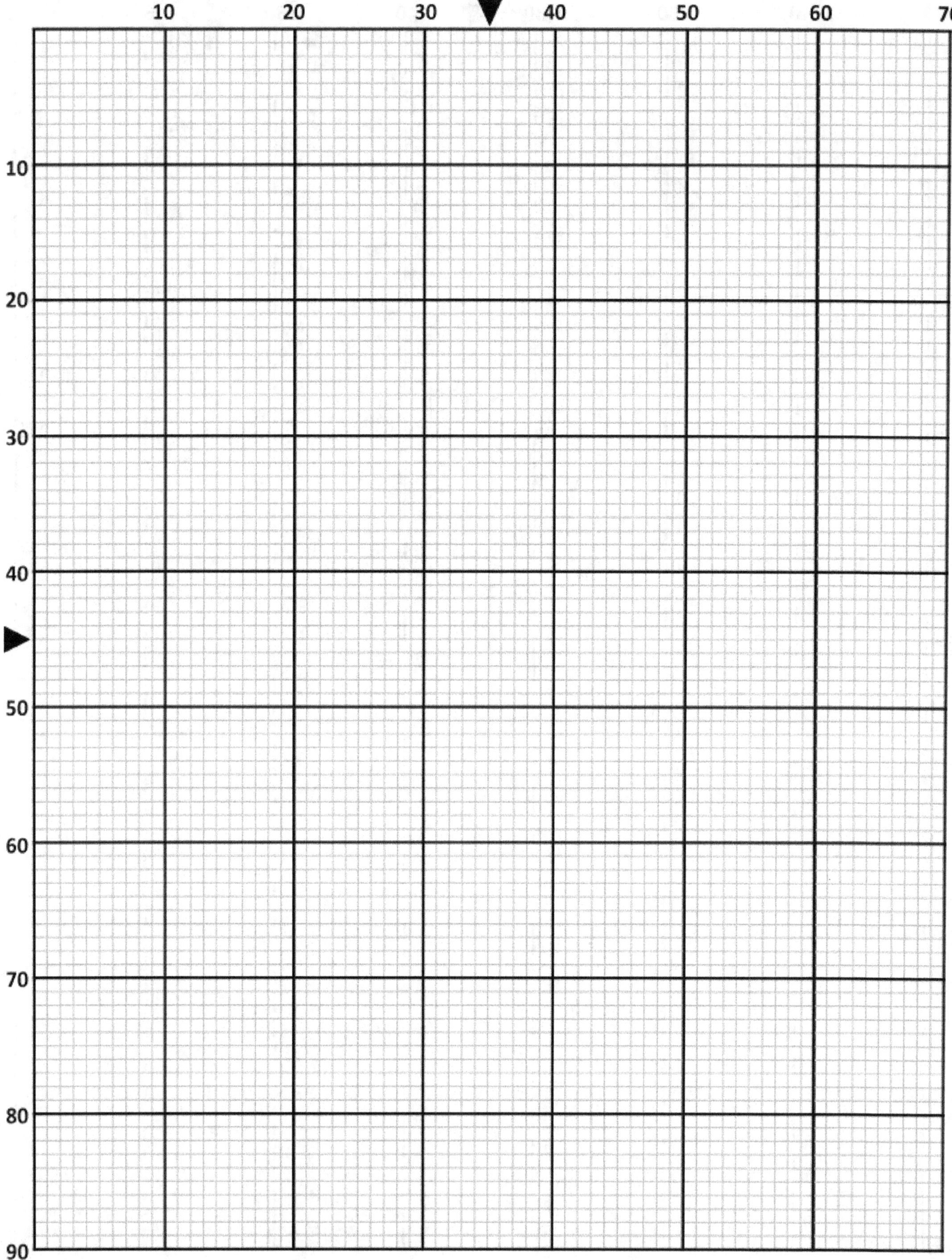

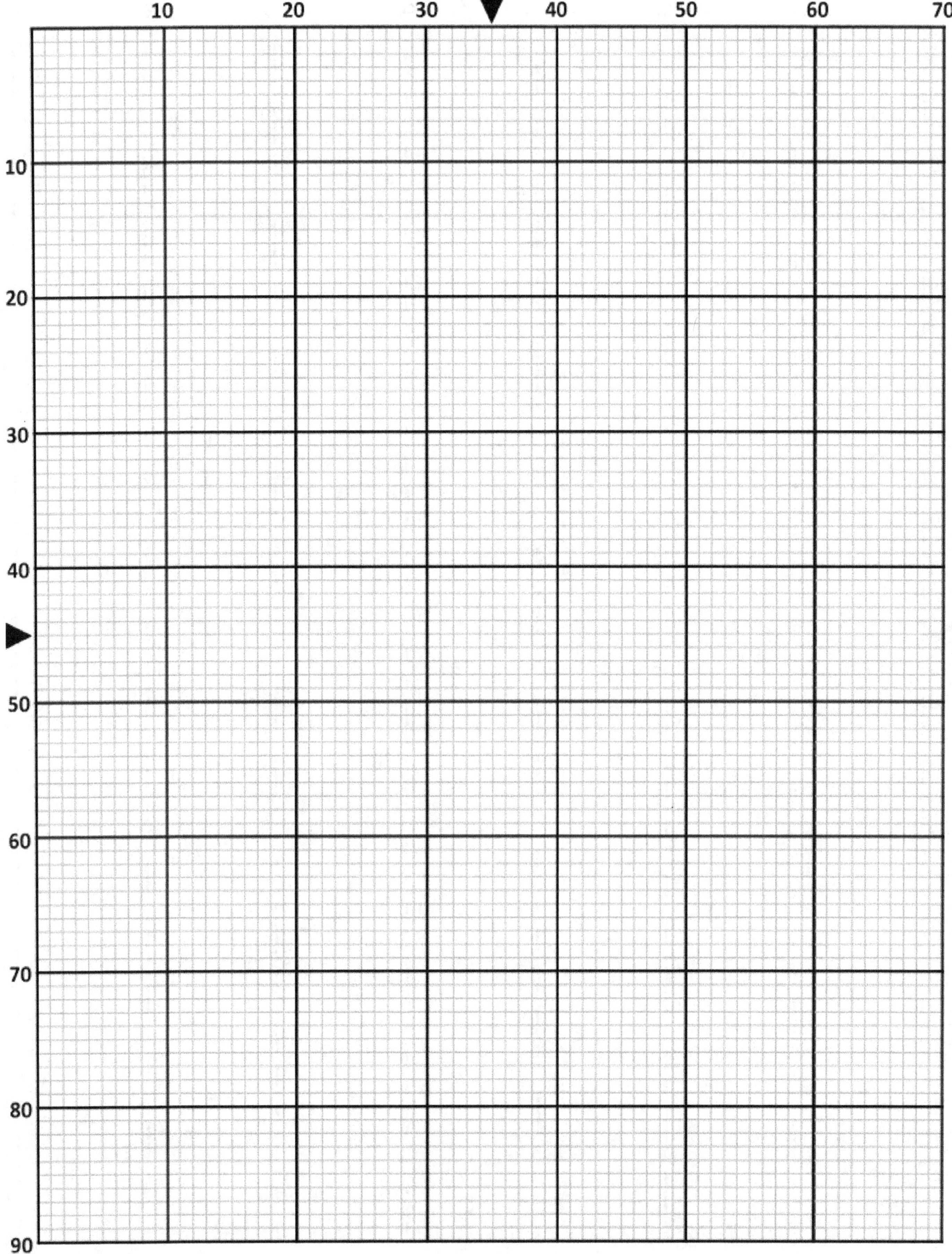

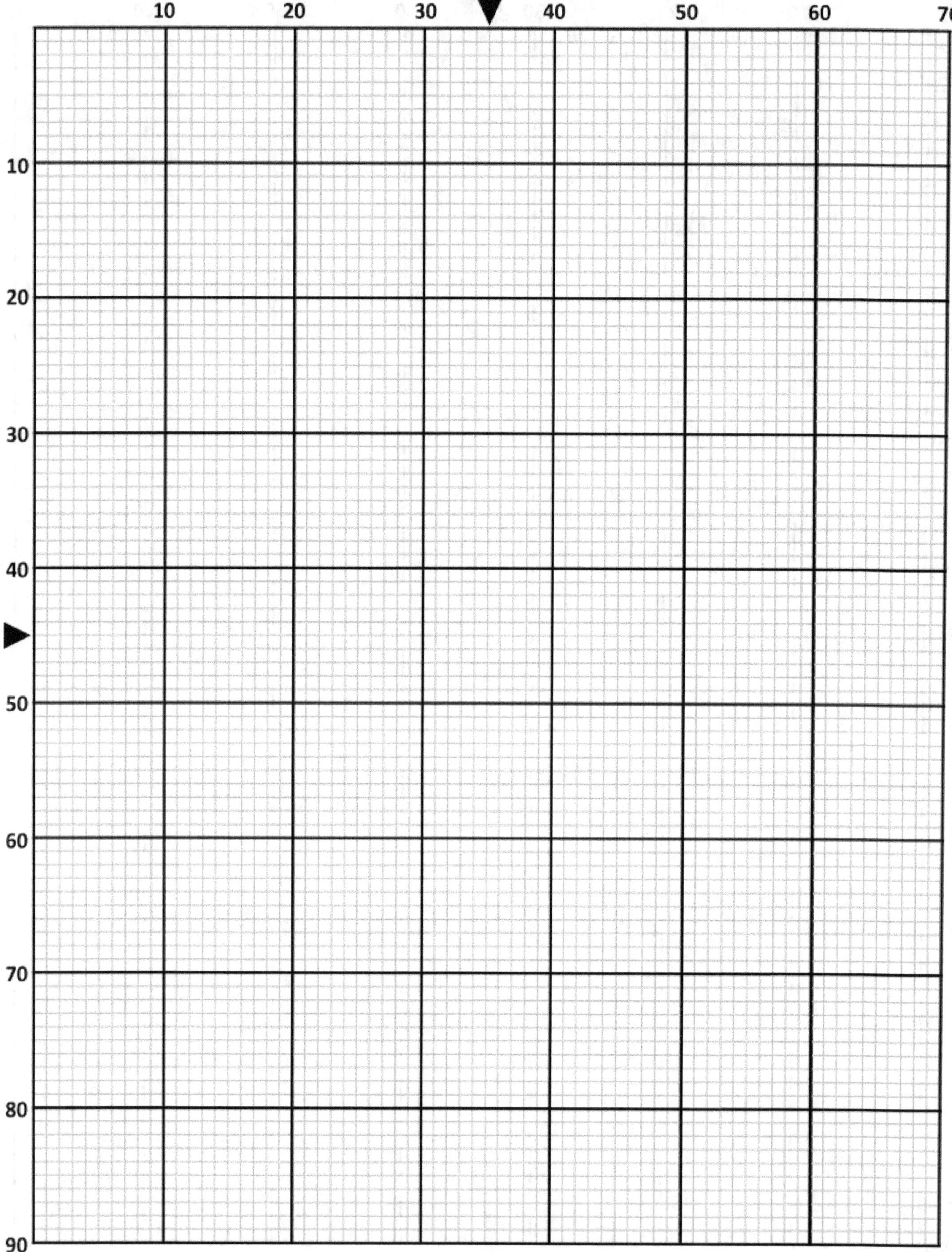

Thank You

We hope you enjoyed

As a small family company, your feedback is very important to us.

Please let us know how you like our notebook at:

mirelaheljbook@yahoo.com